Jung on Art

In this book, Tjeu van den Berk examines C. G. Jung's personal perspective on art and how his work intensely engages with this theme. It analyses Jung's profound reflections on artistic considerations such as how we experience art, the specific qualities in the perception of beauty, the nature of the creative process and the aesthetic attitude.

Jung on Art considers Jung's feelings about art simply being 'art' rather than reducing it to a moral, political, religious or psychological product. It also discusses Jung's notion that the artist is only a breeding ground for a piece of art, and once complete, the piece has an independent existence.

Topics covered include:

- symbolism
- the difference between art and aesthetics
- Jung's ideas about himself as an artist
- the psychology of art
- Jung's perspective on modern art and surrealism.

This book will be of great interest to all Jungian scholars, as well as those interested in the meeting of Jung and art.

Tjeu van den Berk was director of the C. G. Jung Society of the Netherlands. He has written widely on Jungian psychology.

Jung on Art

The Autonomy of the Creative Drive

Tjeu van den Berk

Routledge
Taylor & Francis Group
LONDON AND NEW YORK

Originally published in Dutch as *Eigenzinnig kunstzinnig: De visie van Carl Gustav Jung op Kunst*. Meinema, Zoetermeer (2009)

Authorised translation by Dr Petra Galama

First published in English 2012 by Routledge
27 Church Road, Hove, East Sussex BN3 2FA

Simultaneously published in the USA and Canada
by Routledge
711 Third Avenue, New York NY 10017

Routledge is an imprint of the Taylor & Francis Group, an Informa business

British Library Cataloguing in Publication Data
A catalogue record for this book is available from the British Library

Library of Congress Cataloging in Publication Data
Van den Berk, Tjeu.
[Eigenzinnig kunstzinnig. English]
Jung on art / Tjeu van den Berk. — 1st ed.
p. cm.
Includes bibliographical references and index.
ISBN 978-0-415-61027-8 (hardback) — ISBN 978-0-415-61028-5 (pbk.) 1. Jung, C. G. (Carl Gustav), 1875–1961. 2. Creative ability. 3. Psychology and art. I. Title.
BF410.V36 2012
701'.15—dc23

2011033991

ISBN: 978-0-415-61027-8 (hbk)
ISBN: 978-0-415-61028-5 (pbk)

Typeset in Times by RefineCatch Ltd, Bungay, Suffolk
Paperback cover design by Andrew Ward

To Kasper
(b. 8 June 2008)

> The creative work arises from unconscious depths – we might truly say from the realm of the mothers.
>
> (Jung 1922/1978: 75)

Like every true prophet,
the artist is the unwitting mouthpiece
of the psychic secrets of his time,
and is often as unconscious as a sleep-walker.
He supposes that it is he who speaks,
but the spirit of the age is his prompter,
and whatever this spirit says
is proved true by its effects.

(Jung 1932/1978b: 122–123)

Contents

Plates

Preface

> In reality, the work of art grows out of the artist as a child from his mother. The creative process has a feminine quality, and the creative work arises from unconscious depths.
>
> (Jung)

A psychology of art

The psychiatrist and cultural philosopher Carl Gustav Jung (1875–1961) never wrote a monograph on art. Nonetheless, throughout his work he intensely engaged with this theme on many occasions.[1] In this study, it is my intention to distil a consistent and comprehensive perspective on art from all his contributions.

Therefore, this study deals with a psychology of art. It encompasses the entire discipline of art, but concentrates on one specific perspective; that is, it engages the question of how we experience art. This study is not concerned with the 'what' of art, but rather with the 'how' of its operations. What are the specific qualities in the perception of beauty? How does a creative process work? What is an aesthetic attitude? Jung devoted profound reflections to these themes.

1 In *Psychological Types*, published in 1921, there are three sections where Jung engages extensively with the subject, each time within the context of the themes "extraversion" and "introversion". In Chapter 2 he deals with it in relation to Friedrich Schiller's thoughts on "naïve and sentimental poetry" (Jung 1921/1990: 130–135); Chapter 5 looks at "the type problem in poetry" (ibid., 166–272); in Chapter 7 he applies his typology to the entire field of aesthetics as well as examining Wilhelm Worringer's art theory of "empathy" and "abstraction" (ibid., 289–299).

In 1922 and in 1930 Jung wrote two elaborate articles about the relationship between analytical psychology and literary art, which for the most part can be applied to art in general (Jung 1922/1978; 1930/1978). On 4 May 1925 he gave a seminar on "modern art" (Jung 1926/1989: 50–57). In 1932, he published an insightful study about James Joyce's *Ulysses* (Jung 1932/1978b). In the same year, he wrote a sharp article in the *Neue Zürcher Zeitung* in reaction to an exhibition of Pablo Picasso's work (Jung 1932/1978). In *Flying Saucers: A Modern Myth*, published in 1958, he dedicated an entire chapter to "modern art" (Jung 1958/1964: 383–400). In his letters he often paid attention to the theme of art. Here, I give only two examples: during a correspondence with Herman Hesse, in 1934, Jung stressed the autonomy of the artistic drive (Jung 1973: 170–171; 173–174) and in 1960, one year before his death, he wrote an elaborate letter to the art critic Herbert Read expressing his concern about certain tendencies in "modern art" (Jung 1990: 586–592).

Jung considered psychology the most appropriate scientific approach for interpreting art, because art belongs primarily to the realm of experience. In 1921 he wrote: "Aesthetics by its very nature is applied psychology."[2]

However, he was well aware that this perspective has restrictions. The secret of the creative process is unattainable by whichever method of conscious analysis. Only those elements of art which appear in our consciousness during the creative process, rather than the essence of art, can be the subject of psychology.[3] "The creative act, being rooted in the immensity of the unconscious, will forever elude our attempts at understanding."[4]

Jung was strongly convinced that the essence of art cannot be approached by any scientific methodology. Not even a (more) art-scientific method.[5] This is simply because when we are reflecting upon art, we are placed outside its secret: "One can hardly suppress a doubt as to whether art really 'means' anything at all. Perhaps art has no 'meaning' (…). Perhaps it is like nature, which simply *is* and 'means' nothing beyond that. (…) Art, as it has been said, is beauty, and that is its fulfilment and purpose. It needs no meaning, for meaning has nothing to do with art. Within the sphere of art, I must accept the truth of this statement. (…) For the purpose of cognitive understanding we must detach ourselves from the creative process and look at it from the outside; only then does it become an image that expresses what we are bound to call 'meaning.'"[6]

It is my opinion that Jung's perspective on art is of major importance and worthy of being included into the field of contemporary art criticism. However, it is as good as non-existent in this field. In general, art critics are apprehensive of a depth psychological approach. Usually one knows only the Freudian perspective, which is considered reductive; it is still unknown to most that Jung's view is radically different. Even in leading studies, Jung is regularly quoted in a superficial and incorrect way and/or simply grouped together with Sigmund Freud (1856–1939).[7]

Moreover, irrespective of a depth psychological approach, artists as well as art critics are generally apprehensive of a psychological approach to art. They are open to a philosophy of art. But a psychology of art is generally looked upon with suspicion, as if one fears that considering something psychologically means to declare its non-existence! Theologians are well aware of this: God no longer exists when it is ascertained that He is also something psychological. And one has to

2 Jung 1921/1990: 289.
3 See Jung 1922/1978: 65.
4 Jung 1930/1978: 87.
5 See Jung 1922/1978: 77.
6 See Jung 1922/1978: 77–78.
7 For instance, David Maclagan wrote in the introduction to his *Psychological Aesthetics*: 'The influence of the association of aesthetics with decadence and perversity on both Freud's and Jung's disqualification of aesthetic properties is also explained' (Maclagan 2001: 14; see ibid., 22, 25). To me, his remark concerning Jung seems incorrect. I will treat this subject extensively in Chapters 5, 6 and 7.

admit, there is a psychology which *reduces* reality to its own premises and subsequently tolerates, as it were, its evaporation.

In *Voer voor Psychologen* (*Food for Psychologists*), the Dutch author Harry Mulisch (1927–2010) sneers: 'Psychologists? Barren, intelligent people, who think they can reduce the work to the writer. They still do not know that Shakespeare is created by Hamlet, Beethoven is composed by his symphonies, Rembrandt looks like his self-portraits, Marx was born from socialism, the son gives birth to the mother, the sun has created the eye, love creates the lovers and the egg lays the hen.'[8]

Jung certainly cannot be counted amongst these barren psychologists. Mulisch could even have been his apprentice. In 1930 Jung wrote: "It is not Goethe that creates *Faust*, but *Faust* that creates Goethe. And what is *Faust*? *Faust* is essentially a symbol. By this I do not mean that it is an allegory pointing to something all too familiar, but the expression of something profoundly alive in the soul of every German, which Goethe helped to bring to birth."[9]

There exists another psychology other than just the reductive! In the past decades, Christian Allesch, professor of psychology at Salzburg University, devoted interesting studies to the history of 'psychological aesthetics'. These studies make clear that there has been and still is a tribal conflict between two types of psychology.

Psychology became an independent area of research in the middle of the nineteenth century. Until then, it was a daughter of philosophy. It was a relief that a psychological perspective on art strongly relativised well-known idealistic and normative theories. Beauty was no longer thought of as a reality of metaphysical speculations or of eternal values, but as a subject of everyday life that could be studied through empirical research. Psychology counted itself enthusiastically among the natural sciences. The founding father of experimental aesthetics was Theodore Fechner (1801–1887). He demonstrated empirically, for example, that the senses naturally experience certain abstract proportions, like the golden ratio, as beautiful.

But it soon became clear that this methodology had a major disadvantage, as this approach to the aesthetic experience only registered what was statistically measurable and what was generally approved as valid. The strictly individual aspect of the aesthetic experience, which was instinctively experienced as fascinating, stayed in the background. Researchers either looked diligently for 'refined' instruments that would enable them to measure these impressions, or denied the significance of such 'romantic' affections.

This drawback did not prevent empirical psychology from becoming a great success during the twentieth century. Allesch showed this extensively. The leading predisposition within universities is still that it needs to be a 'hard' science. 'Cognitive theories' are de rigeur. Emotions are described as cognitive functions.

8 Mulisch 2001: 87.
9 Jung 1930/1978: 103.

That reason is a function originating *from* experience is no longer considered a possibility within scientific discourse. Everything which cannot be causally reduced to measurable principles is (still) unimportant. In his ideas about art, Freud maintained this type of hard causality, irrespective of the fact that he took unconscious urges into consideration.

However, in the nineteenth century another type of psychology originated which was described as 'phenomenological'. Its adherents valued the empirical perspective, but only as one next to others. They did not approach the aesthetic experience in a reductive way, but saw it as a *phainoumenon*, a phenomenon which appears to us as essentially immeasurable and which certainly cannot be 'discovered' by us. It is impossible to analyse the object from a distance, because the seer and the seen can never be separated. All one can do is try to research the particular nature of original experience. It is impossible to do anything beyond this.[10]

Jung stands entirely in this second movement. His psychology goes a long way towards resolving the conflict between the experimental and the phenomenological schools of thought in psychology. He greatly valued the empirical methodology. Before he met Freud, he was already famous for his almost behaviouristic approach to association experiments. However, these experiments pointed him above all towards the existence of psychic dimensions which are immeasurable. It was clear to Jung that the artist finds his inspiration in these dimensions of the psyche and he wrote extensively about this subject.

The art philosopher Eliseo Vivas (1901–1993) wrote: 'There can be no doubt that Freud's views are more lucid than Jung's; but Jung does not drag the amateur from his serious interest in art. But more important is the fact that Jung has a better grasp of the nature of art than any of his rivals; for this reason the psychological instruments he puts at the disposal of aestheticians and critics allow a deeper penetration into the nature of art than rival views.'[11] These 'psychological instruments', meaning Jung's well-known hypotheses about the operation of the unconscious in relation to consciousness, are central themes in the chapters of my book.

Outline of this book

The theme of the first chapter is *cryptomnesia*, the psychic process of 'hidden memories'. This process happens in everyone's life. One thinks one is presenting something new, when it is in fact an old and forgotten truth. Jung thought it possible to 'forget' something individually or collectively. In particular an artist is sensitive to cryptomnesia.

The central theme in the second chapter is the driving force behind these 'hidden memories': the *complex*. According to Jung, a *specific* autonomous complex forms

10 See Allesch 2006: 183–186.
11 Vivas 1974: 247–248.

the basis of a creative process. Art is not a sublimated sexual complex, as was Freud's opinion, but a specific drive with roots reaching into our animal instincts.

The third chapter is concerned with the unconscious root system out of which the complexes arise. Jung called this *participation mystique*. Here, psychic and physical processes permeate each other, and the subjective and objective coincide. The artist becomes submerged in it, he becomes enthralled and resurfaces with his enchanting instrument: a work of art.

When it has crossed the threshold of consciousness, the work of art appears to us as a *symbol*. This centrepiece of Jung's thinking is the theme of the fourth chapter. The symbol is the connecting chain between the unconscious and conscious psyche; it is the great transitional reality.

Chapter 5 explicitly deals with *aesthetics*. The artistic and the aesthetic are of course closely related, but for Jung they are certainly not identical. At all times, he is apprehensive of everything which has to do with a purely aesthetic view of life. Nevertheless, he is aware that aesthetic formulation is a necessary tool for the artist.

Chapter 6 discusses how *Jung considered his own artistic creations*. Jung was an architect, sculptor, mandala drawer and painter. However, he regularly asserted that his artistic work had nothing to do with art. Why did he hold this opinion? He was ambivalent about his artistic creations. I will pay extensive attention to the cubic stone he sculpted, and to the many mandalas and pictures he drew and painted.

In Chapter 7 all aspects from the previous chapters will be placed in a *comprehensive perspective on art*. Here, the fundamental Jungian themes will be attuned to each other.

In Chapter 8 this perspective will be tested by and illustrated with one specific theme: Jung's thoughts about "*modern art*". This art originated in Western Europe around 1900 and was characterised by abstract, absurd, surrealistic and cubist forms. Jung closely knew and experienced this art. Zürich was a centre of this movement. Of course, Jung had no idea of what we call now, at the beginning of the twenty-first century, 'modern art', as he died in 1961. So, I will write "modern art" (between double quotation marks), except in Jung's own quotes, to refer to art which was modern to Jung. Jung had a kind of love/hate relationship with "modern art". He did not doubt its artistic value, but considered it morbid at the same time.

Central in the ninth and final chapter is Jung's *analysis of a "modern" work of art*. We will explicitly see him applying his own theory. This concerns the painting of the Surrealistic painter Yves Tanguy (1900–1955), *Noyé indifférent*. Jung bought it in 1929 at an exhibition in Zürich. Three years before his death, in 1958, he dedicated an intriguing discourse to it.

In the epilogue, I will summarise Jung's perspective on art by describing it as a *synchronistic* phenomenon. I consider the essential characteristics of Jung's hypothesis of synchronicity relevant to art.

Some demarcations of the theme

This book is concerned with Jung's personal perspective on art, rather than the question of whether Jungian psychology can be meaningfully employed in the analysis of art. The latter is undoubtedly true, but that does not mean that Jung himself developed a perspective on art. Perhaps Karl Marx (1818–1883) did not develop a perspective on art, but his philosophy can certainly be used in the evaluation of art and works of art.

In the past years many Jungian books and articles have been published, in which important concepts from analytical psychology are applied to the analysis of art. Recently, Christian Gaillard, a former professor at the École Nationale Supérieure des Beaux-Arts in Paris, has published an extensive and differentiated survey of these types of studies.[12] Of course, all these authors reflect from time to time on Jung's personal opinions on art, but to them that theme is subordinate. Their preoccupation lies with the influence of certain Jungian notions. The research of Susan Rowland, a former lecturer in Jungian Studies at the University of Greenwich, takes an in-between position. The main theme of her books is the effect of the Jungian body of thought on art criticism, but she is also attentive to Jung's own reflections on art.[13]

There is remarkably little literature on the specific theme of this book: Jung's own ideas on art. I only know of two studies which have taken a similar viewpoint. These are *An Outline of Jungian Aesthetics* by Morris H. Philipson (1994) and *Jung and Aesthetic Experience* by Donald H. Mayo (1995).[14] Both Philipson and Mayo use Jung's symbol theory as point of departure; both studies elaborate upon the differences between Jung and Freud; both are excellent studies; and without a doubt the symbol is the *uniting factor* in Jung's ideas. However, I think that more factors are clearly playing a role. The themes of cryptomnesia, the complex and *participation mystique*, as well as the difference between aesthetics and art, are as good as absent in Philipson and Mayo's studies. Also, Jung's attitude concerning "modern art" is hardly mentioned.

Apart from these two monographs, there are some articles[15] and chapters which explicitly focus on aspects of Jung's ideas on art. An important author in this area is Paul Bishop, professor of German Studies at Glasgow University. His standard work on Jung's reception of Friedrich Nietzsche (1844–1900) assigns an important chapter to Jung's theory of art.[16] An extensive article written by Christian Gaillard, entitled "The arts", deserves special attention. I consider the first part of it, dedicated to Jung's perspective on art, to be among the best texts on this subject.[17]

12 See Gaillard 2008: 362–369.

13 See Rowland 1999, 2005, 2008.

14 See Philipson 1994; Mayo 1995.

15 See Vivas 1974; Gorsen 1994.

16 See Bishop 1995: 156–186. Furthermore, Bishop has written several ingenious articles about Jung's understanding of art against the background of the thoughts of major classical German authors. See Bishop 1998, 1999, 2008.

17 See Gaillard 2008: 324–376. Furthermore, Gaillard is the author of the well-known work *Le musée imaginaire de Carl Gustav Jung* (see Gaillard 1998).

Nearly all other articles which more or less discuss the theme of Jung and art approach it as is discussed above. The authors take Jungian concepts as point of departure and apply them to some or other form of art.

As much as possible, I will make use of the sources employed by Jung to further his thinking. There are several. He was inspired enormously by his female co-workers; the Dutch Maria Moltzer (1874–1944) made him aware of the importance of intuition, and the Russian Sabina Spielrein (1885–1942) broadened his understanding of the complex and the libido. But there were also renowned authoritative sources. For instance, the art critic Wilhelm Worringer (1881–1965), the anthropologist Lucien Lévy-Bruhl (1857–1939) and the philosopher Nietzsche. Jung knew them through and through and quoted them frequently. I will not discuss here whether he always understood them correctly. Maybe he used their ideas out of context, and maybe they would not have recognised themselves in Jung's report, but I don't think this is important to this study. I am concerned with the consistency of Jung's borrowed understanding within his own frame of reference. Considering whether he adequately quoted his sources does not take this study further. Of course it is possible that Jung did not understand correctly what Nietzsche meant by 'apollinian' and 'dionysian'. But the same question can be asked of Nietzsche himself; maybe he did not understand the ancient Greeks at this point. We can establish, at least, that Jung thought that Nietzsche understood them incorrectly! In the context of this book, it is of little importance who is right. What matters is what Jung intended to say when he used this vocabulary, and how he fitted these concepts into his own vision. We must be careful, for instance, when regarding 'dionysian' as a Nietzschean concept, because then we might miss a part of Jung's perspective!

Autonomy of art

Rounding off this introduction and at the same time serving as a beginning of this book, I want to say the following. If there is one central idea in Jung's perspective on art, it is the more or less complete autonomy of a work of art. The artist was not central in his reflections; nor the beholder of art; nor even social influences or psychic drives; no, what determines art is only the work of art as a *work of art.* Jung never reduced art to a moral, political or religious product, nor to a psychological product. Art is not a sublimated drive nor a social neurosis nor something similar. A work of art exists as an autonomous being.

The artist is 'only' the breeding ground of a work of art. The irrational, creative drive which finds its expression in a work of art is in fact *impersonal* in nature. A work of art, as it were, escapes the artist, and once born, leads an independent existence: "The essence of a work of art is not to be found in the personal idiosyncrasies that creep into it – indeed, the more there are of them, the less it is a work of art – but in its rising above the personal and in its speaking (…) to the mind and heart of mankind. The personal is a limitation, yes, even a burden to art."[18]

18 Jung 1930/1978: 101.

Jung separated the artist from all excessive psychic silt and trickery, and as such approached the 'genius throw', the work of art. He was concerned with the primaeval experience, which is called the creative force. He strongly relativised psychological categories, and this is of course remarkable for a person like Jung. He sometimes wrote with irony about artists who were troubled about their creativity because of his psychology: "These would-be artists, however, develop one characteristic symptom: they all shun psychology like the plague, because they are terrified that this monster will devour their so-called artistic ability. As if a whole army of psychologists could do anything against the power of a god! True productivity is a spring that can never be stopped. Is there any trickery on earth which could have prevented Mozart or Beethoven from creating? Creative power is mightier than his possessor. If it is not so, then it is a feeble thing, and given favourable conditions will nourish an endearing talent, but no more."[19]

Final remarks and acknowledgements

Before expressing my gratitude to those who carefully read this manuscript and discussed it with me, I first want to make a few typographic remarks.

In this book, the footnotes containing references to Jung's work mention two dates: the first date is the publication of the first edition year; the second date refers to the edition which I used for this study. This is in order to give the reader an idea of the period during which Jung developed a certain concept.

To indicate quotations, I generally use a single quotation mark. Except when quoting Jung. To clearly mark those, I use a double quotation mark. They occur regularly and often as part of my own text; so one could easily overlook them and lose sight of who is speaking.

When a person is mentioned for the first time in this book, both first and last names are recorded and this is followed, if possible, by date of birth and death. Afterwards, the person is only named by their surname.

The translator sometimes modified and, if necessary, corrected existing translations of Jung's work. Jung was very careful in the use of his terminology. Because this subject does not yet have a standardised vocabulary in literature, as for example Jung's concept of religion, translators are still free in their choice of words. However, in translating Jung one cannot translate the same word, for instance '*artistisch*', with 'aesthetic' in one place and in another place 'artistic'. In Jung's thinking, there is an essential difference between '*künstlerisch*' and '*ästhetisch*'. Some parts of Jung's work are translated here for the first time. Several times Jung corrected, edited, shortened or made additions to his writing. For instance, his three lectures *Analytical Psychology and Education* were held in 1924 and published in 1927. In the English translation of this work, published in 1946, he included many changes and additions but he also erased some sentences. Some of these sentences are relevant to his perspective on art.

19 Jung 1946/1954: 115.

Finally, I want to dedicate some words of profound thanks. Johan Reijmerink, a Jungian and an expert in language, had the thankless task of studying the 'chaotic draft' of this text (without even a preface or a conclusion!). He did this with the utmost care and competence, which resulted in a conscious elimination of superfluous sentences and a change in chapters.

Inger van Lamoen-Dommisse, a physician and Jungian analyst, and Aart van Lunteren, a theologian, read the 'first neat draft'. Inger had a sharp eye for therapeutic and artistic formulations and made me aware of how Jung wrestled with himself as an artist. Aart had an eye for philosophical and mythological implications, and as a 'man of the Word' has a great sense of formulations.

Five years ago, Marjeet, my beloved partner, inspired me to write this book. As it progressed, we had long conversations about its rich themes, such as *cryptomnesia* and *participation mystique*. With utmost care she studied the final draft and encouraged me to write a separate chapter on 'Jung as an artist'. My sincerest thanks!

Breda, February 2011

Chapter 1

Art originates from 'hidden memories'

> It would never occur to an intelligent layman to mistake a pathological phenomenon for art, in spite of the undeniable fact that a work of art arises from much the same psychic conditions as a neurosis. This is only natural, because certain of these conditions are present in every individual whether in the case of a nervous intellectual, a poet or a normal human being.
>
> (Jung 1922/1978: 67)

In the hallucinations of his mediumistic niece, Jung encountered for the first time a "world behind the conscious world", the "hidden memories" (cryptomnesia) of a person. He realized that these memories not only constitute the reservoir of a somnambulist, but that creative processes, in everyone, exist by the grace of impulses which, independent of our will, arise from the unconscious. This is particularly true for the artist! The ego-consciousness regards them as "abnormal". Nonetheless, creativity exists by the grace of an "unrestrained" spirit.

Jung's discovery of the unconscious via cryptomnesia

In 1900, after having completed his education at the University of Basel, Jung started his first employment as an assistant doctor at the renowned Burghölzli psychiatric clinic in Zürich. At the time, he did not have his doctorate, but he had material for doctoral research. That material consisted of the accounts he had written about the spiritist séances wherein his niece, Hélène Preiswerk (1881–1911) (see plate 1), was a medium. Jung had attended these meetings, as had his mother. Several men and women in Jung's family on his mother's side had mediumistic gifts, Jung's mother in particular.

He finished his doctoral thesis one and a half year later and graduated on 17 July 1902. In his dissertation, he used an empirical methodology in order to find plausible explanations for the fact that his niece heard voices, received insights and acted out personalities during the séances.

On the face of it, paranormal phenomena do not easily lend themselves to empirical research. Nonetheless, Jung regarded these phenomena as his first unshakeable evidence of the existence of something like the unconscious in the human psyche. In 1925 he conducted seminars on the history of analytical psychology and he began his first seminar almost immediately with the following account: "In 1896 something happened to me that served as an impetus for my future life. (…) The thing that started me off in my interest in psychology was the case of a fifteen-and-a-half-year-old girl. (…) This girl was a somnambulist, and it was discovered by her sisters that she could obtain extraordinary answers to questions put to her when she was in a sleeping state. (…) I was impressed with the fact that, notwithstanding appearances, there must be a hidden life of the mind manifesting itself only in trance or in sleep. (…) During the trance several personalities would manifest themselves and, little by little, I found I could call up by suggestion one personality or another. (…) I said to myself, however, that there must be some world behind the conscious world, and that it was this world with which the girl was in contact. I began to study the literature of spiritism but could find no satisfaction there. Then I turned to philosophy, always seeking for a possible clue to these strange phenomena."[20]

It was in psychiatry where he eventually found constructive knowledge about "some world behind the conscious world". Because he encountered a similar kind of hallucinating mind in the psyches of his patients. After his doctorate, he pursued the matter further. The following ten years were marked by feverish and ingenious research into the relationship between the unconscious and this 'paranormal' mind. His first masterpiece on the subject was published in 1912: *Transformations and Symbolisms of the Libido.* The hallucinations of a medium are again central in this work. In this research he definitely chose his own direction. At this point Freud broke with him.

According to Jung, there was only one teacher who had a formative influence on him during those years: the Swiss professor of psychology Théodore Flournoy (1854–1920). He was a leading scientist. In 1892 he was offered the first Chair of Psychology at the University of Geneva. Jung often visited Flournoy in Geneva on his free days. He appreciated his advice. Flournoy was a major support to him, in particular during his crisis with Freud. In *Memories, Dreams, Reflections* nothing equals the warm-hearted gratefulness he expressed towards Flournoy. "Flournoy's ideas were completely in line with mine and they stimulated me. I adopted his concept *imagination créatrice* because it interested me significantly."[21] For Jung it was a fortunate coincidence that Flournoy's book was published in 1900, since it also included an account of the paranormal gifts of a medium.[22]

In his dissertation, Jung explored the functioning of his niece's psyche in trance. He postulated that, among other things, she was subjected to 'cryptomnesia'.[23] He

20 Jung 1926/1989: 3–4.
21 Jung 1962/1997: 378–379.
22 See Flournoy 1900. Jung was so enthusiastic about the book that he asked Flournoy to allow him to translate it into German. Flournoy, however, had already given the rights to someone else.
23 See Jung 1902/1957: 81–84.

adopted this concept from Flournoy, who had given it scientific status as well as a name. The phenomenon of cryptomnesia opened a decisive perspective in Jung's reflections on the unconscious. The term is composed of two Greek words: *kruptos* – hidden – and *mnèmè* – memory. What happens in cryptomnesia, meaning 'hidden memory', is the following: one remembers something without realising that it is a recollection. One is convinced that it is an original thought or intuition. For example, a musician hears a popular folk tune in his youth and this tune becomes a motif in one of his symphonies. However, he is unaware of this connection and thinks he has created something original. Through someone's persuasive investigation it is not only ascertained that the tune already existed, but it is furthermore established that as a child he certainly heard it. Nonetheless, the composer is unaware of any 'malevolence'. Douwe Draaisma, an associate professor of the history of psychology, succinctly described it thus: 'Cryptomnesia means to store the message and to forget its source.'[24]

The fact that these 'hidden memories' resurface leads us to the conclusion that they continued to exist in an unconscious dimension of the psyche. Jung saw this as evidence of the existence of the unconscious! In his view, cryptomnesia has strong evidential value. The subject never ceased to interest Jung. Three years after the publication of his dissertation, in 1905, he wrote a separate article on cryptomnesia; he again discoursed on this phenomenon in his *Tavistock Lectures* in 1935; and again in 1946; and in 1961, shortly before his death, he finished a lengthy text in which he once more extensively discussed this psychic phenomenon which he considered of major significance.[25] I will include three telling examples of cryptomnesia.

The first example Jung personally discovered in Nietzsche's *Also sprach Zarathustra*. He was proud to have found an occurrence of cryptomnesia in this work of art. He refers to it at least four times in his work.[26] Because of its simplicity it provides strong evidence. In the chapter 'On great events', Nietzsche narrated Zarathustra's stay on 'the Isles of the Blest'. One day a ship dropped anchor before one of these islands, called 'smoking mountain'. Nietzsche writes: 'and its crew went ashore in order to shoot rabbits.' Around noon, when the captain and his crew were reunited, they suddenly saw a man floating towards them through the air whilst shouting: 'It is time! It is high time!'[27] That man is Zarathustra.

When Jung read *Also sprach Zarathustra* for the first time in 1899, he became aware of the déjà vu-like character of the 'captain', the 'shooting of rabbits' and the 'man flying through the air'. At first, he could not locate this feeling. He thought about it for several days, until he remembered that he had read something

24 Draaisma 2005: 3.
25 See Jung 1905/1957: 95–106; 1935/1977: 15; 1946/1954: 110; 1961/1977: 198–202.
26 Jung 1902/1957: 82–83; 1905/1957: 102–103; 1961/1977: 200; 1988: 1217–1219.
27 Nietzsche 2005: 113.

similar several years before in the extraordinary stories written by the physician Julius Kerner. It was a sailors' story, published in 1686. It reads: 'The four captains and a merchant, Mr. Bell, went ashore on the island of Mount Stromboli to shoot rabbits. At three o'clock they mustered the crew to go aboard, when, to their inexpressible astonishment, they saw two men flying rapidly towards them through the air.'[28] Everyone realises immediately, remarked Jung, that those similarities can not be coincidental, but we also understand straight away that Nietzsche had no intention to plagiarise. Moreover, the 'shooting of rabbits' is not even meaningful nor does it embellish the story.

The prospective doctor decided to write a letter to Nietzsche's sister to ask for clarification. At the time Nietzsche had become mentally ill. She confirmed that she and her 12-year-old brother had indeed read the extraordinary stories by Kerner. Then it all became clear to Jung. This story was stored in Nietzsche's unconscious. And when the firemountain island of Zarathustra's descent into hell came to his mind, suddenly the 'hidden memory' of the Stromboli story also arose. Nietzsche, however, had no conscious recollection of the sailors' story. Jung even thought that if he had had any recollection of it, he would never have enacted the story of a captain who shoots rabbits!

The second example, in my view even stronger than the first, is narrated by Jung in the text he wrote in 1961, shortly before his death. It is the story of a professor who, during a walk, had a serious conversation with his pupil: "Suddenly he notices that his thoughts are interrupted by an unexpected flow of memories from his early childhood. He cannot account for it, as he is unable to discover any associative connection with the subject of his conversation. He stops and looks back: there at a little distance is a farm, which they had passed a short while ago, and he remembers that soon afterward images of his childhood began to surge up. 'Let us go back to the farm,' he says to his pupil; 'it must be about there that my fantasies started.' Back at the farm, the professor notices the smell of geese. Instantly he recognises it as the cause of the interruption: in his early youth he had lived on a farm where there were geese, whose characteristic smell had formed a lasting impression and caused the reproduction of the memory-images."[29] Jung realised that the 'accidental' recognition of cryptomnesia in this story must be a regular event in daily life. Even if we do not consciously retrace our footsteps, the unconscious will inhale the 'odour'.

I derive the third example from *Poetry and Truth* by Johann Wolfgang von Goethe (1749–1832). He describes an incident which he experienced as a hallucination and which evidently contains an element of cryptomnesia. It happened during the period in Goethe's life when the 22-year-old poet decided to end a love affair with the 20-year-old Frederica Brion. He visited her one more time: 'Those were painful days, whose memories had not remained with me. When I held out my hand to her from my horse, the tears stood in her eyes, and

28 Quoted in Jung 1961/1977: 200.
29 Jung 1961/1977: 199.

my heart was heavy. I rode along the footpath towards Drusenheim, and here one of the most singular forebodings took possession of me. I saw, not with the eyes of the body, but with those of the mind, my own figure coming towards me, on horseback, and on the same road, attired in a dress which I have never worn; it was pike-grey with some gold about it. But as I shook myself out of this dream, the figure had entirely disappeared. It is strange, however, that eight years afterward, I found myself on that very road, on my way to pay one more visit to Frederica, wearing the dress of which I had dreamed, and that, not from choice, but by accident. Whatever one may think of such matters in general, in this instance my strange illusion helped to calm me in this farewell hour. It softened for me the pain of leaving forever lovely Alsace, with all that it had brought me, and now that I had at last put behind me the painful strain of parting, I regained my peace of mind and had a pleasant journey.'[30] A beautiful example of cryptomnesia. Goethe had stored this dream-experience in his creative mind – apparently it was not suppressed – and it reappeared at this important moment without him realising it. 'By accident' and 'not from choice' he is again dressed in the dream-costume from eight years before. It is only at the end of his life that he understood the enigmatic logic of these events.

Implications of cryptomnesia for art

What, according to Jung, are the implications of these examples of cryptomnesia? In the first place, the conviction that not only can contents of human consciousness disappear into the unconscious, but they can resurface without one being aware of it. Jung identified many kinds of such contents: desires, impulses, intentions, affections, observances, intuitions, etc. All this material can be unconsciously stored, either fully or partially, temporarily or permanently.[31] On all kinds of occasions it can again disclose itself to our consciousness. Most of the time we remain unaware of this. Jung wrote about how he once told a friend that apparently he had recently ended an unhappy relationship with his girlfriend. When his friend, astounded, asked him how he knew, Jung answered that during the past ten minutes he had heard him whistle three tunes (of which one was: *Abandoned, abandoned am I!*) which had made it quite obvious. His friend had not even been aware that he was whistling these tunes![32]

Sometimes we accidentally notice some 'intruders from the unconscious', but it is apparent, said Jung, that our unconscious must 'swarm' with these 'strange intruders'. We do not know where they come from and most of the time we are not even aware that they are present! We are ignorant of the hundreds of associations and combinations we create each day. "By far the greater part of the psychic elements in us is unconscious. Our consciousness therefore finds itself

30 Goethe 1913, Vol. 2: 48.
31 See Jung 1961/1977: 203.
32 See Jung 1905/1957: 97.

in a rather precarious position with regard to automatic movements of the unconscious that are independent of our will."[33]

Second, Jung thought that these examples suggest a close connection between cryptomnesia and creative processes. He was convinced that the so-called surprising novelties of an artist, his originality, can for an important part be explained by cryptomnesia. An artist's 'hidden memory' functions optimally, even though he usually does not realise it.[34] Just like the professor in the example, his stream of daily thoughts will suddenly be interrupted. He receives what is called inspiration. This happens because his 'nostrils' are wide open and he unconsciously smells all significant odours. When images, forms, sounds, etc. resurface through cryptomnesia, they are at the same time 'strange' and 'original'. But strangeness and originality are not far apart. Jung wrote: "Strangeness and original creation are (...) closely allied to one another, if we remember the numerous witnesses in *belles-lettres* to the 'possessed' nature of the genius."[35] Subsequently, if it is true that the personal unconscious contains forbidden feelings, desires and thoughts, it means that a work of art can be experienced as liberating or taboo-breaking when the artist allows the release of forbidden material.

It is common to speak of 'possession' when thinking of artists. But possession is not an exclusive characteristic of artists nor is it extraordinary. In fact, the professor was also unconsciously 'possessed' by experiences from his childhood. Nonetheless, it has become a specific term with respect to artists, exactly for the reason that works of art come across as 'strange' and 'original'. There are artists who are surprised that they somehow unconsciously understood the 'signs of the times'. Hence, they must have the feeling that they are 'somehow' driven by a demon or a muse! In the case of the professor, Goethe 'in love' and the whistling friend, the unconscious obviously 'knew' what was desired.

Whether an artist is aware of it or not, according to Jung, the creative process always operates in such a way that it unconsciously drives the artist. When trying to give words to this experience, one usually says that one is driven by 'higher powers'. However, it is actually the 'powers from below' which are operating, arising from the unconscious.

33 See Jung 1905/1957: 98.

34 "What poet or composer has not been so beguiled by certain of his ideas as to believe in their novelty? We believe what we wish to believe. Even the greatest and most original genius is not free from human wishes and their all-too-human consequences" (Jung 1905/1957: 99): In 1946, Jung wrote: "For, in the last resort, we are conditioned not only by the past, but by the future, which is sketched out in us long beforehand and gradually evolves out of us. *This is especially the case with a creative person who does not at first see the wealth of possibilities within him, although they are all lying there already.* So it may easily happen that one of these still unconscious aptitudes is called awake by a 'chance' remark or by some other incident, without the conscious mind knowing exactly what has awakened, or even that anything has awakened at all. Only after a comparatively long incubation period does the result hatch out" (Jung 1946/1954: 110, italics mine).

35 Jung 1902/1957: 82.

Is the 'insane' mind a source of creativity?

Jung frequently established how powerless the mind is against the violence of unconscious impulses when 'hidden memories' manifest themselves. Each day, he recognised this in his psychotic patients. It was wondrous to observe that when their brains sometimes sank into almost complete twilight, unimpaired fragments of 'hidden memories' could suddenly surface. Jung gave several examples. There was a woman who could, for hours uninterruptedly, portray in great detail all the porters she had met during her life (including their families, children and the design of their room): if people had consciously asked her to perform this task she would not have been capable of this achievement. Jung stated: "The work of genius is different in the way that it fetches up these distant fragments *in order to* build them into a new and meaningful structure."[36] The mentally disturbed person is not capable building fragments into a new and meaningful structure. But the artist is. Nonetheless, the layer of the psyche from where the 'porters' resurface is the same layer that generates a work of art.

In his 1905 article on cryptomnesia, Jung noticed how close the relation between 'abnormal' and 'normal' psychic phenomena is and asked the question: Does the genius have similar traits as the insane? Are art and insanity perhaps related to each other? With respect to this issue, Jung took a position which he would essentially never change, even though he had to pay a high price for it. Most of the time, however, critics did not understand his real intention. For example, in 1932 he stated: "Picasso's psychic problems, so far as they find expression in his work, are strictly analogous to those of my patients."[37] His critics not only overlooked the word 'analogous', but furthermore could not grasp that Jung absolutely did not say that Picasso was a schizophrenic, nor understand that he certainly did not say that his paintings were psychiatric products.

What Jung intended to say was the fruit of his depth-psychological insights, which he had already formulated in 1905. In his article on cryptomnesia he wrote about the relationship between insanity and art. He asked himself: "What kind of people seek new combinations? They are the men of thought, who have finely differentiated brains coupled with the sensitivity of a woman and the emotionality of a child. They are the slenderest, most delicate branches on the great tree of humanity: they bear the flower and the fruit. Many become brittle too soon, many break off. Differentiation creates in its progress the fit as well as the unfit; wits are mingled with nitwits – there are fools with genius and geniuses with follies, as Lombroso has remarked."[38]

At present, no one risks referring to Cesare Lombroso (1835–1909). He has an exceptionally bad scientific reputation. Lombroso was the founding father of the positivistic movement in criminology. He was stigmatised because of his opinion

36 Jung 1905/1957: 105 (italics mine).
37 Jung 1932/1978a: 135.
38 Jung 1905/1957: 99.

that there exists something like a 'born criminal' and that one can determine someone's nature, for instance, by the size of the skull. It did not make a difference that it gave Lombroso a reason to treat prisoners humanely (essentially they were not to blame!) or that he adjusted his theory by including social factors. Lombroso became taboo. However, in 1905, the professor in medical law and psychiatry at Turin still had a worldwide reputation. Lombroso was compulsory literature for every student of psychiatry. Jung did not indicate which work by Lombroso he had in mind in his 1905 article. That was unnecessary. Every reader knew: *Genius and Insanity*, published in 1882. In that book, as well as in others, Lombroso elaborated upon his view that artistic genius is a form of inherited insanity and that products of insane people are similar to those of artists. He collected a large amount of work created by psychiatric patients.

What did Jung discover in Lombroso's work? Although he never adhered to his positivistic trend in psychiatry, Jung always stayed sensitive to empirical facts. He placed this material within his own analytical context. In one of his speeches as a student, in May 1897, he called Lombroso "the renowned anthropologist and psychiatrist". He referred to him as an example of a grand empirical psychologist and quoted his "classical confession": 'I pride myself on being the slave of facts.' This appealed to Jung. Nevertheless, unlike Lombroso, he would never be content merely with sensorial facts and emphasised that the psyche knows its own 'facts'. Moreover, Jung always avoided metaphysical speculation. And for this reason he felt at home with Lombroso, particularly because as an empiricist he had spoken in favour of a "belief in spiritualism".[39]

Jung did not want to have anything to do with a 'floating' spirit. He would never separate psychical phenomena from their physical component. "Psychology, though formerly counted a discipline of philosophy, is today a natural science and its subject-matter is not a mental product but a natural phenomenon, i.e. the psyche. As such it is among the elementary manifestations of organic nature, which in turn forms one half of our world, the other half being the inorganic."[40]

In his *Transformations and Symbolisms of the Libido*, published in 1912, Jung referred to Lombroso and inserted an elaborate quote from his work. This quotation is important with respect to our subject: the relationship between psychiatry and art. It is taken from *Genius and Insanity*. According to Jung, Lombroso described in this passage "the pathological fantasy concerning two insane artists". Lombroso wrote: 'One of these artists was endowed with a true artistic sense. He painted a picture in which he was just in the act of creation; the world came forth from his anus; the membrum was in full erection; he was naked, surrounded by women, and with all insignia of his power.'[41] The manner in which Jung analysed this information and adopted it within the context of

39 Jung 1983: 35.
40 Jung 1946/1954: 89–90.
41 Quoted in Jung 1912/1944: 117.

his own psychology is of great importance to us. In the following I will expand upon this. Lombroso would hardly have recognised himself within this depth psychological vision.

As was mentioned above, *Transformations and Symbolisms of the Libido*, just like Jung's dissertation, deals with hallucinations. The hallucinations were experienced by an American student of Flournoy. She relayed her paranormal fantasies under the pseudonym Miss Frank Miller. Flournoy translated the English survey into French and published it in 1906.[42] This article formed Jung's point of departure for his first *magnum opus*.

In one of Miss Miller's hallucinations, her great hero, the Aztec Indian Chiwantopel, played a main role. This great warrior became involved in a great drama, ending with his decomposition. Whilst he was decaying into dirt and shit, a smoking volcano erupted and an earthquake took place. How is it possible, Jung wondered, that this potent, heroic spirit was so closely affiliated with the 'out-of-the-way regions of the body' which fart and defecate? In other words, why did all this filthy piss and shit occur exactly at this point in Miss Miller's fantasy? Which psychic mechanism was at work here? Jung wrote: "In order to understand this [i.e. Miss Miller's 'out-of-the-way regions of the body' – fantasies] we have to realise that when something is produced from the unconscious, the first thing to come up is the infantile material that has long been lost to memory. We have, therefore, to adopt the points of view of that time, when this material was still on the surface. So if a much venerated object [here Chiwantopel] is related by the unconscious to the anal region, we have to conclude that this is a way of expressing respect and attention, such as the child feels for these forbidden functions. Naturally traces of this infantile interest still linger on in the adult."[43]

How should we understand Jung's words? To begin with, we ascertain that this case (again) concerns a case of cryptomnesia. The "infantile material that has long been lost to memory" resurfaces as 'hidden memories'. Miss Miller was unaware of this. She could not imagine that this 'filth' came forth from her. However, Jung established that for a child anal processes are normal. He gave multiple examples of the importance a child attaches to the process of defecation. It is of great productive value, especially because for many children defecation and reproduction are closely linked. "The child thinks: that is how things are produced, how they 'come out'".[44] Furthermore, Jung showed how many fairy tales and myths, especially in religious stories, include elements which are connected to 'the anal'. "The toilet is well known as the place of dreams where much is created that would later be considered unworthy of this place of origin. Lombroso recounts a

42 Flournoy's article is entitled: 'Some facts of the subconscious creative imagination' (see Jung 1952/1956: 446).

43 Jung 1952/1956: 189. I quote from the edition published in 1952: it is almost the same formulation as the one in the 1912 edition, but Jung improved the final sentence in the 1952 edition (see Jung 1912/1944: 116).

44 Jung 1952/1956: 190.

pathological fantasy..."[45] What follows is the Lombroso quotation about the painting of the insane artist cited above.

On the painting one sees the artist creating the world from his anus. Once more, we must acknowledge that it concerns cryptomnesia. 'Normal' adults almost completely censure the lust and assertiveness they experienced during the anal phase of their lives. But neither in the medium Miss Miller nor in the pathological artist does this censure function. The artist portrayed the process of creation analogous to the way he defecated as a child, and in the same way Miss Miller erupted a volcano in Chiwantopel.

"A much venerated object is related by the unconscious to the anal region." This is what it is about. In our childhood we were still *conscious* of these anal processes and experienced them as 'creating something', 'achieving' and 'being creative'. But as we grew up, also because of culturally defined feelings of shame, these experiences disappeared into the unconscious where they live a dormant life. But as a result of some strong 'impulse' the censure is broken and the 'hidden memory' becomes a fact.

Time and time again the unconscious is *triggered*. Anal drives are attracted by the painting, memories of youth by the smell of geese, songs by heartache, a children's story by Zarathustra, a grey mantle by the beloved. This core mechanism is activated during the creative process of the artist. With respect to each theme, the *open mind* of the artist gives the unconscious all space to stage 'hidden memories' in sound, speech or image.

At this point it is important to ascertain that, even though the mechanism of 'hidden memories' plays a role in a mentally disturbed person as well as in an artist, Jung thought that there is *no direct causal relationship* between mental illness and an artist's fervour when he is in the process of creating. A mental ailment in itself is not a breeding ground for the creation of art and being a genius is not per definition coupled to a mental illness. In this respect, there can be no doubt about Jung's view. Central in all these different examples is the phenomenon of cryptomnesia. At numerous moments the unconscious brings 'hidden memories' into the conscious spotlight. On all these occasions we notice that the censure of the conscious is played down in one or way or another. The source of the memory remains hidden! This phenomenon is present in the professor, the lover, the artist, the mentally ill, the hallucinator and the genius. In all these examples, consciousness is deceived and has a great sensitivity and receptivity. The reason is that all of them somehow have an *unrestrained consciousness*. This means that art and insanity in themselves are *not* related to each other. However, both the artist and the person with a mental illness have a kind of unrestrained consciousness and the floodgates to the unconscious are open so that 'hidden memories' arise more easily.

This does not imply that there are (have been) no mentally ill artists. Lord Byron (1788–1824), Robert Schumann (1810–1856), Vincent van Gogh

45 Jung 1952/1956: 190.

(1853–1890), and the Dutch authors Gerrit Achterberg (1905–1962) and Maarten Biesheuvel (b. 1939) are certainly mentally ill according to the present criteria. But it needs to be acknowledged that they are artists *despite* their mental illness, not because of it.[46] We also know that some artists used opium and cannabis to loosen the control of their consciousness. The poets Charles Baudelaire (1821–1867), Paul Verlaine (1844–1896) and Arthur Rimbaud (1854–1891) are famous examples. One can accept that drugs facilitated the creative process; but it did not necessarily improve or cause the quality of the creative process itself, the poetic echelon of their poems. Without a doubt, one can be a great artist without being mentally ill or without using opium. When a psychiatric patient knows how to create a work of art, and there are many examples of this, the reason is that he or she is an *artist*. What is created is not a psychiatric product but an artistic product.

In 1932, Jung said in a lecture: "it would never occur to an intelligent layman to mistake a pathological phenomenon for art, in spite of the undeniable fact that a work of art arises from much the same psychological conditions as a neurosis. This is only natural, because certain of these conditions are present in every individual (...) whether in the case of a nervous intellectual, a poet or a normal human being."[47] Certain psychical conditions are always present. Of course, Jung said in the same lecture that one can subject an artist to medical treatment and study for instance his neurotic fantasies. In this way one can research Nietzsche's brain: "But what would this have to do with *Zarathustra?* Whatever its subterranean background may have been, is it [the work of art] not a whole world in itself, beyond the human, all-too-human imperfections, beyond the world of migraine and cerebral atrophy? (...) In order to do justice to a work of art, analytical psychology must rid itself entirely of medical prejudice; for a work of art is not a disease, and consequently requires a different approach from the medical one."[48]

It is likely that artists in general, because of their predisposition to relax control of their consciousness, are more mentally vulnerable and more open to mood changes than persons without this predisposition. When an artist suffers from a psychosis now and again, it will scarcely foster the process of art. Research on the creative episodes of the composer Schumann ascertained that he hardly composed anything during times of severe depression.[49] In our present time, he probably would have had much less hindrance of these mood disorders through the use of anti-psychotics. However, there is the question of whether this would have caused a loss of his creativity. Because these medications resist the release of the control of our consciousness! What would Schumann have done if a medicinal treatment had led to a flatness in his creativity?

Therefore, Jung refused to consider a direct relationship between insanity and art. He even considered it dangerous for art to stigmatise the artist as neurotic and

46 See Kortmann 2000. Some information in this paragraph is derived from this survey.
47 Jung 1922/1978: 67.
48 Jung 1922/1978: 69, 71.
49 See Kortmann 2000: 561.

was suspicious towards neurotics who present themselves as artists. In 1926, he said in a lecture at London: "Disease has never yet fostered creative work; on the contrary, it is the most formidable obstacle to creation."[50] When he republished these lectures in 1946, strongly improved and with additions, he added certain thoughts (which I partially quoted in the preface). If one fails to distinguish between the creative and the insane person, Jung wrote: "the creative individual immediately suspects himself of some kind of illness. While the neurotic has lately begun to believe that his neurosis is an art, or at least a source of art. These would-be artists, however, develop one characteristic symptom: they all shun psychology like the plague, because they are terrified that this monster will devour their so-called artistic ability. As if a whole army of psychologists could do anything against the power of a god! True productivity is a spring that can never be stopped. Is there any trickery on earth which could have prevented Mozart or Beethoven from creating? Creative power is mightier than his possessor. If it is not so, then it is a feeble thing, and given favourable conditions will nourish an endearing talent, but no more."[51]

But what exactly did Jung mean when making the above mentioned statement "that Picasso's psychic problems, so far as they find expression in his work, are strictly analogous to those of my patients"? Are art and insanity not suspiciously alike in this statement? To begin with, Jung does not say that Picasso is mentally ill. After he was heavily criticised because of these words, he unambiguously stated: "I regard neither Picasso nor Joyce as psychotics."[52] Jung is saying that an artist can use certain 'psychic problems' as *themes* for his work. For certain (contemporary) reasons, one can depict the schizophrenic or split human personality on canvas. In other words, the artist can elaborate upon morbid themes. This does not imply that the work of art itself is a morbid product, nor that it was a morbid mind which portrayed these themes. Again, this does not imply that Picasso could not have had a morbid mind. But that does not have anything to do with his art. Furthermore, Jung rightly ascertained that the psychic problems which Picasso depicted are "strictly analogous to those of my patients". Picasso's paintings occasionally bring us eye to eye with the "modern" split human person.

The collective unconscious and cryptomnesia

One important idea is missing in the 1905 cryptomnesia article: the "collective unconscious". In Jung's theory, it became the psychological reservoir of the artist. He was already developing this key concept in those years. Nonetheless, there was a surprising complication regarding the idea of cryptomnesia.[53] The reason is that

50 Jung 1946/1954: 115.
51 Jung 1946/1954: 115.
52 Jung 1932/1978a: 137, f. 3.
53 In Chapter 4, I will elaborate upon the collective unconscious. Here I will outline this phenomenon only in its relationship to cryptomnesia.

cryptomnesia exists by the grace of a *personal* unconscious (the composer personally heard a tune as a child and has forgotten it); if Jung wanted to prove that images which could not possibly stem from the personal unconscious can arise into consciousness, he had to demonstrate that these images could not be the result of cryptomnesia.

The famous story of Jung's discovery of the collective unconscious took place in those years. It is the story of the 'Solar Phallus Man'.[54] The severely mentally ill Emile Schwyzer was admitted into the Burghölzli clinic in 1901. In his delusions – Schwyzer thought he was God – he thought he could move the 'Solar Phallus'. By shaking his head up and down, he propelled the wind, which caused an upward movement. In 1902 Jung became interested in the hallucinations of this man. In his view, this man could not know that his hallucination was related to a universal mythological image. He was keen to prove that Schwyzer had not previously seen an image of the Solar Phallus in a magazine or in a painting nor had read something about it.[55] Hence, he could not have stored the image of the Solar Phallus in his personal unconscious. Subsequently, there had to be a collective unconscious from which such images originate spontaneously.

Taking everything into consideration, this, too, is a case of cryptomnesia, although with a collective nature. It is a collective storage of messages, whereby the memory of its source is lost collectively. Jung historian Sonu Shamdasani wrote in *Jung and the Making of Modern Psychology*: 'In essence, what Jung was proposing was a radical extension of Flournoy's concept of cryptomnesia. He was claiming that it wasn't only memories of impressions gained during one's lifetime that reappeared in unrecognised forms, but also memories of the race. This concept forms an important stage in the development of his thinking. It could be termed 'phylo-cryptomnesia.'[56] Shortly before his death in 1961, Jung wrote that "really new thoughts and creative ideas can appear which have never been conscious before. They grow up from the dark depths like a lotus, and they form an important part of the subliminal psyche."[57]

At the end of this chapter one question becomes pressing: What is the reason that at a certain moment *this* 'hidden memory' arises rather than another? The answer to this question determines the subject of the next chapter. The answer is: Because *this* memory is *imbued with more affect* than another and is therefore

54 See Bair 2003: 171–190.

55 I am well aware that this whole episode is only briefly and superficially mentioned here. An exceptional amount is written on its historical and theoretical importance. I am concerned with only one aspect of this hallucination: its character of collective cryptomnesia.

56 Shamdasani 2005a: 218. 'Phylo' (not to be confused with 'philo' = loving) is derived from the Greek *phulon* = tribe, dynasty, species. 'Phylo-genesis' means *the development of a species*, for example that of the human species. 'Onto-genesis' means the development of one particular being within that species, from ovum to adulthood. Therefore one can speak of an onto- and a phylo-cryptomnesia. The first describes the 'hidden memories' of a particular human individual, the second describes those of the whole human species.

57 Jung 1961/1977: 198. Subliminal literally means 'underneath the threshold' of consciousness.

more forceful. Why did Jung's friend unconsciously whistle his songs? Because his feelings of 'abandonment' were so forceful that they could not be suppressed. They arose unbidden; one has to say, with compulsion. This strong affect plays a role in all the examples cited. Strong experiences from one's youth (the professor), strong experiences of love (Goethe), a thrilling children's book (Nietzsche): they all have a strong libido.

Jung called this compound of strong affects searching for an outlet a 'complex'. Complexes can have different natures, including an artistic nature. During his years at the Burghölzli, Jung became famous for his complex theory. For a while, his psychology was called 'complex psychology'. I will elaborate upon this key concept in the next chapter.

Chapter 2

Art, a product of an 'autonomous complex'

> "We would do well, therefore, to think of the creative process as a living thing implanted in the human psyche. In the language of analytical psychology this living thing is an autonomous complex."
>
> (Jung 1922/1978: 75)

Complexes are "the living units of the unconscious psyche". The creative process is such a living unit, implanted in the soul of the human person like a tree in the earth from which it draws its nourishment. Art is an autonomous complex rather than a derivative of the sexual complex. Jung's Russian patient Sabina Spielrein exercised a major influence on him with respect to this subject. The artistic qualities of the human person have animal roots, this was already established by Darwin, and are not the result of some infantile repression. In and through the "artistic drive" the creative process is propelled "from below upwards" and receives within the psyche a "radiating" numinous aspect.

A difficult start to a career

In 1900, it was hard for Jung to adjust to his first employment at the Burghölzli. He soon realised that it was not only he who knew little or nothing about what was going on in the tormented minds of his patients; his colleagues were equally ignorant in this respect. However, this did not seem to trouble them nor did they consult any research. Jung worked frantically through all 50 volumes of the *Allgemeine Zeitschrift für Psychiatrie*, but found little of value in them.[58] Furthermore, he could not share his broad interests in *Weltanschauung*. He missed the lively discussions about theological, philosophical and literary subjects that he had been accustomed to in Basel. His first period at the Burghölzli was therefore marked by psychic confusion. When his mother came to visit him once and found his room completely covered with graphs, charts and lists of his word association tests, she asked him with her inscrutable voice (his mother

58 See Hannah 1977: 78.

had two voices; an everyday one and a primaeval one): 'And, do you think this means something?' He really did not know. His mother was one of the few people who could upset him.[59] In many respects, Zürich was like a cold shower for the graduate from Basel.

Jung needed a sabbatical. He asked his director, Eugen Bleuler (1857–1939), to allow him to attend the classes of the professor of psychiatry Pierre Janet (1859–1947) in Paris, during the winter seminar of 1902–1903. He wanted to study the unconscious psyche of the psychiatric mind. At the time, Paris was famous for its progressive research on this subject. Freud also went to Paris to study with Janet's predecessor, Jean-Martin Charcot (1825–1893). However, his director did not give him permission and to everyone's astonishment, Jung resigned. Everyone knew how much he needed a salary, but no one knew that he was about to be engaged (on 6 October 1902) to his future wife, Emma Rauschenbach (1882–1955), daughter of one of the wealthiest manufacturing families in Switzerland. His chronic lack of money was soon to belong to the past.

He went to Paris in October 1902 and furthered his insights there. Back in Switzerland, he married Emma on 14 February 1903. After their honeymoon, in April 1903, he returned to work at the clinic. First he replaced several physicians who had been called to serve military duty. Gradually, he became immersed in all kinds of scientific research and worked fanatically. Emma helped him to work on his notes. In the spring of 1904, they moved into an apartment that was walking distance from the Burghölzli. He began to feel at home in the clinic, Basel fading into the background, and he asked Bleuler for permanent employment, which he took up in October 1904. From then until 1907, Jung applied himself to the study of the theme which would make him famous, even before he became acquainted with Freud.

A major discovery: The complex

Jung's complex theory was a result of his research with word-association tests, which he carried out together with his young colleague Franz Riklin (1878–1938) from the spring of 1901. This test examines conscious streams of thoughts. Jung took it very seriously, refined the technique and discovered methods to qualify and quantify reactions more precisely. During the experiments, a person was given some 'incentive words' and was asked to react to each of them with a spontaneous 'responsive word'. Jung was intrigued and irritated by the *disturbances* in the clients' flow of thoughts. There were hindrances which at first sight seemed inexplicable. Because the instruments were so refined (measuring pulse, blood pressure and perspiration), he could accurately measure the differences in reaction and the reaction time. 'Suddenly' a client would have difficulty articulating a word or would be blocked by what seemed to be a common word. For one or another dark reason, the sequence of associations would stop, the client would become

59 See Bair 2003: 66.

tense, what he was saying would no longer make sense, and he would utter explanations or fall silent. At first sight, there was no explanation for this behaviour. This intrigued Jung and he wanted to 'discover' its meaning. One day, he realised he had encountered the reality of the unconscious; the exact reason why he had chosen this occupation.

In a seminar in 1925, Jung recalled this period. He talked about the derogatory response from those around him regarding his choice of psychiatry. Their comment was: 'Well, we always thought you were crazy, and now we know it!' Jung continued: "I told nobody that I intended to work out the unconscious phenomena of the psychoses, but that was my determination. I wanted to catch the intruders of the mind – the intruders that make people laugh when they should not laugh, and cry when they should not cry. When I developed my association tests it was the defects that the tests brought out that held my interest. I made careful notes of the places where people could not accomplish the experiments, and out of these observations I came to my theory of autonomous complexes being the cause of the blockage in the flow of libido."[60]

Jung noticed that series of answers could form a certain pattern. He was not interested in the fact that clients responded differently to the same word, but he saw that these differences showed a symptomatic pattern. As if there were focal points in the psyche which caused a clustering of certain drives. Jung began to call these focal points 'complexes', literally 'compounded units'. The concept of the complex had already been introduced in 1898 by the professor of psychiatry Theodor Ziehen (1862–1950), but Jung appropriated the concept in such a way that Ziehen did not recognise his own ideas. Whereas for Ziehen the complex was merely a conscious phenomenon, Jung discovered that the word association tests opened a door to the unconscious. He realised that the complex was the same as what Janet called an *idée fixe subconsciente* (unconscious fixed idea).

A client was usually unaware of such drives and even if he was aware he could still not prevent them from resurfacing repeatedly. The reactions were autonomous, unintentional, fused with affect and bound to the individual. Psychic energy was compounded into a focus which was specific to that person. Reactions were also stereotyped. For example, the aspect 'father' could resurface arbitrarily. Jung spoke of this as a 'father complex'. An 'inferiority complex' was when a dark feeling of inferiority was attached to all kinds of situations.

A complex can be described as a collection of ideas and images which are clustered around unconscious drives. "Complexes are not entirely morbid by nature but are *characteristic expressions of the psyche* (...) they are in truth the living units of the unconscious psyche."[61] They are not only reactive, but can also be creative on certain occasions. Our conscious logic always perceives complexes as ambiguous, illogical and sometimes unmanageable. They can either decelerate or stimulate consciousness. But they are necessary for life, as they prevent psychic

60 Jung 1926/1989: 7–8.
61 Jung 1934/1960: 101.

activity from coming to a standstill. They start to move when the psychic system is without equilibrium. Through a fantasy or a wish they can force themselves upon consciousness from the inner world, whereas at other times the outer world gives rise to this energy. The ability of the ego to deal with this surge of energy is important for one's psychic health. When it is strong enough, it can organise the stream of energy into an orderly structure, put boundaries to it and realise ideas. But the ego can also be flooded by a complex.

Complexes are 'parts of the psyche' in the dark realms of the unconscious where they exist independently from consciousness. Nonetheless, they are related to our conscious personal experiences. For example, a mother complex arises on the one hand from the many experiences of the physical mother (and mother-figures), but on the other hand from the mother-images stored in the unconscious. Its strength will increase when the conscious I has a positive relationship with such a complex and knows how to integrate its powers. But psychic tensions will manifest themselves when there is a negative relationship. Hence, the complex positively or negatively colours an experience.

In 1906, Jung recorded his discoveries in *Studies in Word Association* and sent a copy to Freud in Vienna. Freud was pleased and also thrilled that there was another explorer of the unconscious. He replied that he had already bought the book. Jung himself had found, independently from Freud, the unwavering clue for the existence and the functioning of the unconscious psyche. For the rest of his life, the complexes would pave, alongside dreams, the royal road to the unconscious.

The main subject of Jung's inaugural lecture held at the Technical School of Advanced Education in Zürich, on 5 May 1934, was his complex theory. He presented a comprehensive exploration of the subject. He said: "Where the realm of the complexes begins the freedom of the ego comes to an end, for complexes are psychic agencies whose deepest nature is still unfathomed. For they are part of something that directly affects all that is uncontrolled in man – the *numinosum*, to use an apt expression of Rudolf Otto."[62]

In 1917, the theologian Rudolf Otto (1869–1937) wrote in *The Idea of the Holy* that the basis of all religion is found in an irrational experience of a 'fascinating and terrifying mystery', which he called 'numinous'. Otto's vision influenced Jung throughout his entire life. The 'numinous', he thought, is not only a source of religion, but also of sexuality, science and … art. In his work as a doctor of souls, this numinous reality was close to his heart. On 28 August 1945 he wrote in a letter to the British psychologist P. W. Martin: "You are quite right, the main interest of my work is not concerned with the treatment of neuroses but rather with approaching the numinous. But the fact is that approaching the numinous is the real therapy and inasmuch as you arrive at numinous experiences you are released from the curse of pathology."[63]

62 Jung 1934/1960: 104.
63 Jung 1973: 377.

The complex is not caused by an arbitrary, conscious personal deed; no, it seizes a person on the inside and controls him; he becomes 'possessed' by it. This is true for the mystic, the beloved and the scientist. And for the artist. From the very start, Jung realised that artistic creative processes are also clustered around a specific complex. In 1912, he wrote about theatre: "From the viewpoint of analytical psychology, the theatre, besides any aesthetic value, may be considered as an institution for the group-treatment of the complex. The enjoyment of the comedy, or of the dramatic plot ending happily is produced by an unreserved identification of one's own complexes with the play. The enjoyment of tragedy lies in the thrilling yet satisfactory feeling that something which might occur to one's self is happening to another."[64]

A work of art is an aesthetically formulated artistic complex. An artist is not necessarily conscious of this. Whereas the mentally ill person is flooded by a complex from time to time, the artist's ego is strong enough to channel the energy of a complex into an artistic structure without succumbing to it. As early as 1905, in Jung's cryptomnesia article, one can find a passage about the complexes that drive an artist: "The genius, too, has to bear the brunt of an outsize psychic complex; if he can cope with it, he does so with joy, if he can't he must painfully perform the 'symptomatic actions' which his gift lays upon him: he writes, paints, or composes what he suffers. This applies more or less to all productive individuals. Tapping the depths of the psyche, the instinctively functioning complex sends up its unknown and inexhaustible treasury of countless thoughts to its slave 'consciousness', some old and some new, and consciousness must deal with them as best as it can. It must ask each thought: Do I know you, or are you new? But when the daemon drives, consciousness has no time to finish its sorting work, the flood pours into the pen – and the next day it is perhaps already printed."[65]

Comparing Jung and Freud

A good way to get a sharp view of Jung's ideas about the complex is to compare them with those of Freud. Freud acknowledged the existence of only one complex: the sexual complex. It could change shape and, for example, form the concealed drive of the *caritas* of a nurse or the creative process of an artist. It could also be found in the enjoyment of a good meal. But on the whole it was always the operation of a disguised sexual complex. Jung had always considered this position too one-sided, even before he personally knew Freud.

Of course, Jung realised that the sexual complex is one of the strongest 'separated partial psyches' in a person, capable of affecting everything. Take for instance 'falling in love'. When a person falls in love, he experiences almost all his other drives as 'stained' by the sexual libido. Such a complex can control the

64 Jung 1912/1944: 22.
65 Jung 1905/1957: 100.

entire psyche, but this does not necessarily imply that the other drives are simply reductions of the sexual drive. When a poet writes a poem, the sexual drive can provide a tremendous surplus of libido, especially when it is a love poem, but Jung could never accept that the *process of making a poem* itself was essentially a sexual affair. In his view, the drives of a creative process are clustered in *an autonomous complex*. As such, he thought, a person also possesses an autonomous complex for religiosity. The general core of these complexes is not their sexual but their numinous nature.

In his study on schizophrenia, published in 1907, Jung distanced himself from Freud. He had written it before he became personally acquainted with Freud. In its preface, dated July 1906,[66] he said that "this does not mean that I attribute to the infantile sexual trauma the exclusive importance that Freud apparently does. Still less does it mean that I place sexuality so predominantly in the foreground, or that I grant it the psychological universality which Freud, it seems, postulates." He added: "Nevertheless, all these things are side issues."[67] In this respect he was mistaken. Or rather, he mistook Freud. Because Freud did not discern a main issue among many, but just *one* issue.

Notwithstanding this preface, in this study Jung showed himself to be a follower of Freud. His Freudian approach is noticeable when reading, for example, the following quotation on the relationship between the sexual complex and art. However, a closer reading reveals that he also relativised Freud's viewpoint: "*The complex must under all circumstances assert itself.* Since, for many people, the sexual complex cannot be acted out in a natural way, it makes use of *by-ways*." He subsequently gave many examples of these by-ways. One of them is the creative process of the artist: "Artistic natures in particular are wont to benefit by such displacements [of the sexual drive]." And in a footnote Jung added: "Freud calls this 'sublimation'."[68] Freud, who probably raised his eyebrows when reading the preface, must have consented with these last sentences. But it is clear that, even in this early text, Jung already differed considerably from Freud.

In the footnote mentioned above, Jung referred to one of Freud's classic works, published a year earlier (1905): *Three Essays on the Theory of Sexuality*. In this study, Freud described the normal development of the 'natural and general ability of the libido'. This meant, he thought, undergoing a process of maturation via psychic inhibitions.[69] This is his classic treatise on the oral, anal and genital phases in the development of the sexual libido. But Freud stated that there are also 'abnormal dispositions' of this urge. He expanded upon three dispositions: perverse sexual behaviour, repression and sublimation. He thought that sublimation could be applied to creative processes. He described 'sublimation' as a process in

66 Their first encounter took place in Vienna on 2 March 1907.

67 Jung 1907/1960: 4.

68 Jung 1907/1960: 49, 50.

69 See Freud 1930: 134.

which 'powerful excitations from individual sources of sexuality are discharged and utilised in other spheres', and added that it results in 'a considerable increase of psychic capacity'. This is followed by the passage to which Jung referred: 'This forms one of the sources of artistic activity, and, according as such sublimation is complete or incomplete, the analysis of the character of highly gifted, especially of artistically disposed people, will show any proportionate blending between productive ability, perversion and neurosis.'[70]

On which points did Freud and Jung differ? Jung did not write that sexuality can be a *source* of artistic activity. Neither did he consider the artistic temperament to be essentially of a sexual nature, let alone of a suppressed nature. However, he had no difficulty accepting that the sexual drive can 'flow over into', can 'shift' (the poet in love, for example), but that is different from reducing the artistic process to a sexual phenomenon. And Jung certainly did not think of artists as 'abnormal' people. Not only in patients, he wrote, is it possible that images and words can appear in the mind or pass through consciousness, "we find something similar in *normal* people who are dominated by an unusually strong complex, for instance in poets and artists."[71] By contrast, Freud always considered artists as people who are projecting in an 'abnormal' way.

In the above mentioned footnote, Jung was probably not (yet) aware of the 'narrow' scope of Freud's concept of sublimation. Otherwise he would have been more careful to quote him with consent. Jung and Freud met each other in person after this publication, and, with time, Jung began to see more clearly how much they differed in their understanding of the complex. Jung increasingly underlined these differences.

For example, ten years later, in 1917, he wrote with annoyance about Freud's one-sided sexual perspective on the artist. Their friendship had ended four years earlier, they had each taken their own position, and it had become unthinkable that Jung would refer to Freud's notion of sublimation. Jung considered artworks as creations originating from a complex which has its own nature, not a sexual one. He wrote to the psychoanalyst Sabina Spielrein that, according to Freud's theory, *Also sprach Zarathustra* was merely the result of Nietzsche's repressed sexuality, while he regarded it as an authentic creation. He thought it impossible to explain such a work of art using Freud's theory. Naturally, Nietzsche will have repressed his sexuality in some way. Is there one poet or thinker, is there one human being who does not suffer from repressed sexuality? But this knowledge will never further our understanding of the unique character of someone's creation.[72]

It is not coincidental that Jung wrote about his annoyance to Spielrein. In the previous years she had played an important role in the development of his ideas, particularly in regard to this specific subject.

70 Freud 1930: 138.
71 Jung 1907/1960: 85 (italics mine).
72 See Covington and Wharton 2003: 52.

Spielrein and Jung

The 19-year-old Sabina Spielrein (see plate 2) was admitted to the Burghölzli clinic on 17 August 1904. She was Jung's patient. Diagnosis: hysteria.[73] She frequently tormented her caregivers to the utmost because of her ailments. However, her behaviour stabilised when they allowed her to join the physicians in their daily hospital rounds. They also allowed her into the hospital laboratory. She became interested in the word-association tests and was enthusiastic when Riklin asked her to assist with measuring. It soon became clear that they were dealing with a highly gifted woman. She felt much better when Jung allowed her one day to observe him whilst he executed a test. She only had her fits when she was expelled from Jung's laboratory. No one seemed to notice that her admiration for him was changing into adoration and her adoration into passion.

Jung saw her several times a week during the summer of 1905, either because he was treating her or because she assisted him with measuring. During that time, Jung's ideas about complexes developed into a full-grown theory. Spielrein was closely involved in this process. That same year, she started to study medicine at the University of Zürich. A passionate relationship developed between them. They wrote each other letters and read each other's diaries. When Spielrein quoted Jung's words, she wrote 'your words' between quotation marks.

No one knew about this relationship until the end of the Seventies, when a box full of papers containing her texts was discovered in a basement in Geneva. Since then the press has not been silent, of course in part because of her intimate relationship with Jung (Emma Jung complained about it to Freud!), but more importantly because of her ideas. She evidently influenced Jung and later also Freud. Jung acknowledged this in a letter written on 25 March 1912. He wrote to her: "Perhaps I borrowed from you too; certainly I have unwittingly absorbed a part of your soul, as you doubtless have mine. What matters is what each of us has made of it."[74]

Spielrein kept a diary in 1906/1907 and excerpts from it were published in 1983.[75] These texts are fascinating, because in them she also developed thoughts about the 'art complex'. Jung will have introduced these ideas to her to some extent, but she undoubtedly discussed these with him. Spielrein wrote: 'Art is only a complex which has found its independence or which "having turned wild, wants to express itself fully" (your words) or "wants to be transformed" (my

73 I use the term 'hysteria' as it was generally used at the beginning of the twentieth century. Patients suffering from paralysis whereby no physical cause could be established were diagnosed with 'hysteria'. They frequently acted excessively emotionally. Currently the term is no longer used. Apart from having a negative connotation it is also too vague. This specific form of paralysis is now diagnosed as Briquet's syndrome whereas the other characteristics of 'hysteria' are now diagnosed as 'borderline personality' or 'theatrical personality' disorders (see van der Molen 1997: 220, 577, 872).

74 Quoted in Covington and Wharton 2003: 46.

75 See Covington and Wharton 2003: 15–31. Spielrein did not date her diary entries. Careful comparative research has shown that they are from 1906 or 1907 (see ibid., 16).

words). When the artist creates, it is not the manifestation of the needs to communicate something to the world. It is rather that the complex itself simply *wants* to emerge!'[76]

No sexual connotations can be found in this description. There are forces operating in the artist which function independently and which are stronger than personal (possibly sexual) needs. One notices from her diary that she considered Jung to be too Freudian. Again and again she pointed out to him at what she considered to be his short-sighted viewpoints. She wrote (her italics): '*All things considered, it is wrong to apply the term "libido" (that is "sexual feeling" in a limited sense) to art or science: the root of affectivity is not a special sexual feeling, but (...) an instinct of transformation which can eventually verge on the sexual side. (...) I must adopt an extreme position where you are concerned because you never admit, in the enthusiasm of your new theories, the possibility of non-sexual transformation.*'[77]

This last sentence is remarkable. It is of course Jung who always underlined the possibility of non-sexual transformation. Obviously not yet in those years – Spielrein is still encountering in him a full-blooded Freudian.

The above quotation was written at the beginning of 1906.[78] This is important, because, as we have seen, one month later, in July 1906, Jung distanced himself from Freud's 'totalitarian' standpoint in the preface of his study on schizophrenia. Did Spielrein influence his views? It certainly looks like it.

Consider, for example, the following lines from her diary in which she quoted Jung (I have italicised that citation): 'As I have already said, complexes that necessitate transformation are not necessarily linked to the sexual complex; thus a painter who has just experienced a storm at sea can eternalise it in a painting without sexual feeling having anything to do with it; but if it intervened nevertheless, it is not the sexual feeling that would have made the artist paint: it is simply the "*complex gone wild which had to emerge, which needed to find full expression*". (...) We are totally ignorant of the cause of feelings, and it is impossible for us ever to know it. One could at the most discuss the foundations of feelings; it is clear to me that the foundation, or the alpha and omega, of feeling is the transformation instinct.'[79]

Spielrein's thoughts must have been appealing to Jung. In 1912, in his first important study, he called this transformation instinct 'libido', thus distancing himself definitively from Freud, for whom the libido was of an exclusively sexual nature. For Freud, 'sexual libido' was a pleonasm. Jung gave his study the telling title *Transformations and Symbolisms of the Libido*. In this study, like Freud, he does not doubt that the sexual instinct, in the strict sense of the word, has the

76 Quoted in Covington and Wharton 2003: 19.

77 Quoted in Covington and Wharton 2003: 27. In her diaries, Spielrein forcefully underlined these sentences with a blue pencil.

78 See Covington and Wharton 2003: 31, footnote 13.

79 Quoted in Covington and Wharton 2003: 24.

tendency to 'flow over into the libidinous'. No one will doubt that, for example, lips whilst kissing are 'overflowing' with sexual potency. But this still does not imply that lips are sexual organs. There are of course many more such examples. No one will doubt that in the case of hysteria[80] there can be an element of strongly suppressed sexuality. But Jung thought that in the case of schizophrenia (in those years still called *dementia praecox*) one can no longer speak of such an 'overflow'. The schizophrenic patient loses all contact with reality during their psychosis and their hallucinations do not seem to have any relationship with personal sexual suppression or anything like it. The fantasy is suddenly and in an astounding manner filled with archaic material. It is difficult to accept that, for example, light, fire or solar symbols are always expressions of a repressed sexual instinct. Several years later, Jung put forward the hypothesis that these instances are the outcome of inherited primaeval impressions: the archetypes. In schizophrenic patients, a general energetic tension is operative in order to work its way out. But it is not necessarily a sexual energy. Jung called this general energetic tension 'libido'.

Spielrein clearly inspired him in this respect. Against the background of her diary entries it is not surprising that Jung, elaborating upon his 'broadening of the understanding of the libido' in *Transformations and Symbolisms of the Libido*, was supported by Spielrein's study of the hallucinations of schizophrenic patients published in 1911. This study was her doctoral thesis.[81] Jung referred to it 17 times. According to him, Spielrein showed that the hallucinations of patients suffering from schizophrenia contain certain material even though it was impossible that they personally could have had previous knowledge of this material. This material has 'obvious characteristics of archaic thinking'. She stated that the most extraordinary images arise in these patients; images belonging to mythical and superstitious thinking.[82] We also recognise them in the symbolism of alchemy. Patients see people being 'boiled' in the niches of an altar, have cosmological visions of the sun and the moon which defy any scientific understanding, use 'mother' images such as 'earth' and 'water', depict alcohol as a 'flood of semen' and so on. Nevertheless, for the patient these symbols adequately express the state of their unconscious. Spielrein found no reason to explain this sexually. She found that these symbols do not bear any relation to actual personal events or repressions. They are surreal. Jung was convinced that they are archaic psychic remains stored in an unconscious which he later described as 'collective'. Spielrein asserted that they are symbols originating from complexes. Jung quoted the following crucial passage from her study: 'Thus a symbol seems to me to owe its origin in general to the tendency of a complex for dissolution in the common totality of thought. The complex is robbed by that of the personal element. This tendency towards dissolution (transformation) of every individual complex *is the motive for poetry,*

80 For the term 'hysteria' see footnote 73.
81 See Spielrein 1911.
82 See Jung 1912/1944: 85.

painting, for every sort of art.'[83] Jung totally agreed with her. He merely corrected her by stating that it is not the complexes which dissolve themselves into libidinal activities such as art (complexes are too strong to be dissolved), but that the libido dissolves itself into complexes. Not an unimportant correction, incidentally.[84]

In Jung's view, the libido is the great, neutral, transforming energetic force. He proposed to understand the libido as 'psychic energies in general'. Psychic energy is a concentrated amount of cosmic energy. One cannot sense or taste energy itself; it is a force/power which relates objects/subjects to each other, attracts them to each other and operates in them. Jung gave an analogous example from the physical world: gravity. Gravity does not say anything about the objects themselves, but about the way they are attracted and rejected.

The libido, this awesome mysterious force keeping the whole universe in motion, also 'comes to the surface' in the psyche of a living human being. It is a powerful irrational force which can either implode or explode. In myths, this primaeval engine received many names: for example, the 'Spirit' which blows where it wants, the 'Logos spermatikos' which fertilises everything, or the androgynous 'Eros' which vibrates within the whole cosmos and sustains it. In humanity, Eros is so explicitly at work between the sexes that it possesses its own form in the winged child of Aphrodite and Ares. This god knows how to 'erotically' move and subdue gods and humanity. Plato's famous dialogue in the *Symposium* mentions the primaeval Eros, the drive for beauty, and we read that it is one of the primal instincts of creativity. In mythology, we constantly perceive a transformation, a metamorphosis of this libidinal force, this lust. In view of the great force of the sexual drive, it is understandable that afterwards the term 'erotic' began to be used in a strictly sexual context. However, the sexual drive is only one aspect of the universal Eros, which permeates the entirety of reality like a dark irrational power, from the sub-atomic world to the cosmic realms. In his *Transformations and Symbolisms of the Libido*, Jung repeatedly quoted from myths which portray the diversity of this force.[85] Myths were his main source for the discovery of the broad range of this force. When he recognised that large parts of these myths arose in the hallucinations of his patients, he became intrigued with the meaning of this correlation.

The libido, he wrote in 1952, "denotes a desire or impulse which is unchecked by any kind of authority, moral or otherwise. Libido is appetite in its natural state. From the genetic point of view it is bodily needs like hunger, thirst, sleep, and sex, and emotional states or affects, which constitute the essence of libido. All these factors have their differentiations and subtle ramifications in the highly complicated human psyche. There can be no doubt that even the highest differentiations were developed from simpler forms."[86]

83 Quoted in Jung 1912/1944: 85 (italics mine).
84 See Jung 1912/1944: 86.
85 See Jung 1952/1956: 137–138.
86 Jung 1952/1956: 135–136.

The 'art complex' has animal roots

Jung saw art as one of those "highest differentiations", one of the "subtle ramifications" which reach back far into evolution. In 1912 he wrote in *Transformations and Symbolisms of the Libido*: "Thus we discover the first instincts of art [Kunsttriebe] in animals used in the service of the impulse of creation, and limited to the breeding season."[87] Reading this sentence, one initially thinks that Freud slipped back in through the back door. Nothing could be less true. At this point, Jung was in discussion with Freud. If it is true that animals have 'instincts of art', this implies that art is not a pure human phenomenon nor a phenomenon of repressed infantile sexuality. We can hardly imagine that animals repress their sexuality. Jung broadened the scope of artistic ability and gave it an animal-biological context. He did not want to get caught in the 'narrow' area of Freudian sublimation.

But what was Jung intending to say in the above quotation? He thought that the mating behaviour we see in animals shows almost all the artistic variations that humanity developed into the fine arts. Theatre, applying colours, producing sounds and dancing. He did not suggest that animals are artists and that they produce art. However, they possess artistic anchors which the human artist will incorporate into the creative process. In whatever way this affiliation may be described, one thing is certain: we have our instinctive sense for the aesthetic in common with animals.

In *The Descent of Man*, Charles Darwin (1809–1882) had already ascertained that there is no separation between the human person and the animal in this respect. He wrote: 'This sense [of beauty] has been declared to be particular to man. (...) When we behold a male bird elaborately displaying his graceful plumes or splendid colours before the female (...) it is impossible to doubt that she admires the beauty of her male partner. (...) If female birds had been incapable of appreciating the beautiful colours, the ornaments, and voices of their male partners, all the labour and anxiety exhibited by the latter in displaying their charms before the females would have been thrown away; and this is impossible to admit.'[88] Darwin showed that animals have preferences for shapes and colours, for order, proportion and symmetry.

Famous is the example of the bower bird which lives in the woods of Australia and New Guinea. The courtship place constructed by the male bower bird exhibits remarkable characteristics that we associate with art. Its construction ('bower') is built with twigs and branches and can rise up to three metres in height. It is not intended to serve as a nest or a shelter, but as a place to attract female birds for the purpose of mating. The bowers are outwardly adorned with flowers, berries and brightly coloured lichens, and smeared on the inside with colours and shiny resins. 'The bird even appears to do a form of painting. It will masticate grass, ash or

87 Jung 1912/1944: 80.
88 Darwin 1877: 92.

berries to generate a coloured slime, which is then spread by beak over the entwined bower walls.'[89] A variety of bottle tops, clothes pegs, shells, glass, shards of porcelain are 'exhibited' in a circle. Dressed up in its feathers, the male bird parades around its bower. Full of bravado, athletic, hissing and stamping about, it tries to impress the grey-brown female that is hiding somewhere and weighing up its options. Of course, the male sings a song. Similarly, the male peacock shows off its feathers. But this is a physical ornament, whereas the bower bird creates something like a 'work of art' that functions independently of its physical appearance.

Darwin is of course right when he states that the male must have good genes in order to have the time and energy to build such a construction. And of course the female bird instinctively looks for good genes when it weighs up whether or not to answer the advances of the male bird, and probably also considers the beautiful items. However, Jung questioned whether the need for good genes *causes* the sense of beauty. Nigel Spivey, whose 'artistic' portrayal of the bower bird I summarised above, asks the following question: 'The bower bird in action is a marvel to behold. But is it a marvel of *art* or sheer reproductive energy?'[90] I think Jung would have given the following answer: neither the one nor the other. The bower bird does not create art (that is a human activity), but neither are its 'creations' merely causally explicable *by* the reproductive urge.

Why does a bird sing its song? Is its song caused by the force of the reproductive drive? Jung answered: "Even if there can be no doubt about the sexual origin of music, still it would be a poor, unaesthetic generalisation if one were to include music in the category of sexuality. A similar nomenclature would then lead us to classify the cathedral of Cologne as mineralogy because it is built of stones."[91]

We can understand Jung as follows. Certainly, in the animal world the 'art drive' surfaces *within* the realm of mating. However, it is the libido 'behind' the mating, the 'psychic energy in general' which *brings* the 'music' *into play* during mating. In the same way, a higher power is operative in the supply of stones for the construction of a cathedral. The cathedral is built from stones, but does not find its artistic reason of existence in the stones and the stones themselves are of a different nature, which is mineral. Music is essentially asexual in nature. But their sexual disposition causes birds to sing, it somehow *triggers* the singing.

Jung could have read this formative thought in Spielrein's diary. She wrote: 'Music, that is again nothing but the "personal expression" or rather more accurately the *expression of the rhythm* of a complex.' And she added: 'I have felt on innumerable occasions that an affect provokes a rhythmic movement: one walks up and down, one rubs one's hands together, one dances or sighs in a rhythmic sequence.'[92] Spielrein knew exactly what she meant. Music is an

89 Spivey 2005: 13.
90 Spivey 2005: 13.
91 Jung 1912/1944: 80.
92 Quoted in Covington and Wharton 2003: 25, 26 (italics mine).

autonomous 'complex' event which is provoked by its own yearnings. This lust-for-rhythm is not only felt in sexual passion. On all kinds of other occasions one can feel this rhythmic impulse, for example during a walk or at a party. On these occasions one does not conclude that walking is the cause of music; it stimulates it. She in fact said that the influence of all the complexes can be so full of libido that a certain rhythmic behaviour flows from it. We cannot resist it. In this way (the art of) music reveals itself.

Libido flows *in* the channels of mating, feeding, and sexual inclination, but does not flow *from* it. There is no *causal* relationship between the sexual drive and for example the drive to music; there is only an *intermediary* or *facilitative* relationship.

Not repression but transformation of the drive

During lectures held in London in May 1924, Jung extensively discussed the subject matter of the relationship between art and instinct. He started with the remark that we do not have any clear ideas with respect to the instincts. How must we distinguish them? How many are there? What are they? He asked for modesty. In any case, he thought it too simplistic to state that all instincts are 'nothing more than' sexuality (Freud) or 'will to power' (Adler). Sometimes one falls from one extreme into the other. "Before Freud nothing was allowed to be sexual, now everything is nothing but sexual."[93]

Jung wondered whether it is possible to start from the hypothesis that there are several instincts. "Consider religious experience, for instance. Can science be so sure that there is no such thing as a 'religious instinct'? (...) The same is true of art, which is likewise supposed to be the result of sexual repressions, although even animals have aesthetic and artistic instincts."[94]

If art is the result of sexual repression then it is sick. That can certainly not be true. Moreover, if the creative force is the result of repression, then there would be no artistic inclination when a person is liberated from repressions. Because there would be nothing left to sublimate. Jung thought this kind of reasoning absurd.[95]

In 1946 Jung republished these lectures, but he edited some parts and made substantial additions. He extensively elaborated upon the different drives of the unconscious. Of course, he stated that the unconscious contains elements which are repressed by our consciousness. That is Freud's truth. But there exists so much more within the unconscious which is not repressed. Jung wrote: "It is not, in my experience, justifiable to assume that the unconscious consists wholly or for the greater part of repressed materials. Repression is an exceptional and abnormal process."[96] He did not deny the reality of repression and even reminds us that he

93 Jung 1946/1954: 84.
94 Jung 1946/1954: 83.
95 "No breaking down of repressions can ever destroy true creativeness" (Jung 1946/1954: 115).
96 Jung 1946/1954: 109.

himself discovered repression through his association experiments. But he considered it ridiculous to conclude from this evidence that the unconscious consists only of repressed material. Once again, he referred to the phenomenon of cryptomnesia.[97] Turning Freudian reasoning around, Jung said: "Why do we not simply accept, what we experience daily anyway, that the unconscious is a living and creative process, and that the unhealthy process of repression is not necessary for the creation of something. (...) Must we really assume that all beauty and magnificence of the human creative act is merely a poor surrogate of infantile primitivity?"[98]

In his discussion with Freud, Jung constantly emphasised the following: art has its own instinctive foundation, it is not a derivative of sexuality and it is certainly not a sublimated, repressed sexuality. Its instinctive roots reach into the animal-biological realm. In and through the complexes, the creative process is propelled from 'below' towards 'above' and receives within consciousness a 'radiant', numinous perspective.

In a striking way Gaillard writes: "It is here, in Jung and Freud's respective relationship to the arts, that the most radical difference between their concepts and respective practices of the unconscious is made apparent. While Freud approaches the unconscious through repression (...) for Jung the unconscious is the constantly renewed origin of consciousness, from which it only partially and provisorily breaks off and disengages; it is an original state always present and highly impersonal. (...) We can always return and re-evoke this state, unexpectedly or in a more deliberate manner, especially when we encounter the arts or when we ourselves are involved in a creative process.'[99]

Art, an autonomous drive

Jung was never as outspoken about the autonomous drive of creativity as in a correspondence with Herman Hesse (1887–1962) in 1934. Hesse responded to an article written by Jung, in which the latter accused Freud of wrongly applying the ancient alchemists' term *sublimatio* in his reductive psychoanalysis. Sublimation is the ancient alchemical art of transforming something without value into

97 "It sometimes happens that even important contents disappear from consciousness without the slightest trace of repression. They vanish automatically, to the great distress of the person concerned and not at all on account of some conscious interest which has engineered the loss and rejoices over it. I am not speaking here of normal forgetting, which is only a natural lowering of energy-tension; I am thinking rather of cases where a motive, a word, image, or person, vanishes without a trace from the memory, to reappear later at some important juncture. These are cases of what is called cryptomnesia" (Jung 1946/1954: 109–110).

98 Jung 1927: 66. Also: "If you assume that the unconscious consists mainly of repressions, you cannot imagine any creative activity in the unconscious. (...) Causalism is exaggerated out of all proportion and the creation of culture is interpreted as a bogus substitute activity" (Jung 1946/1954: 111).

99 Gaillard 2008: 337.

something precious.[100] Hesse thought that Jung was fault-finding, because, in Hesse's view, Freud was close to the ancient alchemists. Repressed sexuality is also something poor, and behold: the nobility of the fine arts arises from it. Jung answered agitatedly:[101] "You do me an injustice with your remarks on sublimation. It is not from resentment that I fight this idea."[102] He emphasised that Freud understands sublimation in terms not of elevation but of repression.

Hesse responded in that same month. His response is interesting, because the theme of art is central to his argument. He was not concerned, he wrote, with defending Freud's view at any cost, because he also considered its scope too narrow. But when it comes down to it, sublimation is related to repression. Of course there is a lot of unhealthy repression, but there is also the case of 'successful repression'. A repressed drive can move itself towards a different but culturally elevated realm, such as art. He included examples from the history of classical music. Generations of masters have offered all their drives, their entire soul, to bring classical music to life. 'Such a classic art is worth every offer.' A gifted person offers part of his instincts to these subjects. Hesse considered this kind of existence of the highest worth even if an individual artist might become pathologically ill because of it. Psychoanalysis might be valuable and fruitful to non-artists, but 'for an artist it is very difficult and dangerous, because, when he takes it seriously, his creative powers might become a forbidden area for the rest of his life. When this happens to a dilettante, that is fine – but when it happens to someone like Händel or Bach, then I would prefer not to have any analysis and keep Bach. Within our category of art, we artists perform a true sublimatio, not by will or from ambition, but by grace.'[103]

Jung responded to Hesse on 1 October: "Naturally we shouldn't quarrel about words. Nevertheless I would note in all humility that the expression 'sublimation' is not appropriate in the case of the artist because with him it is not a question of transforming [Wandlung] a primary instinct *but rather of a primary instinct (the artistic instinct) gripping the whole personality to such an extent that all other instincts are in abeyance, thus giving rise to the work of divine perfection.*"[104]

Jung held a plea for the autonomous operation of the creative process in a human person. It is an autonomous process. This was an outstandingly eccentric and courageous view within a psychoanalytic culture which reduced almost all cultural behaviours to sublimations, projections and illusions.

In conclusion, I will give another beautiful quote which summarises this chapter: "The creative urge lives and grows in him [the artist] like a tree in the

100 See Jung 1932/1978c.
101 See Jung 1973: 171, footnote 2.
102 Jung 1973: 171.
103 Jung 1972/1990: 224–225. The German edition includes a more extensive quotation of Hesse's letter (see Jung 1973: 173).
104 Jung 1973: 173 (italics mine).

earth from which it draws its nourishment. We would do well, therefore, to think of the creative process as a living thing implanted in the human psyche. In the language of analytical psychology this living thing is an *autonomous complex*. It is a split-off portion of the psyche, which leads a life of its own outside the hierarchy of consciousness. Depending on its energy charge, it may appear either as a mere disturbance of conscious activities or as a supraordinate authority which can harness the ego to its purpose."[105]

105 Jung 1922/1978: 75.

Chapter 3

Art is rooted in *participation mystique*

> This re-immersion in the state of *participation mystique* is the secret of artistic creation and of the effect which great art has upon us.
>
> (Jung 1930/1978: 105)

The human person is merely the blossom and fruit of one season, sprung from a centuries old system of roots of which he is an intrinsic part by means of *participation mystique*. The artist in particular knows how to descend into these roots and to excavate the prima materia from the underworld like a true alchemist and to transform it into a work of art. He does this in two ways. Either he enchants this prima materia in abstract forms or he is inebriated by it in organic forms. According to Jung both motives are present in each work of art. The artist descends into the primaeval chaos, but he is not allowed to drown in it.

Empathy and abstraction

Throughout his work Jung was particularly influenced by one theory of art, developed by the art historian Wilhelm Worringer (1881–1965). In 1907, Worringer graduated in Bern with his thesis *Abstraction and Empathy: A Contribution to the Psychology of Style*. When the commercial edition was published in 1908, the book was immensely popular. It became a classic. Jung bought the third edition, published in 1911. Worringer's views were close to his own ideas, even more so because he described works of art from a psychological perspective. Jung was convinced that the subject of art belongs to the study of psychology rather than philosophy. "Aesthetics by its very nature is applied psychology", he writes in 1921.[106] He was certain that important themes in psychology should also be central in the study of aesthetics, for instance the crucial opposites of extraversion and introversion. Worringer explored precisely these opposite attitudes. He called the extraverted attitude *Einfühlung* (empathy) and the introverted attitude *Abstraktion* (abstraction).

106 Jung 1921/1990: 289.

Jung discussed Worringer's theory on two occasions. The first was in a lecture given at the Psychoanalytical Congress in Munich on 8 September 1913. On this occasion Jung and Freud encountered each other for the last time.[107] The second occasion was in 1921, when he devoted an entire section of his *Psychological Types* to this theory.[108] One notices that Jung consented almost completely with Worringer's perspective on art. However, he would further develop this theory with respect to one specific point. He therefore introduced a concept which would determine his thinking until the end of his life: *participation mystique*. It remains a question whether Worringer would have recognised his own theory in Jung's argumentation. But for Jung this concept became the cornerstone of his perspective on art. Later in this chapter, I will extensively expand upon it. First, I will present a summary of Worringer's theory.

Worringer's theory of art

In his book, Worringer explored the motives behind art. Take for instance a landscape which a painter portrays on canvas. What motivates him to transform that landscape into an aesthetic product? A 'beautiful landscape' is not in itself a work of art. He argued that from prehistoric times people have alternated between two motives. Either people feel the need to *empathise* with reality (*Einfühlung*), or they tend to *distance* themselves from this reality (*Abstraktion*). Naturally there are transitional forms and both motives can alternate within one culture or even in one person, but the motivation behind art always involves this double tendency.

'Empathy' gives aesthetic pleasure, because the artist can completely identify himself with the object. 'Abstraction' gives that pleasure because he subdues the object to his will by means of abstract, geometrical forms and is able to distance himself from the object. Empathy finds fulfilment in the beauty of organic life, surrendering itself to it and having confidence in it. Abstraction finds satisfaction in the inorganic movement away from life by keeping it at a distance through abstract law. In the first situation reality is fascinating, in the second it is tremendous.[109]

These extraverted and introverted attitudes produce two forms of art: realistic and abstract; one of them will prevail in any given epoch. Abstract art products are without a natural shape, consisting of lines, one or more dimensional figures, rectangles, triangles, circles, braiding, colours etc. Abstract art was immensely popular in Egypt, Byzantium, Persia and in almost all primitive cultures. A prime

107 See Jung 1913/1990: 871.

108 See Jung 1921/1990: 289–299.

109 Jung summarised it thus: "Empathy is a movement of libido towards the object in order to assimilate it and imbue it with emotional values; abstraction withdraws libido from the object, (...) leaching out, as it were, its intellectual content, and crystallising from the lye the typical elements that conform to law, which are either superimposed on the object or are its very antithesis" (Jung 1913/1990: 504).

example of this type of art is the pyramid, but there are numerous others, such as the obelisk, totem pole or mandala. In Europe, this type of art was reinvested with appreciation at the beginning of the twentieth century.

Whether in the form of sculptures or tapestries or mosaics or the braiding of a basket, abstract art tries to create a contemplative sphere by means of schematics and repetitive motifs. It is essential that all references to an existing reality are eliminated. It is made of inorganic forms. In the creation of realistic art, the artist works in a very different style. This art intends to bring to mind and portray the vividness, the forms and colours of tangible existence. It wants to paint the threatening sphere of a pine tree forest, the texture of human blood, the rounding of a tear or the ferocity of a lion. This form of art is completely absorbed in the experience of organic reality. It marked the ancient Greek and Roman cultures and that of Renaissance Europe in particular. In Europe it continued to be the major form of art until the end of the nineteenth century.

According to Worringer, precisely those values which are lacking in a society are expressed in art: this is the decisive factor with respect to the question of which motive predominates. We designate as beautiful only those things we are missing, we appreciate the style that carries us away from everything which does not give us contentment or which scares us. Abstract art – when drenched with harmony, serenity and rhythm – speaks to those societies which long for calmness; societies which are fighting for law and order, where major ideological changes are taking place and chaos threatens. Through its art, the Egyptian culture enchants a land which has been flooded every year since ancient times and is always threatened by a barren desert and a scorching sun. Societies which have reached a high level of internal and external order, in which life is predictable and delineated dogmatically, long to escape this structure and want to entrust themselves to intense, elusive feelings. During the Renaissance, people wanted to be released from medieval church and feudal patterns. We need art because we continually fear losing our equilibrium and cannot bear a one-sided viewpoint.

According to Worringer, the majority of art originated from the tendency to abstraction. Empathic art is less common. Historically, the majority of art is abstract in nature. Nearly all primitive cultures are familiar with this form of art. 'Thus the urge to abstraction stands at the beginning of every art.'[110] In 1913, Jung quoted this remark with approval, as he considered it a "meaningful sentence" and added: "This idea finds weighty confirmation in the fact that schizophrenics produce forms and figures showing the closest analogy with those of primitive humanity, not only in their thoughts but also in their drawing."[111] The schizophrenic person obviously has an immense need for abstraction in order to get a grip on reality.

Worringer emphasised that we should not think that the artist is free to decide whether to work with 'abstraction' or 'empathy'. That would be a serious

110 Worringer 1980: 14.
111 Jung 1913/1990: 506.

misconception. Unconsciously he is *driven* to a certain styling and cannot escape it. An abstract painter is not unable to paint realistically; he can do this, but does not want to. Many objects from ancient Egypt have been preserved which show that Egyptian artists were capable of depicting an object organically. But the artist was driven, irrationally, to work in an abstract way. Of course a medieval sculptor was enough of a craftsman to be able to make Greek statues, but instinctively he created his Roman and Gothic icons. Picasso was able to paint romantically, but he did not want to. The artist does not feel free with respect to this will. During the Renaissance, people felt attracted, as if inebriated, to the organic world and could not escape its fascination. Artists who portray reality with triangles and squares are not doing this because they are dilettantes, primitives in comparison with for instance the Dutch masters, they do this because they feel a *different drive* within themselves.

In the western society of the past centuries, people have assumed too often that only one type of art can be designated as real art, that is 'empathic art', and that each artist, if he wants to be worthy of the title, *must* feel the need to work in a way that is true to nature and *must* experience pleasure from beautiful natural forms. Worringer argued that this prejudice leads to a second misunderstanding. Because the 'empathic' artist generally portrays as precisely as possible what he perceives – for instance Albrecht Dürer (1471–1528), Leonardo da Vinci (1452–1519), Michelangelo Buonarroti (1475–1564) and Jan van Eyck (1390–1441) – one could assume that 'imitation' is his artistic aim. However, according to Worringer, the drive to imitate has nothing to do with art. This drive is of course present in all ages and is innate in each human being, but even in the so called 'primitive' cultures it was completely distinct from the pure drive to create art. That the 'empathic' artist takes nature *as a model*, and therefore lovingly portrays the blade of grass as precisely as possible, *results from* his empathy. He wants to portray accurately what he enjoys or abhors. It is not that he simply wants to imitate.

Because these two misconceptions were cherished for generations, people subsequently began to appreciate as beautiful what was valued as beautiful in realistic art, and finally reached the point where only realistic art could be appreciated as true art. However, beauty is capable of attaching itself not only to a realistically portrayed world, but also to one which is portrayed in an unnatural way. We can appreciate a pyramid as being really 'beautiful', even though it is 'only' an object built from a square and triangles. In principle it is not different to, say, the cubist forms in a painting by Georges Braque (1882–1963). A "modern" artist has no immediate need for beauty; first and foremost he has an unconquerable need for abstraction. We also experience this when looking, for instance, at a work of art by Wassily Kandinsky (1866–1944). We instinctively experience that there was no drive to identify with nature. Here, the opposite drive was operative.

The two motives correspond to the two attitudes to life which, according to Worringer, are operative in all facets of life, including philosophy, religion and ethics. 'Whereas the precondition for the urge to empathy is a happy pantheistic relationship of confidence between man and the phenomena of the external world, the urge to abstraction is the outcome of a great inner uneasiness inspired in man by these phenomena, and its religious counterpart is the strongly transcendental colouring of ideas. We might describe this state as an immense spiritual dread of space.'[112] Jung approvingly quoted this sentence. One could say that by means of 'empathy', reality is experienced as a fascinating mystery, and by means of 'abstraction' it is experienced as a tremendous mystery.

According to Worringer, apprehension is the beginning of the realisation of consciousness within all cultures, a fear which wants to seize reality in the shackles of art. When we are increasingly in control of that reality, there begins a phase in which we are more inclined to entrust ourselves to it. But when, after a while, we again lose our grip on our existence for some reason – for instance in nineteenth-century Europe, when enlightened reason encountered its limitations – we see the return of a kind of 'primitive' art. Reality becomes maya: enchanting, magic, dangerous. The drive to abstraction resurfaces and finds expression in, for example, the 'black square' by Kazimir Malevitch (1878–1935). *Instinctively* the artist favours geometrical shapes. He passionately tries to delineate reality with a few vertical and horizontal lines. The reality of everyday life is withdrawn from time and space and receives an almost sacred character.

In Jung's days, people were astounded by the fact that Worringer introduced his ideas several years before the origination of abstract art in the twentieth century, a form of art which had little in common with 'empathy'. Worringer showed that the tendency to abstraction in someone like Piet Mondriaan (1872–1944) or Paul Klee (1879–1940) or Kandinsky was nothing new and had already existed for centuries. Moreover, he provided insight into these abstract works of art.

Participation mystique

What appealed to Jung was Worringer's understanding that art is motivated by an *absolutes Kunstwollen* (absolute artistic volition), a drive which precedes all art and all kinds of artistic formulation.[113] This was in accordance with his own idea that art is an autonomous complex. Worringer described the 'artistic drive' as such: a 'latent inner demand which exists *per se*, entirely independent of the object and of the mode of creation, and behaves as will to form. It is the primary factor in all artistic creation and, in its innermost essence, every work of art is simply an objectification of this *a priori* existent absolute artistic volition.'[114] This *a priori* was close to Jung's heart.

Jung would expand upon this subject and bring it in accord with his own understanding. In his view, Worringer made it appear that the artist stands on one side and reality on the other, separated from each other, and that the artist is motivated to depict this reality in one of two ways: concrete or abstract. Jung

112 Worringer 1980: 15.
113 See Jung 1913/1990: 505.
114 Worringer 1980: 9.

believed that a person cannot be separated from his reality, that he literally partakes in it, originates from it, is rooted in it. Therefore, there is an a priori undivided condition of existence which precedes any kind of projection. Jung wrote: "It seems to me that Lévy-Bruhl's *participation mystique* is more descriptive of this condition, since it aptly formulates the primordial relation of the primitive to the object."[115] What was Jung saying exactly?

The masterpiece of the French anthropologist Lucien Lévy-Bruhl (1857–1939), *The Mental Functions in Inferior Societies*, was published in 1910. Jung immediately bought it. His notes taken in preparation for his *Transformations* contain several quotations from this book.[116] One idea stayed with him for the rest of his life: *participation mystique*.[117] He considered it a brilliant intuition and, according to him, its importance reached much further than the narrow context in which it was described by Lévy-Bruhl.

In short, the difference in opinion between Lévy-Bruhl and Jung can be described as follows. Lévy-Bruhl was concerned with the way the primitive human being engages with reality, but Jung was concerned with the most primitive engagement of each human being with reality. Lévy-Bruhl was an anthropologist who (still) distinguished between 'primitive' and 'civilised' cultures. He thought that there were still some archaic remains of this *participation* within our culture, but that a 'civilised' person should be freed from it as much as possible. In this respect, Jung held a very different opinion.

According to Jung, Lévy-Bruhl was correct in his observation that people from so called *inferior societies* do not generally see themselves as independent individuals, as this is what the concept of *participation mystique* means. In their awareness, they almost merge with the things around them. The outside world and the interior world are merged in an awareness of unity. Stars, trees and animals are not separated from the 'I' and are mentally just as close as the tribe, children, parents and ancestors. A mysterious bond unites 'beneath' and 'above', the closest and the furthest, the divinity, the animals and the tribe. In this primitive awareness all objects are considered to be alive. The psychic spheres of the inner and outer world permeate each other to such a degree that it is impossible to decide what belongs to whom. There is a minimum of self-consciousness and a maximum of

115 Jung 1921/1990: 291.

116 See Jung 1977/1978: 214–215. Jung became personally acquainted with Lévy-Bruhl in 1932, when the latter stayed with him in Küsnacht for several weeks.

117 When, towards the end of his career, Lévy-Bruhl was not strong enough to withstand the sharp criticism against this notion and dropped it, Jung stubbornly continued using it. This proves the importance Jung attached to it. He criticised Lévy-Bruhl for being unfaithful to his own ideas. For Jung it was simple. All these erudite scientists were ignorant about the operations of the unconscious, including Lévy-Bruhl. They did not realise how valuable this idea was (see Jung 1955–56/1963: 488, footnote 106). He realised that it was a complicated subject. In 1951, he wrote extensively to the English translator of his work, explaining how he wanted this notion to be translated and which terminology should be consistently used (see Bair 2003: 582–583). The correct formulation was of major importance.

attachment to the object.[118] They are unable to distance themselves in an intellectual way. Lévy-Bruhl described this participation as 'mystical'. This is not a well-chosen word. His critics (including Jung) thought that 'unconscious' or 'irrational' would have been a more accurate term.

Before I discuss Jung's further development of this idea, I want to draw attention to the fact that Jung personally knew how to live a 'primitive' life. He seems to have had a natural penchant for this *participation mystique*. His Bollingen project was characterised by his participation in such a primitive way of life. In 1922, after the death of his mother, Jung bought a wild, isolated piece of land in the village of Bollingen on the northern shore of the Obersee. One year later he built a tower to live in. Initially he had in mind to build an African hut with a fireplace in the middle. In Bollingen, Jung was completely indifferent to physical comfort. He did not want electricity, only the warmth of a fire. In winter, ice sometimes froze to the door. Half in jest and half seriously, he regularly said that the tower had to be a dwelling place for ancestral souls. In 1934, he wrote about his lifestyle to the psychologist G. A. Farner: "As you know, in olden times the ancestral souls lived in pots in the kitchen. *Lares* and *penates* are important psychological personages who should not be frightened away by too much modernity."[119] Jung literally built a relationship with the pots and pans in the kitchen in Bollingen. He greeted them every morning, and asked his visitors to do the same. Each day he washed himself using a hard brush, sunbathed in the open air, took long walks through the hills and washed all his pans and cutlery in the lake. He could find everything in the dark as long as it was in the right place. He could spend hours sitting motionless. There is a story about a bird which used his hair to build a nest and of another bird sitting on his head for ten minutes. Ronald Hayman (b. 1932) wrote in Jung's biography: 'He was motivated by faith in the collective unconscious. Given silence that was almost tangible, it seemed possible to make contact with thoughts that were centuries old, to experience trees and birds as an extension of himself. It was easy to feel humble when chopping wood or carrying water from the lake to the fire.'[120]

We have to keep this aspect of Jung's life in mind. When he was in Bollingen he lived, so to speak, in an uninterrupted *participation mystique*. Of course there is a huge difference between the animistic native and Jung. The major difference is, obviously, that 'primitive people' are unaware of this participation, whereas Jung *realised* the extent of his participation in the reality surrounding him. Jung was aware of his primaeval union, whereas most likely the 'primitive' person is unaware of this union.

In his *Psychological Types*, published in 1921, Jung introduced his idea of *participation mystique*. In the list of definitions at the end of this book, he described

118 See Timmer 2001: 571–572.

119 Jung 1973: 168. *Lares* and *penates* were Roman house gods, glorified spirits or souls of good ancestors who provided protection (see Timmer 2001: 423).

120 Hayman 1999: 251–252.

the concept: "It denotes a peculiar kind of psychological connection with objects, and consists in the fact that the subject cannot clearly distinguish himself from the object but is bound to it by a direct relationship which amounts to partial *identity*. This identity results from an *a priori* oneness of subject and object."[121] Whether a person is aware of it or not, he simply *exists* as a participating being.

To understand the further development of his thinking, it is important to realise that Jung distinguished two forms of *participation mystique*: a healthy and an unhealthy one. It is healthy for a person to realise that he *is* an intrinsic part of reality. Jung continually emphasised that the *participation mystique* wherein a human being is born forms the unconscious dimension in which all individuals are both without boundaries and identical. There is unity in multiplicity, there is the one human being in all.[122] But something detrimental takes place when, at an adult age, this *participation mystique* slows down a healthy process of individuation and a person misses out on important aspects of his individual independence. Jung noticed this again and again in the people around him.

According to Jung, many so called civilised people have no clue how much they are controlled by unconscious cultural motives (which are different to the drives of the collective unconscious). Their entire life, they stay caught in unhealthy forms of 'participation'. This can be a simple thing like owning a car. When their car is criticised, they themselves are criticised. When something happens to their car, they themselves get sick. How many people experience their families with the same kind of 'mysticism'? What is of crucial importance within the first phase of our life – an almost complete (unconscious) symbiosis between mother and child – becomes a serious handicap at a later age. The baby, who is unaware where it 'ends' and where its mother 'begins', has an authentic experience of a 'shared identity'. But as an adult, a person should be detached from this experience, be liberated. Many adults, however, still belong to their family in the same way as a primitive person belongs to his tribe, but they *are unaware of this*. Jung called attention to the fact that people can lose their own identity in church and societal organisations, which is all but positive. One can also get completely lost in the marital bond. "We are still in a primitive state of *participation mystique* in the relation between the sexes; we have not discovered that only different things can enter in relationship."[123]

Lévy-Bruhl would agree with these unfavourable characteristics of the modern person and subsequently emphasises this as the reason why a civilised person should liberate himself from his *participation mystique*. But Jung thought differently about it. He argued that during his individuation process a person should follow a path which not only unconsciously begins in *participation mystique*, but which, after having gone through all kinds of phases, should also end there. But this time with full consciousness.

121 Jung 1921/1990: 456.
122 Agnel *et al.* 2005: 67–68.
123 Jung 1938/1984: 301.

The five phases of the individuation process

Jung called the inner transformation of a human person in becoming a mature individual "the individuation process". Throughout the years, Jung crystallised this process into five phases. He elaborated upon these phases in several studies. I will concisely discuss them here. Seeing clearly the process of these phases will enable us to outline the function of art more accurately.[124]

But perhaps a warning needs to be put in place. What is so clearly distinguished in the following theory is not as clearly distinguished in daily life. It hardly ever happens that we progress entirely to another phase. Phases constantly flow over into each other. Perhaps only the first two phases show a similar process in everyone. At some points we get stuck, whereas at others we progress. It is possible that one aspect of our personality can be in phase three, whereas another aspect is in phase five. Complexes can play a major role in this regard. In particular an artist can be in phase five with respect to his art, but still in phase three during his daily life. It is also possible to relapse into a previous phase. However, this does not imply that the following process of the five phases is inaccurate. It provides a reliable measuring point. It shows us, for instance, whether and where there are signs of relapse or progress.

The first phase in every human life is thus marked by *participation mystique*. It is the phase in which individual consciousness is merged with its surrounding environment. One can hardly speak of an individual consciousness. Subject and object are identical in a concealed way. It is important to repeat that, according to Jung, this identity is not a projection but a fact. We *are* united with everything and everyone. It is only in the second phase that a person starts projecting and subsequently differentiates between himself and reality. But in whatever way he is projecting, in the end, in the final stage, he *realises* that his a priori identity still exists. After many years of 'extraversion' one can then speak of 'introversion'.

In the second phase, when the person is still literally a child, he starts projecting. Projection is an unconscious, automatic psychic phenomenon in which an unconscious content is transferred onto an object in such a way that this content seems to belong to the object. In the person's consciousness he differentiates between an inner and an outer world. In his projections he differentiates, localises and selects the objects within it; parents, parts of his body, colours, animals, toys, etc. Because those projections are accompanied with intense feelings of lust (libido) they are powerful. The parents are like gods. No one can completely go beyond this stage. Many people will find carriers of their projections in institutions (churches, sports, art). Falling in love, getting married, having children: these acts are built on powerful projections. Each time we allow ourselves to be enchanted, such a mechanism has come into play. For many people their personal development

124 I am here closely following Murray Stein's clear discourse on this theme (see Stein 2006: 179–189).

ends here. We project the good and the bad onto objects in such a way that we are convinced that those qualities are *within* these people or things.

In the third phase, projections can be abstracted. Suddenly we see clearly the difference between the projections and the concrete carriers of the projections. The parents *are not* gods, Santa Claus does not exist, etc. The projections are withdrawn. Usually they are subsequently attached to abstract, higher values. The parents may no longer be gods, but we continue to project a god, a truth, an ideology. In daily life we feel liberated and less anxious (because God is present, my reason will deal with it, I am in control of nature), but the projections are still directed at all kinds of -isms. We can still be deeply touched by the ideals of a visionary person and be driven by grand moral imperatives. We can still believe that God will reward the good after this life and punish the bad. Projection is still present, but it is turned towards a mythological representation.

In the fourth phase a person can, sometimes suddenly, see through those ideological, moral or religious projections and then radically try to get rid of all of them in order to trust only his own credible and sensible ego. 'God is dead', 'soul', 'meaning of life', 'infinity', and 'good and bad' have lost their 'primitive' force and are replaced by utilitarian, pragmatic, agnostic and hedonistic ideas. We are only the small parts of a cosmic machinery, dust in an anonymous cosmos, clouds in an eternally silent sky. 'Gods' and 'devils' are expressions of mental disorders. There are no longer heroes and bad guys. Reality consists of coincidences and we are played with by impersonal forces. Only the rational (healthy) mind prevails.

In Jung's view, most modern people cannot avoid this phase. Suddenly they see themselves completely naked and realise that it was nothing more than a fairy tale. *Jung calls the person who has arrived in phase four 'the modern person'.* In almost all his writings he addressed this secular, agnostic person. It is the person who, on the one hand is able to see through his projections and realises that his supernatural ideas have no objective experiential foundation, but on the other hand is unable to see that these projections reveal important truths about himself and his existence. When someone is stuck in this phase, his life becomes meaningless. The problem is that the 'modern person' does not know how to connect all these metaphysical ideas with universal psychic events. This is exactly the core of the modern person's spiritual crisis. "The man who has attained consciousness of the present is solitary. The 'modern' man has at all times been so, for every step towards fuller consciousness removes him further from his original, purely animal *participation mystique.* (...) Every step forward means tearing oneself loose from the maternal womb of unconsciousness in which the mass of men dwells."[125]

The *unconscious* mind of this modern person functions in the same way as it did for millions of years. The people from ancient times and for the most part also our own great-grandparents were unconscious of their projections, but they knew how

125 Jung 1928/1964: 75.

to channel their unconscious drives by means of their projections. They were in touch with the devilish and divine depths of the unconscious. The modern person, who is predominantly engaged with rational consciousness, represses this unconscious world rather than integrating it into his consciousness. This integration is central to the fifth and final phase.

The first four phases are all related to the growth of ego consciousness. In the fifth phase, the ego returns to its own unconscious roots and becomes conscious of its *participation mystique.* In this phase the 'major work' is to recognise that one is still attached to one huge projection; that of the rational ego as almighty God, as carrier of good and evil, as judge of truth, goodness and beauty. The modern person needs to know that the source of all his projections is not outside himself but within, in his unconscious. He needs to realise that although he no longer believes in 'the devil', this does not imply that evil has disappeared. If he does not realise this, he will not be strong enough to resist the forces of his own shadow. The ideal of the *Übermensch* will destroy him. Many modern people are incapable of coping with this 'godless' phase and remain stuck in their projections regarding the many issues which they see as fundamental. Others judge the modern person and retreat into phase three or two. They frequently are the fundamentalists amongst us.

The fifth phase is the reunion of consciousness with the unconscious, it is a rebirth out of the waters of the unconscious; the classic 'rebirth' and 'initiation'. This phase is concerned with the acknowledgement of the boundaries of the ego and the experience of the irrational 'higher' forces which constitute the drives of our psyche. Overall, phase five is a regression and an *a posteriori* awareness of our *participation mystique.* The archetypes that have a grip on us should not be identified haughtily with functions of our conscious ego. When a symbol reconnects the conscious and the unconscious, we usually experience this as numinous. *A work of art can be such a numinous moment* upon which we project our psyche and its stirrings.

It seems appropriate at this point to make a remark on projections. There is nothing wrong with projection. To the contrary. We constantly project from early in the morning until late at night, irrespective of the phase we find ourselves in. When I say: 'the colour of the wall is green', this is a projection, because there is no green in the object itself. Green only exists in our psyche, as does sound. Colour is a psychic phenomenon which I project onto that wall.[126] Someone who enjoys a painting by Rembrandt, who is dreaming, who is in love, who is watching a film, projects all his affects. To be *aware* of these projections means to realise that the painting, for instance, is a carrier of our unconscious drives. In this way, art can give a huge impulse to processes of symbolisation, which is projection, but the person remains aware that his unconscious comes into play. In Jung's analytical psychology, projection is the most important means through which contents of the inner unconscious world are made tangible to ego consciousness. An encounter

126 See Jung 1935/1977: 137.

between the conscious and unconscious is meaningful. The outer world of things provides the material through which we activate the unconscious.[127]

Art and *participation mystique*

Jung wrote: "The psyche is not of today; its ancestry goes back many millions of years. Individual consciousness is only the flower and the fruit of a season, sprung from the perennial rhizome beneath the earth; and it would find itself in better accord with the truth if it took the existence of the rhizome in its calculations. For the root matter is the mother of all things."[128]

Participation mystique here denotes the "perennial rhizome beneath the earth", the matrix of our existence. Jung stated that it constitutes the soil of the artist's creative process. If there is one person who is connected to this root system, it is the artist. As no other he is in touch with the roots of our reality and receives his inspiration from it. In this region of his psyche resides the artistic drive.[129] The artist is rooted into the collective unconscious of humanity, thus reaching beyond his personal unconscious. This is Jung's credo. A crucial passage from 1930 demonstrates this: "This re-immersion in the state of *participation mystique* is the secret of artistic creation and of the effect which great art has upon us, for at that level of experience it is no longer the weal or woe of the individual that counts, but the life of the collective. That is why every great work of art is objective and impersonal, and yet profoundly moving. And that is also why the personal life of the artist is at most a help or a hindrance, but is never essential to his creative task. He may go the way of the Philistine, a good citizen, a fool, or a criminal. His personal career may be interesting and inevitable, but it does not explain his art."[130]

Art can be of invaluable importance to the "modern person" in the transition from the fourth to the fifth phase in the individuation process. He sees his unconscious drives projected in a work of art. Probably, the modern person is nowhere as distinctively present as in this phase. Whereas the official churches often vegetate on a harmful *participation mystique*, the artist is in touch with his archaic roots in a self-conscious and healthy way. In his "insight" it is as if "eyes in the background" are seeing in an impersonal act of perception.[131] This way of seeing is the secret of all great art. Paradoxically, everyone is personally moved by it. Great art speaks to all of us. But what exactly is happening here? The artist knows how to awaken us from our harmful projections.

I will take the liberty of recalling such a personal moment. When I saw, for the first time, the painting by René Magritte (1898–1967) depicting a 'real pipe' from

127 See Samuels 1987: 113–114.
128 Jung 1952/1956: XXIV.
129 See Jung 1921/1990: 294–295.
130 Jung 1930/1978: 105.
131 See Jung 1961/1989: 50.

his grandfather's time, beneath which the painter wrote the words *Ceci n'est pas une pipe*, a tremendous earthquake took place within me. It is difficult to describe how many of my projections (until then they were like dogmas to me) were shattered. I woke up from the many *cecis* and suddenly understood that underneath each painting one could write: *This is not... a cypress, a man, a wife, Jesus, a tree, an object.* And not just underneath paintings, but underneath every work of art. 'Water' on a movie screen is not water, the 'crucifixion' in the *Matthäuspassion* is not a crucifixion. I suddenly reached the point where I asked myself what *ceci* was, if it was not a pipe. I also remember saying to myself: 'But I do not think this is beautiful!' To regard something as 'beautiful' is not a decisive criterion in beholding art. Suddenly, unconscious forces are breaking free and new constellations are taking shape within our *participation mystique*. Suddenly, a work of art can bridge centuries and affect us in that system of roots from which it sprung.

The philosopher Alain de Botton (b. 1969) gave a telling example in one of his books. 'In his memoirs, the German theologian Paul Tillich (1886–1965) explained that art had always left him cold as a pampered and trouble-free young man, despite the best pedagogical efforts of his parents and teachers. Then the First World War broke out, he was called up and in a period of leave from his battalion (three quarters of whose members would be killed in the course of the conflict), he found himself in the Kaiser Friedrich Museum in Berlin during a rain storm. There, in a small upper gallery, he came across Sandro Botticelli's *Madonna and Child with Eight Singing Angels* and, on meeting the wise, fragile, compassionate gaze of the Virgin, surprised himself by beginning to sob uncontrollably. He experienced what he described as a moment of 'revelatory ecstasy', tears welling up in his eyes at the disjunction between the exceptionally tender atmosphere of the picture and the barbarous lessons he had learnt in the trenches.'[132]

This is an excellent example of how art can affect us. The young man is connected with the German empire and its awful war by means of a harmful *participation mystique*. Literally and figuratively speaking, he got stuck in the trenches of his existence. Because Botticelli (1445–1510) dwelled in the same depth, he knew how to offer the weeping Madonna as a liberating symbol. The work of art compensates, Jung would say, an unhealthy one-sided attitude. A work of art can free someone from such a nightmare by 'moving' him, because its roots are equally deep as those of evil. Furthermore, it is typical for an artist to descend into *participation mystique* without drowning in it. He moves it, brings movement into it. A part of himself identifies itself with it (*Einfühlung*) and another part distances itself from it (*Abstraktion*). Through this dynamic engagement he creates wholesome symbols.

In *Psychological Types*, Jung compared the artist who descends into *participation mystique* to a wizard who returns in the possession of a magical

132 de Botton 2007: 22, 25.

object. He charms reality through magic and at the same time inspires reality with its magic.[133]

Jung refined Worringer's theory. One cannot limit art to two types: one originating from *Einfühlung* and the other from *Abstraktion.* No, both drives are present within each work of art though in unequal measure. "It is evident, therefore," Jung wrote, "that both empathy and abstraction are needed for any real appreciation of the object as well as for artistic creation. Both are always present in every individual, though in most cases they are unequally differentiated."[134] Abstraction protects against the dissolving influence of the outside world, whereas empathy protects against the dissolving influence of the subjective inner world.[135] The artist is neither allowed to drown in the object nor to lose all contact with it.

However, Jung fully agreed with Worringer's statement that a great work of art will be created when the leading culture develops itself one-sidedly: "Whenever conscious life becomes one-sided or adopts a false attitude, these images 'instinctively' *rise to the surface in dreams and in the visions of artists and seers to restore the psychic balance, whether of the individual or of the epoch.*"[136] This is a typical Jungian strain of thought. Psychic energy moves when it becomes unbalanced and searches for a new homeostasis, a new dynamic equilibrium. The artist knows how to get in touch with this wholesome psychic depth in which we all partake, and for this reason a single person's deed influences all of us in a visionary way.

But how does this vision reveal itself to our consciousness? As a symbol. The symbol is the major connecting factor between our consciousness and the unconscious. It is rooted in unconscious *participation mystique* and appears in our consciousness in an aesthetic form. The following chapter deals with the symbol.

133 "Just as the latter [abstraction] is based on the magical significance and power of the object, the basis of empathy is the magical significance of the subject, who gains power over the object by means of *mystical identification*. The primitive is in a similar position: he is magically influenced by the power of the fetish, yet at the same time he is the magician and accumulator of magical power who charges the fetish with potency" (Jung 1921/1990: 295, italics mine).

134 Jung 1921/1990: 296.

135 See Jung 1921/1990: 297. "Abstraction and empathy, introversion and extraversion, are mechanisms of adaptation and defence. In so far as they make for adaptation, they protect a man from external dangers" (Jung 1921/1990: 297–298).

136 Jung 1930/1978: 104, italics mine).

Chapter 4

Art reveals itself in symbols

> It is not Goethe that creates Faust, but Faust that creates Goethe. And what is Faust? Faust is essentially a symbol. By this I do not mean that it is an allegory pointing to something all too familiar, but the expression of something profoundly alive in the soul of every German, which Goethe helped to bring to birth.
>
> (Jung 1930/1978: 103)

Symbols are projections of unconscious contents of the psyche. They are metaphors which move the senses. They are certainly not signs, which can be explained causally. Symbols are driven by archetypes, biological matrixes which structure the psyche that are millions of years old. Archetypes are not images, they show themselves in images, lines, colours, sounds, forms, rhythms, hence in all forms of art. In the artist, the collective unconscious sends symbols to the surface of consciousness, which subsequently has a compensating influence in culture. A new equilibrium comes into existence.

Fantasy thinking

The central thought in *Transformations and Symbolisms of the Libido* (1912), Jung's first masterpiece, is that there are two kinds of thinking: rational thinking and fantasy thinking.[137] The first consists of thoughts, the second of images; in the first the logos is central, in the second the mythos; the first gives knowledge, the second wisdom. In his study, Jung mainly expanded upon the second. He was fascinated by it. In 1911, he wrote about it in a letter to Freud: "Unconscious fantasy is an amazing witches' cauldron. (...) This is the matrix of the mind."[138] This capacity for images is the same as our creative capacity. In all areas of the human mind – science, philosophy, art and religion – it is the engine behind creative processes. Without this capacity, a scientist would not be inspired by new

137 See Jung 1912/1944: 11.
138 Freud and Jung 1994: 188.

intuitions, religions would harden and art would simply be impossible. In ancient times there were no clear boundaries between these areas. We see that in those times artistic formulation attached itself in a natural way to, for instance, religious and philosophical themes. Apparently, these areas have the intrinsic tendency to present themselves artistically. Jung wrote: "Here [in the Grecian sphere] we move in a world of fantasies, which, little concerned with the outer course of things, flows from an inner source, and, constantly changing, creates now plastic, now shadowy shapes. This fantastical activity of the ancient mind created artistically *par excellence.* The object of interest does not seem to have been to grasp hold of the 'how' of the real world as objectively and exactly as possible, but to aesthetically adapt subjective fantasies and expectations."[139]

By means of this fantasy thinking we are connected to the unconscious, "with the oldest foundations of the human mind, which have been for a long time beneath the threshold of consciousness."[140] Jung distinguished three unconscious layers and subsequently three kinds of images. Just underneath the threshold of our consciousness lie our waking-dreams and day-fantasies. Usually we can relate to them consciously. Our night-dreams are in a layer underneath it. Our consciousness perceives them as more enigmatic. "Last, there is a so-called wholly unconscious fantasy system in the split-off complex, which exhibits a pronounced tendency towards the production of a dissociated personality."[141] In Chapter 2 I described extensively how the creative process is such a separate, autonomous creative complex which "lives and grows in him [the artist] like a tree in the earth from which it draws its nourishment." This complex is undisturbed by a logical way of thinking; "it may appear as a supraordinate authority which can harness the ego [of the artist] to its purpose."[142] The core of fantasy thinking is the symbol. Jung saw it as the image par excellence. According to Jung, great art is always composed of symbols. His entire life, he was especially proud of his symbol theory. This theory was to a great extent the catalyst for the divide with Freud.

Symbols and signs

Usually, one thinks of symbols as 'image-codes' referring to something else. For instance, an anchor stands for hope, a peacock stands for pride, armorial bearings stand for a family lineage, etc. It is of great importance to realise that Jung rejected such an understanding of the symbol. In this context he called the anchor, the peacock and armorial bearings 'signs'. A symbol indicates something entirely different.

To start with, in Jung's view, one can never say that something *is* a symbol. It is possible that something *becomes* a symbol. Something becomes a symbol

139 Jung 1912/1944: 13.
140 Jung 1912/1944: 19.
141 Jung 1912/1944: 19.
142 See Jung 1922/1978: 75.

when I *make* a symbol of it. However, this does not happen by means of conscious thoughts but on the grounds of unconscious inclinations. When something has become a symbol to me, this was always preceded by an interior unconscious process of which I became aware at a certain point. I remember the story of the Brazilian theologian Leonardo Boff (b. 1938), in which he told that it was impossible for him to be present at his father's funeral, because the distance from North to South Brazil was too far for him to be there on time. Several days later, his brother sent him a package with half a cigar, which was the last his father had smoked. Full of emotion, he placed it on his desk, where it stayed for years. He conveyed this as if he was talking about a sacrament. His father was 'present in the appearance' of that cigar. Without a doubt, Jung would have called this an authentic process of symbolisation. We need to realise that the cigar *is* not by nature a symbol. It *became* a symbol because Boff projected his entire soul onto this object. He *made* a symbol of it. He did not do this by straight thinking, no, it was instinctive forces which were operative in his imagination.

To us this cigar is not a symbol, but a sign which refers to Boff's father. However, we can sense from his narrative that it is a symbol to Boff. Jung empathetically wrote several beautiful historical studies about processes of symbolisation in many cultures. But this does not imply that they are symbols to him or to us. The living symbols of the alchemist, for example, are to us usually no more than cryptic rebuses. It therefore depends on someone's attitude whether or not something is/becomes a symbol.

Symbols are fascinating sensory images, images which touch the senses. Suddenly we realise that something has become a symbol to us. This tree, this person, this gesture, this colour, this thought, this melody means so much to me that I attach symbolic value to it, because all other things do not have this unique meaning to me. However, we can never rationalise why something or someone becomes a symbol to me. Symbols originate from our fantasy thinking, which is irrational in nature.

Jung thought that in the majority of cases when we are speaking of symbols, we are actually referring to signs. The meaning of signs is bound to a code (a sign can only be explained in one way), whereas the meaning of symbols is free of codes. The sign is transparent and always moves from a general premise or consensus to a specific case. This specific case illustrates the general premise. Furthermore, a sign can be used with different associations: God can be represented as a man, evil as a devil, the blood of Jesus as wine, wisdom as salt, etc. It is a well thought out construct, predictable and conveyable. As the central point in this chapter is the symbolic nature of art, it does not allude to the many 'signs' that might be part of a work of art, for example in a painting. The average museum guidebook can competently explain these signs, but this explanation has little or nothing to do with the question of whether or not this painting becomes a symbol to us. The sign is predictable, whereas the symbol is unpredictable, vague and inscrutable. It reveals itself in a concrete, unique situation, is surprising, uncontrollable in all its implications and personal in nature. It can never be conveyed in general terms. "The living symbol formulates an essential unconscious factor."[143]

Therefore, an essential aspect of a symbol is that "it always presupposes that the chosen expression is the best possible description or formulation of a relatively unknown fact, which is none the less known to exist or is postulated as existing."[144] "For when something is 'symbolic', it means that a person divines its hidden, ungraspable nature and is trying desperately to capture in words the secret that eludes him."[145]

Differences between Freud and Jung

According to Jung, Freud never had an eye for this inscrutable secret; he did not have an eye for the *autonomous* unconscious drive of the imagination: he did not distinguish between symbols and signs; and, in Jung's view, he reduced all fantasy thinking to signs. He used a reductive method with respect to all images, and thought they could all be logically reduced to facts and relations that were in principle known to the person. He thought that all fantasies, myths and creative expressions in truth originated from personally repressed sexuality. In Freud's eyes, projected sublimations should be rigorously confronted with the principle of reality. From the start, Jung considered this theme non-negotiable.[146]

Jung never denied that it regularly happens that our fantasy thinking can be reduced to repressed sexual components and that in those cases the causes are clearly demonstrable. In his association tests he often encountered such fantasies. He said that such imagery goes back to familiar causes "in much the same way as one might regard the red of scarlet fever as a 'symbol' of the disease."[147] However, for Jung the 'red rash' is not a symbol but a symptom. The red rash is a 'symptomatic sign' of a well-known process lying underneath it. The same is true for the dream and fantasy images of hysterical patients.[148] However, symptoms are nothing other than signs.

Jung illustrated Freud's method by means of the famous symbol of 'the cave' in Plato's myth. He saw Plato's 'cave' as a real and proper symbol, because it expresses a situation for which there are no objective words. He wrote: "If we were to interpret Plato's metaphor in Freudian terms we would naturally arrive at the uterus, and would have proved that even a mind like Plato's was still stuck at a primitive level of infantile sexuality. But we would have completely overlooked what Plato actually created out of the primitive determinants of his philosophical ideas; we would have missed the essential point and merely discovered that he had

143 Jung 1921/1990: 477.
144 Jung 1921/1990: 474.
145 Jung 1932/1978b: 123. "So long as a symbol is a living thing, it is an expression for something that cannot be characterised in another or better way" (Jung 1921/1990: 474).
146 See Jung 1927: 66.
147 Jung 1921/1990: 477.
148 For clarification of the diagnosis 'hysteria', see footnote 73.

infantile sexual fantasies like any other mortal. (...) But this would have nothing whatever to do with the meaning of Plato's parable."[149]

The myth of 'the cave' did not originate from Plato's repressed mother bond: to the contrary, it sprang from an *impersonal* source within him. The same sort of processes occur in art. The artist does not move from one known to another known, no, the unknown is manifested in him through its own force. The artist gives it an aesthetic form, the philosopher integrates it into his philosophical vision and the mystic into his religious vision.

In Jung's view, art does not originate from the reservoir of the personal unconscious wherein the libido is poured out in sexual fantasies, whether sublimated or not. This does not really produce great art. To the contrary, the artist is inspired by the impersonal unconscious: "Personal causes have as much or as little to do with a work of art as the soil with the plant that springs from it. We can certainly learn to understand some of the plant's peculiarities by getting to know its habitat. (...) The personal orientation which the doctor needs when confronted with the question of aetiology in medicine is quite out of place in dealing with a work of art, just because a work of art is not a human being, but is something suprapersonal. It is a thing and not a personality; hence it cannot be judged by personal criteria. Indeed the special significance of a true work of art resides in the fact that it has escaped from the limitations of the personal and has soared beyond the personal concerns of its creator."[150]

But which impersonal unconscious forces are operating in the creation of a great work of art, in the processes of symbolisation? Jung's answer has become notorious: those are the archetypal forces, dwelling in the collective unconscious.

The collective unconscious and its archetypal trajectories

In 1918, Jung wondered where mythological fantasies originate if they do not spring from the personal unconscious, and he unfolded his hypothesis of the collective unconscious. "This unconscious, buried in the structure of the brain and disclosing its living presence only through the medium of creative fantasy, is the *suprapersonal unconscious*. It comes alive in the creative man, it reveals itself in the vision of the artist, in the inspiration of the thinker, in the inner experience of the mystic. The suprapersonal unconscious, being distributed throughout the brain-structure, is like an all-pervading, omnipresent, omniscient spirit."[151]

We can never discover the collective unconscious in a direct manner. And in any case, this is impossible with regard to psychic phenomena in general. They do not occur in time and space like physical phenomena. In this sense, the collective unconscious does not even exist. We only know it indirectly and never in its

149 Jung 1922/1978: 70.
150 Jung 1922/1978: 71.
151 Jung 1918/1964: 10.

totality. It consists of inherited regulatory principles within the structure of the brain that contain possibilities of images, visions and creative ideas. The term Jung used to describe these principles was 'archetype'. He said: "Of course this term is not meant to denote an inherited idea, but rather an inherited mode of psychic functioning, corresponding to the inborn way in which the chick emerges from the egg, the bird builds its nest, a certain kind of wasp stings the motor ganglion of the caterpillar, and eels find their way to the Bermudas. In other words, it is a *pattern of behaviour*."[152] The expression 'psychic instinct' comes close to what Jung intended to say here. *Arche* means 'primaeval', *tupos* means 'mark'. When 'typing' a letter, a hammer 'marks' the paper with the letter; in the same way, during our evolution nature pushed buttons which left lasting imprints within our psyche. This is one of Jung's most well-known hypotheses.

Archetypes are the expression of the primaeval experiences of humanity. "They are the precipitate of the psychic functioning of the whole ancestral line; the accumulated experiences of organic life in general, a million times repeated, and condensed into types. In these archetypes therefore, all experiences are represented which have happened on this planet since primaeval times."[153] At birth, they are inherited collectively, just as a bird is born with a pre-existent regulator to build a nest. This regulator also originated from primaeval experiences. Jung detected these archetypes because he saw identical, repetitive motifs of image in myths, fairy tales, literature, fantasies, dreams and delusions. And this at all times and in all cultures.[154]

It is important to realise that, even though Jung discovered archetypes mainly in material consisting of images, the archetypes themselves are not images. They reveal themselves in images. But not only in images. They also reveal themselves in sounds, smells and actions (rituals). What kind of 'images' should we hear when listening to Bach's cello sonata, which is an archetypal experience par excellence?

The archetypes come to awareness, as Jung mentioned in the above quote, in creative fantasy or, put another way, in the symbol. And this takes us again to the central theme of this chapter. What is unconscious can only be brought to consciousness by means of symbolising, and the archetypes are the engines of this process. They facilitate the common human combinations of symbols, both those of the individual as well as those of humanity. "Symbols always derive from archaic residues, from racial engrams [imprints]."[155] Therefore, the archetype is in the first instance a biological trajectory which operates without images. At a certain moment it dresses itself in appropriate symbols, suiting the individual person, and brings him into a state of ecstasy.[156] *In fact it is in this way that an archetype attracts a certain image and makes a symbol of it.* This happened with

152 Jung 1949/1977: 518.
153 Jung 1921/1990: 400.
154 See Timmer 2001: 58–59.
155 Jung 1921/1990: 239.
156 See Jung 1949/1977: 518–519.

Leonardo Boff's cigar. It is an autonomous process. The operation of an archetype is not subjected to a decision of the will. In 1952, Jung described this excellently: "The archetypes are the numinous, structural elements of the psyche and possess a certain autonomy and specific energy which enables them to attract, out of the conscious mind, those contents which are best suited to themselves. The symbols act as *transformers*, their function being to convert libido from a 'lower' into a 'higher' form. This function is so important that feeling accords it the highest values. The symbol works by suggestion; that is to say, it carries conviction and at the same time expresses the content of that conviction. It is able to do this because of the *numen*, the specific energy stored up in the archetype. Experience of the archetype is not only impressive, it seizes and possesses the whole personality, and is naturally productive of faith."[157]

When does the operation of the collective unconscious start, and why does it send symbols to the surface of consciousness? According to Jung, the most important characteristic of the collective unconsciousness is its *compensatory function*. It always searches for a balance in our energies. Our psychic energies are always moving within a bipolar tension. A certain mood relates to another mood in the same way as a low pressure area is attracted by a high pressure area and vice versa. It causes movements, a process. The pole which is repressed will in time cause a pressure to restore the lost equilibrium.

Jung thought that the operation of the symbol gives our consciousness a kind of compensation with respect to unconscious inclinations. A symbol is therefore usually experienced as a violation, a fascination, a shock, a temptation, an enticement, etc. Suddenly you are gripped by something, or you are enlightened. A new mood appears, *a new equilibrium is reached*, even though at first it seems like you are losing your equilibrium and are taken aback. The symbol itself is not a compensation, but it attracts our energy towards a different mood, *it is the third factor which unites the contradictions at a higher level*. It is for this reason a work of art affects us.

Nature and culture

To fully understand the operations of the symbol, we have to take the distinction between nature and culture into consideration. To Jung this distinction was very important. In his view, the symbol was clearly a cultural phenomenon, whereas the symptom was a natural event. What was he trying to say?

According to Jung, a person is subjected to two kinds of processes. The first is experienced as the outcome of instinctive natural laws; the second seems to withstand these determining laws and create something new.[158] In the first, the instincts are operative; whereas in the second, it is dreams, fantasies and creative

157 Jung 1952/1956: 232.
158 See Jung 1921/1990: 478.

ideas. With respect to the first, Jung speaks about nature, whereas with respect to the second he speaks about culture.[159] I will elaborate upon this view and in particular show the crucial place of symbolisation.

With respect to the concept of 'culture', Jung used what is probably the most ancient meaning of *cultura*, that is agri-culture. When we cultivate nature we can speak of culture. When nature is left untouched, it only brings forth natural phenomena and does not lead to any 'accomplishment from manual labour'. Culture provides machines which enable us to use natural processes in order to produce a higher profit. With respect to human consciousness there are two tendencies of the same libido; a tendency which continually follows its *natural* flow and a tendency which provides new *cultural* achievements. Of course, Jung was aware that he distinguished two forces which are essentially one. "That man should ever have invented this machine must be due to something rooted deep in his nature, indeed in the nature of the living organism as such. For living matter is itself a transformer of energy, and *in some way as yet unknown* life participates in the transformation process."[160] This does not weaken the fact that one can perceive two tendencies: regressive and progressive. Not only the human person is capable of cultural achievements. Jung again and again underlined that animals are also capable of this. The nest fabricated by a bird, the waterworks constructed by a beaver bear witness. The 'nature' of a beaver has differentiated itself in such a way that a surplus of energy is transformed into a 'machine' which gnaws through tree trunks and builds dams.

The entire libido is thus able to 'relocate' and 'shift' during the course of evolution. In the previous chapters we encountered this phenomenon several times. 'Surpluses' of energy can accumulate and will find their 'own way'. Jung thought that we can see this everywhere in nature. Take for example the atrophy of the sexual organ of the male bee. After the drone has performed his sexual activities he transforms himself into a 'worker-bee'.[161] Libido relocates itself. Each time 'nature' is cultivated one can speak of a 'machine', in whatever form. Jung wrote: "Similarly human culture (...) is a machine. First of all a technical one that utilises natural conditions for the transformation of physical and technical energy, but also a psychic machine that utilises psychic conditions for the transformation of libido."[162]

It may sound like a technical metaphor, the machine, but Jung knew how to apply it in order to explain perfectly what he meant. In her study of Jung as a cultural philosopher, the professor of literature and culture Véronique Liard summarises it beautifully and leads us to the machine par excellence, the symbol: 'Like warmth is transformed through the medium of the steam engine into pressure and kinetic energy, in the same way the libido is transformed into

159 See Jung 1918/1964: 16.
160 Jung 1928/1960a: 41 (italics mine).
161 See Jung 1921/1990: 239–240.
162 Jung 1928/1960a: 42.

a lucrative culture *whereby the symbol is the psychic machine that transforms the energy*.'[163]

The symbol, the steam engine of culture. It knows how to mobilise and to transform natural energy towards a higher level. "The history of civilisation has amply demonstrated that man possesses a relative surplus of energy that is capable of application apart from the natural flow. *The fact that the symbol makes this deflection possible* proves that not all the libido is bound up in a form that enforces the natural flow, but that a certain amount of energy remains, which could be called excess libido."[164]

The symbol forms the transition between nature and culture

We must be aware that according to Jung the archetypes manifest themselves as *psychic* forces. They belong to the reality of our mind. Therefore Jung claimed that the archetype has not a natural but a cultural character. He wrote: "It [the archetype] is thus the necessary counterpart of instinct."[165] This is a crucial insight. Culture partially counteracts nature. Jung saw a psychic force operating in the realisation of culture (art, religion and science), rather than a physical one. He called this 'spirit'. There are no theological connotations attached. The spirit shows itself as an autonomous *psychic* drive. Whereas the human person as a natural being is controlled by his instincts, as a spiritual being he is driven by his archetypes. By means of a symbol the person becomes aware of these processes.[166]

Art is a cultural-spiritual event par excellence. All kinds of art have occurred within the history and prehistory of humanity's existence: plastic art (masks, totem poles, paintings), musical art (song, dance, instrumental music), theatrical and literary art. They will occur, as it were, effortlessly in order to bring the person from one dimension to another and as such they bend the 'natural flow'. These archetypal forces, Jung said, "force the primitive to act against nature so that he shall not become her victim. That is indeed the beginning of all culture, the inevitable result of consciousness and of the possibility of deviating from unconscious law."[167] In this way he contrasted them: "A cultural attitude as opposed to sheer instinctuality."[168]

Jung reproached Freud and his followers – it is a repetitive tune – for reducing important cultural achievements to mere instinctual processes, to nature. Jung thought that in this way art, religion and philosophy are reasoned 'away'. In Jung's opinion, Freud reduced them by means of causal reduction to a one-sided 'natural'

163 Liard 2007: 29 (italics mine).
164 Jung 1928/1960a: 47 (italics mine).
165 Jung 1921/1990: 447.
166 See Jung 1928/1960a: 58.
167 Jung 1928/1960b: 375.
168 Jung 1928/1960b: 59.

origin. Symptoms belong to the natural world, but symbols to the spiritual world. Symptoms block the natural system. It is good to cure a person from his symptoms, but this is only one side of the coin. A transition to spiritual forces should also be taking place. Jung's entire work was focused on this transition. It is essential to unite nature and culture in a marriage. "This task [to bring both worlds into accord] occupies philosophers, founders of religions and *artists*."[169]

Hence, the machine for this transition is the symbol. The symbol is itself a transitional reality. Above, we read that symbols function as *transformers* of the libido.[170] By means of the symbol an important transition and transformation from a biological disposition towards a culturally minded disposition takes place.[171]

In the previous chapter, we saw how the artist descends into the *participation mystique* of his existence and like a true alchemist extracts a work of art from it and transmutes it into a cultural product. *Ars perficit naturam* is the ancient saying: 'art perfects nature'. We saw how *participation mystique* as a natural, instinctive reality can cause estrangement. We also saw that the *prima materia* of nature contains all the forces used in sculpting 'the philosopher's stone'.[172] However, this can only be done by cultivating nature.

But what art is still remains the question

In the previous chapters, we discussed themes which all belong to the heart of art. We have seen that complexes are the architects of art, that symbols are the building stones, that there needs to be a descent into *participation mystique*, and that cryptomnesia continually comes into play. But all these things also account for so many other psychic realities. It is not only art that is a symbolic reality, but also, for instance, religion; and Plato also worked with symbols, and a child playing with a doll does the same. How should a symbolic reality appear to us in order to make us speak of a work of art? Not as a toy, a mystical experience, a scientific intuition, a dream, etc.

A second point which is given with Jung's understanding of the symbol forces itself to the fore. If it is the case that something never *is* a symbol but can only *become* one eventually, one cannot say that something *is* a work of art separate from the individual who experiences it symbolically. Jung left us little choice, so it seems: "Whether a thing is a symbol or not depends chiefly on the *attitude* of the observing consciousness. (...) It is left to our discretion and our critical judgement to decide whether the thing we are dealing with is a symptom or a symbol."[173] Hence, it depends on the individual person or a group of people

169 Jung 1918/1995: 30 (italics mine).
170 See Jung 1952/1956: 232.
171 See Jung 1928/1960a: 61.
172 *Prima materia* is an alchemistic term. It stands for the primaeval matter from which the cosmos is built. This dark, original, chaotic dust is the rough material used by the alchemist to create the 'philosopher's stone'.
173 Jung 1921/1990: 475, 478.

whether a certain object is (still) an appropriate carrier of a projection. Again and again we notice throughout history how works of art 'disappear' and 'appear'; how one culture is affected by certain concerns to which others are indifferent.

Also against the background of these two points we are now asking the question: 'What is art?' Or should we ask: 'When does something become art?' This much seems certain: the specific perspective with respect to art is an *aesthetic* one: it concerns beauty. What did Jung have to say about this? Valuable insights, as we shall see – even though occasionally eccentric. He considered the aesthetic aspect of art important. This will become clear in the following quotation. In it, Jung delightfully summarised what a symbol is. "To be effective, a symbol must be by its very nature unassailable. It must be the best possible expression of the prevailing world view, an unsurpassed container of meaning; it must also be sufficiently remote from comprehension to resist all attempts of the critical intellect to break it down; *and finally, its aesthetic form must appeal so convincingly to our feelings that no argument can be raised against it on that score.*"[174]

Jung's understanding of beauty is the central theme in the next chapter.

174 Jung 1921/1990: 237 (italics mine).

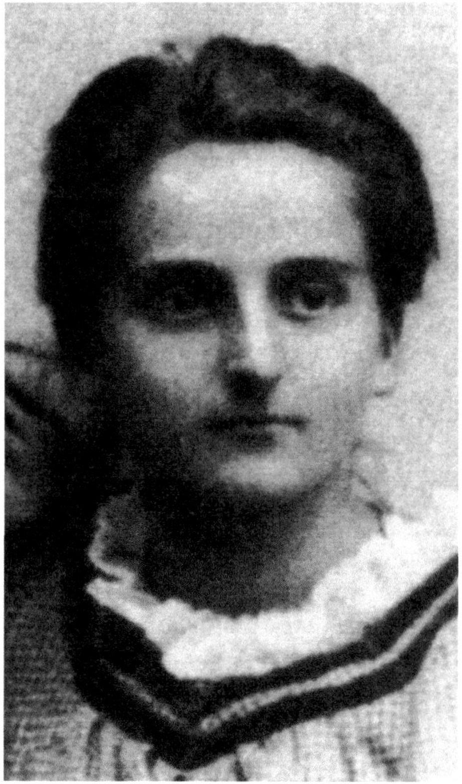

1. Hélène Preiswerk (1881–1911)

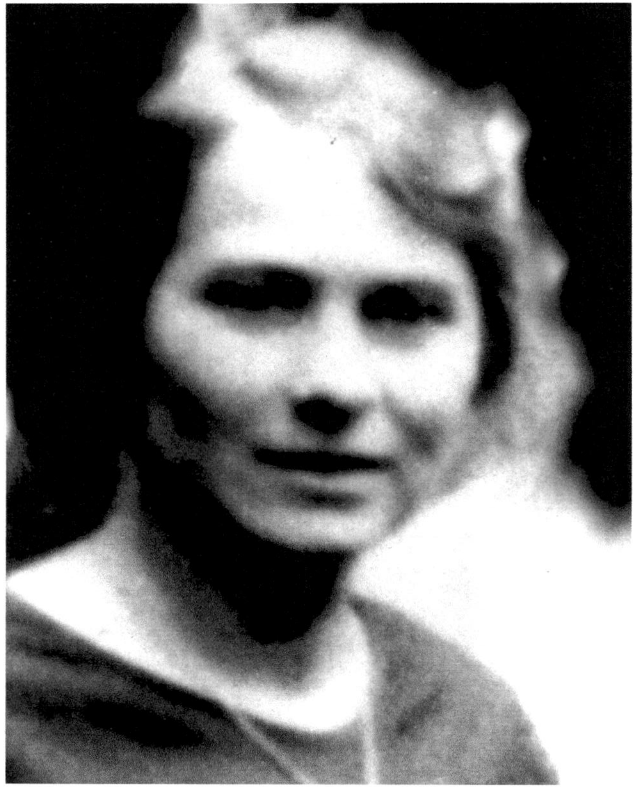

2. Sabina Spielrein (1885–1942)

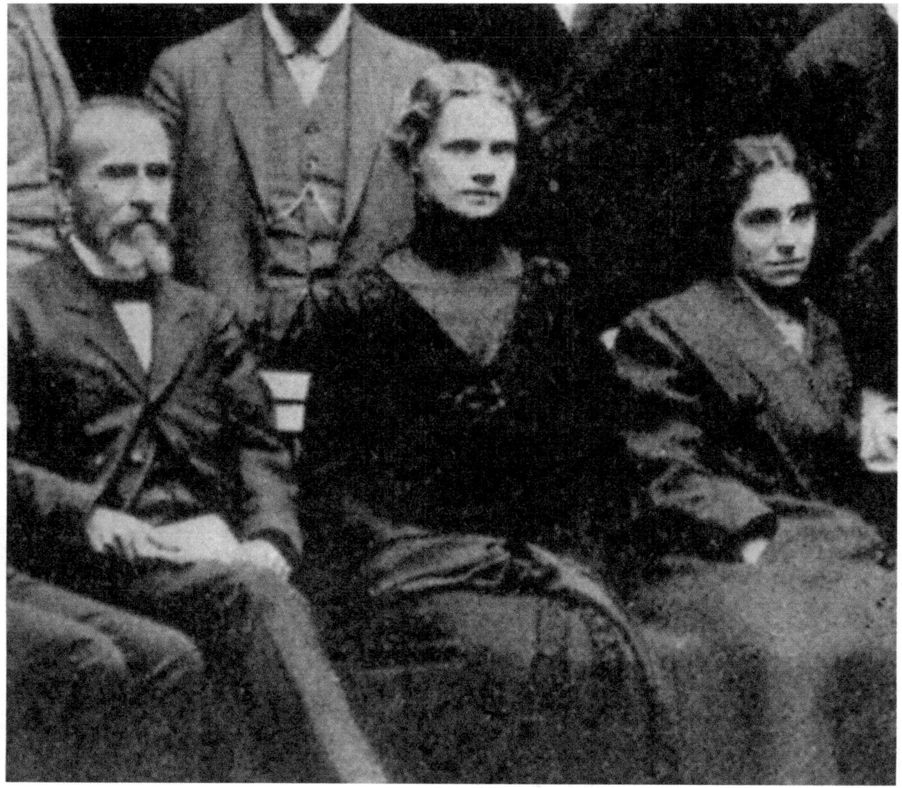

3. Maria Moltzer (centre) (1874–1944)

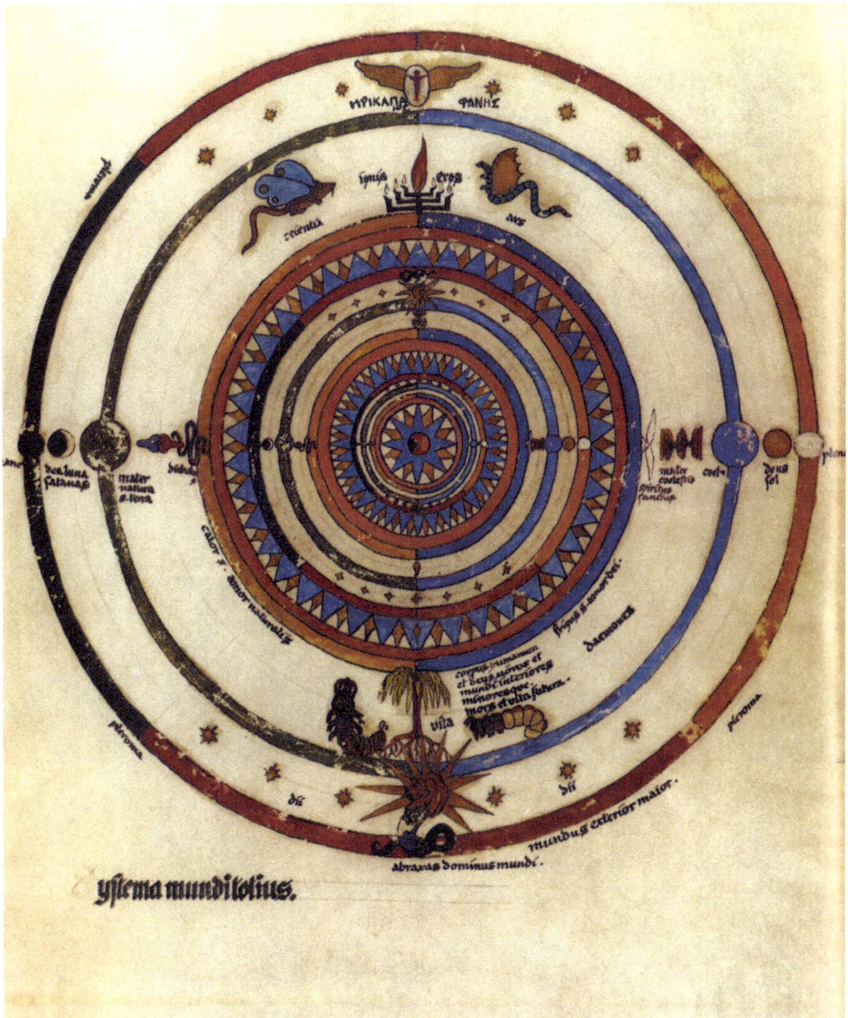

4. Jung's first mandala, *Systema Mundi Totius*, from 1916

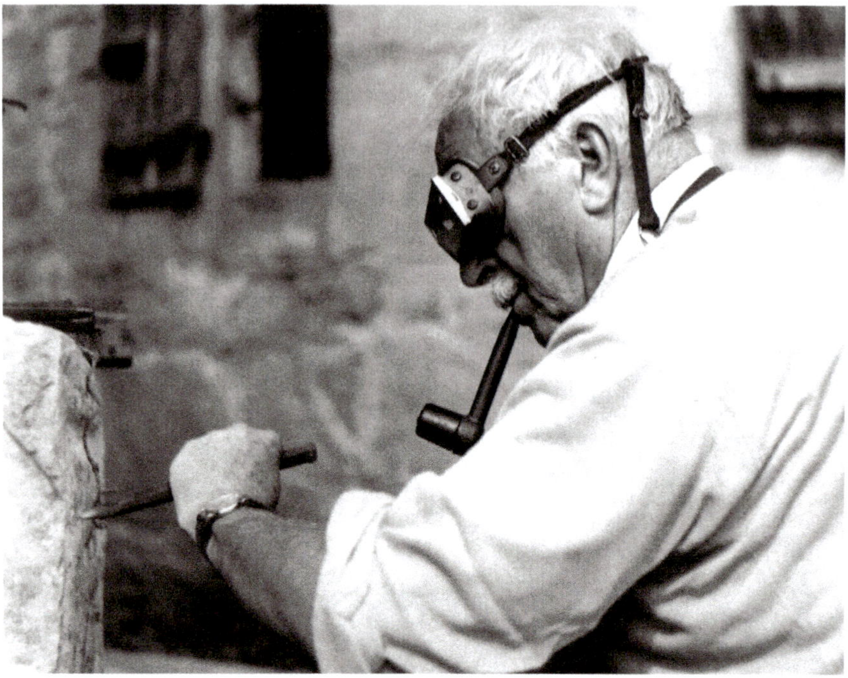

5. Jung working on 'The Stone' at Bollingen, 1950

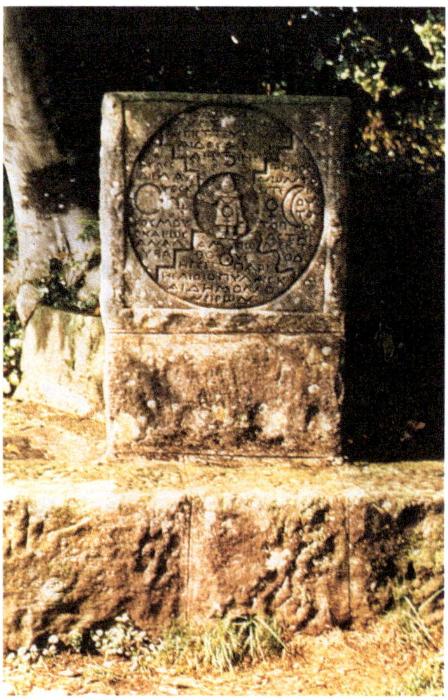

6. 'The Stone' (photograph by Ruth Ammann)

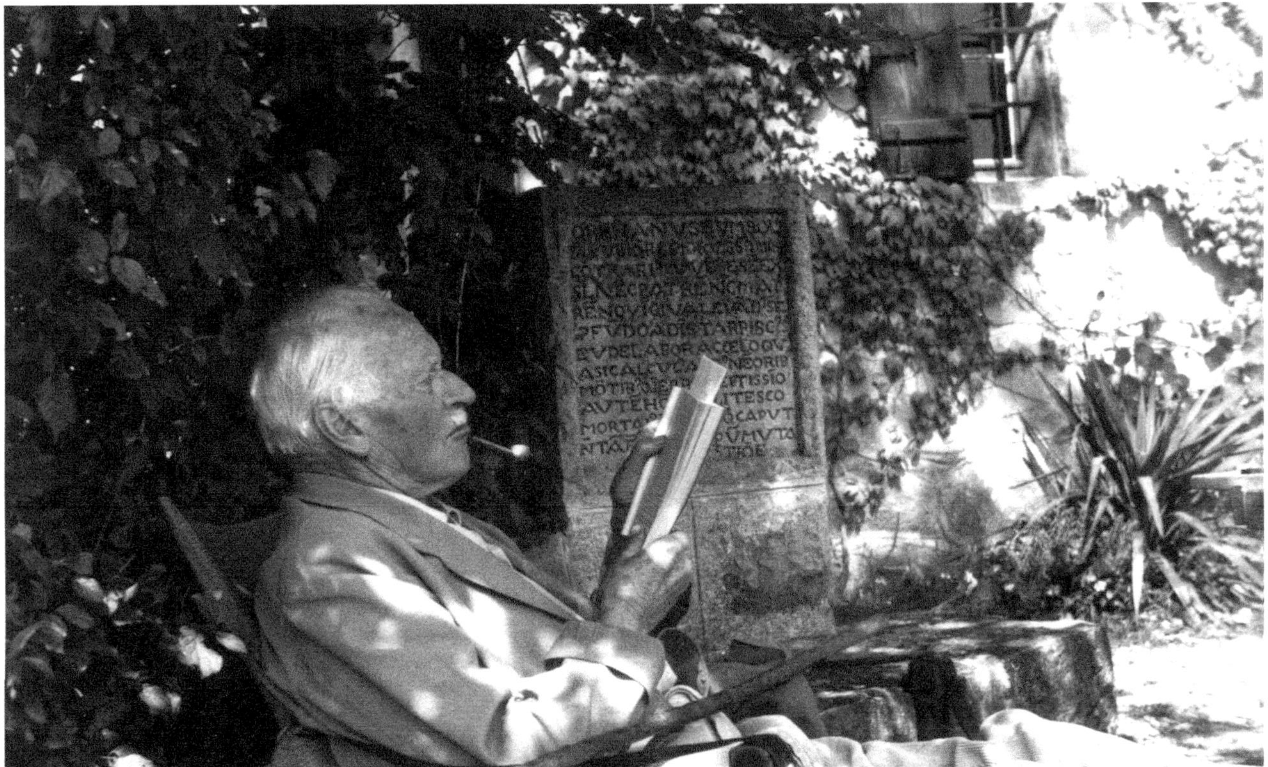

7. Jung reading by his stone at Bollingen (photograph by Aniela Jaffé) © Robert Hinshaw

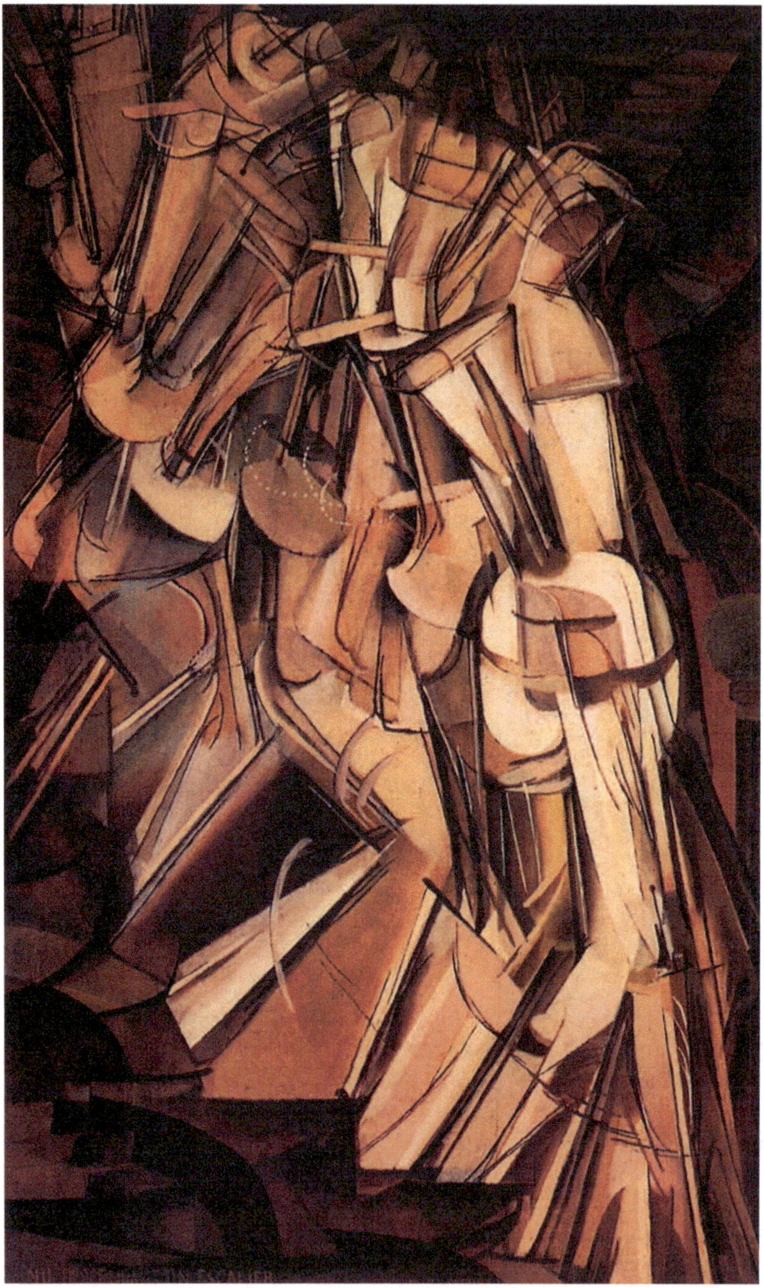

8. Marcel Duchamp, *Nu descendant l'Escalier* (1912) © Succession Marcel Duchamp/ADAGP, Paris and DACS London 2011

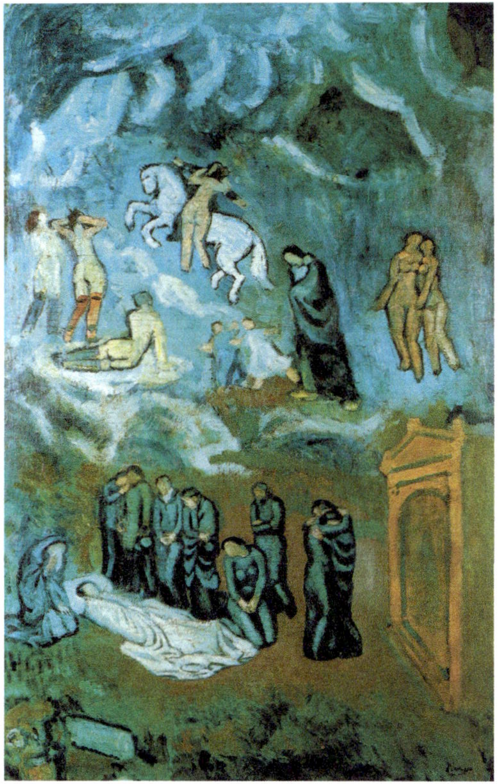

9. Pablo Picasso, *Evocation* (*L'enterrement de Casagemas*) (1901) © Succession Picasso/ DACS, London 2011

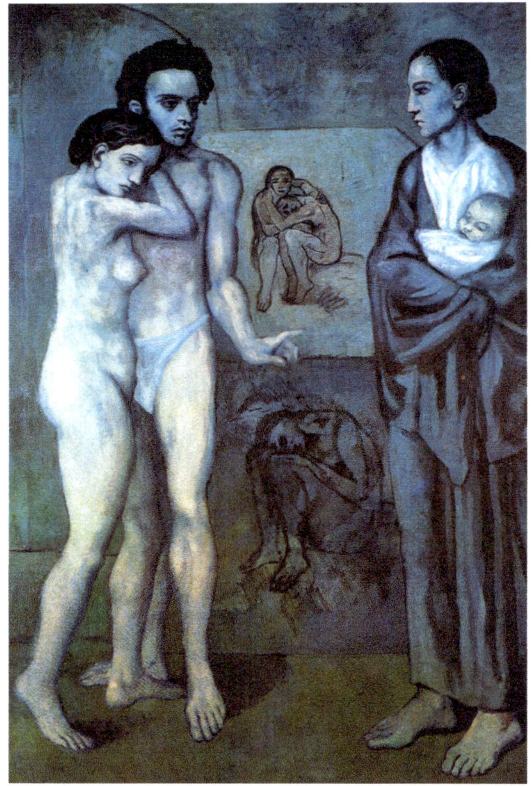

10. Pablo Picasso, *La vie* (1903) © Succession Picasso/DACS, London 2011

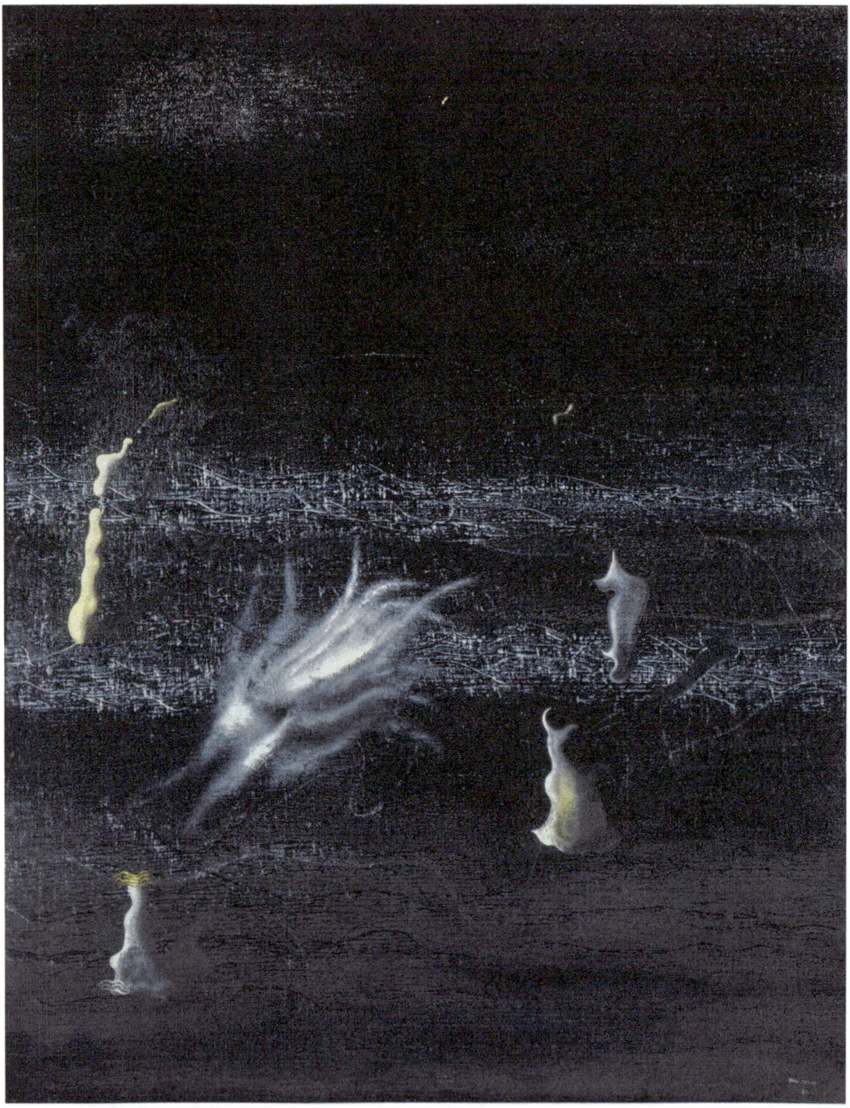

11. Yves Tanguy, *Noyé indifférent* (1929) Reproduced with permission of Galerie Jan Krugier & Cie

Chapter 5

Art and aesthetics are not identical

> Beauty does not indeed lie in things, but in the feeling that we give to them.
> (Jung 1912/1944: 107)

Jung believed that when a person adopts an aesthetic viewpoint, that is to value something as beautiful or not, it is mainly intuition and sensation that are activated in him. Not thinking and feeling. An aesthetic viewpoint is thus not at all the same as an ethical viewpoint. Jung questioned a 'separately' functioning aesthetic attitude and fundamentally disagreed with the opinion that art is the same as aesthetics. It is intriguing that it was the Dutchwoman Maria Moltzer who inspired Jung in this respect. Whereas Jung initially distinguished two psychological functions, feeling and thinking, she discovered intuition. And she realised that the artist in particular is driven by intuition. Jung was indebted to her, even though he left his personal mark on her discovery.

The quality of sensory sensation

By around 1900 the term 'aesthetics' had already gone through a turbulent history, even though it was still a short history. Introduced in the second quarter of the eighteenth century, it rapidly became an important subject studied by famous philosophers in the following one and a half centuries. David Hume (1711–1776), Immanuel Kant (1724–1804), Georg Hegel (1770–1831), Friedrich Schiller (1759–1805), Arthur Schopenhauer (1788–1860) and Nietzsche devoted magnificent passages to it. For sure they sometimes differed hugely in their opinions, but one can also detect a uniformity in their views. Before discussing Jung's ideas, I want to recall some of the main themes in this recent study of aesthetics. It was against this backdrop that Jung developed his own perspective.

Jung remained sensitive to the notion of 'aesthetics' as it was introduced into European culture for the first time in 1735 by the philosopher Alexander Baumgarten (1714–1762). He called it the science of 'the quality of sensory sensation'. He argued that aesthetics is not based on abstract reflection – *noésis* – but on sensation – *aisthèsis*.

If all human beings are mortal, Socrates is a human being and thus must be mortal; we do not smell, hear or see this conclusion, but grasp it through logic. However, we make use of aesthetics when sensory sensation is involved. This fundamental meaning of the word aesthetics is still relevant, for instance in the terms anaesthesia (being sensually numb) and synaesthesia (having different sensual experiences at the same time).

Baumgarten concentrated his research on one particular type of sensation: that of 'beauty'. Almost everyone followed him in this respect, including Jung. But whereas later researchers equated 'aesthetics' with 'art', Jung persistently took a different course. According to Jung, a work of art is not adequately defined as an 'object of beauty'. It is even true that a work of art can look terribly ugly to us. And not everything beautiful is art. No one will call a beautiful landscape a work of art. Furthermore, we can also speak of an aesthetic view of reality. Which is altogether something different than an artistic view. But what is meant by 'aesthetics' or by 'aesthetic judgement'?

"Beauty does not indeed lie in things"

Since ancient times, the question has been whether the aesthetic, beauty, is a quality of the perceived object or whether it is a quality of subjective perception. Why do I call something 'beautiful'? Because it *is* beautiful or because I *appreciate* it as beautiful? One could try to lay the beauty of something *within* that object, but this idea has lost credibility in modern aesthetics. 'To call an object beautiful' is now generally understood as a subjective projection of beauty upon the object. Kant in particular formulated ideas which are still of crucial importance to the discourse of aesthetics. He asserted that aesthetic judgement is not an objective but a subjective judgement, and within this context subjective means that the judgement does not emanate from our reason but from our imagination. Saying 'this is red' means relaying a notion to an object; whereas saying 'this is beautiful' means one's *taste* passes a judgement. We are no longer dealing with the ratio but with the *imaginatio*. We behold with contentment. It is worthwhile quoting the first sentence of Kant's *Critique of the Power of Judgement* (1790); the thoughts which he expressed here are still central in almost all studies on beauty and art. This kind of intricate sentence typifies Kant's style: 'In order to decide whether or not something is beautiful, we do not relate the representation by means of understanding to the object for cognition, but rather relate it by means of the imagination (perhaps combined with the understanding) to the subject and its feeling of pleasure or displeasure. The judgement of taste is therefore not a cognitive judgement, hence not a logical one, but is rather aesthetic, by which is understood one whose determining ground *cannot* be *other than subjective.*'[175]

175 Kant 2000: 89.

When we look closely in order to see what kind of 'pleasure' this is, we can see that Kant thought that it involves two dispositions. An aesthetic perspective gives us great pleasure, but at the same time the pleasure keeps us at a distance from the object providing the pleasure. Taking-pleasure-in as well as keeping-a-distance-from; this contrast experience is always involved. To regard a peach as 'beautiful' and subsequently eating it is a different kind of taste than the aesthetic. The nature of aesthetic pleasure is altruistic, without self-interest. The two attitudes balance each other. Pleasure prevents us from turning away from the object, but the distance ensures that pleasure does not turn into a possessive desire.

In her book *Aesthetics*, the art critic Helen Sheppard dedicated a chapter to 'aesthetic appreciation'. She chiefly elaborated upon the aspect of distancing. 'The detachment arises because we know the emotions [in the work of art] are not "for real". They do not move us to action. This can be seen more clearly if we consider the way we behave before objects we regard aesthetically. We look at them, listen to them, taste, smell, touch, or feel them, as appropriate, but what is striking is what we *do not*. We do not take action to rescue the character in the play who is about to be killed, we do not try to shake hands with statues or walk into pictures. The person who contemplates the fog at sea aesthetically will probably infuriate the sailors who are trying to steer the ship since he just stands there admiring it and doing nothing.'[176]

This does not by any means explain when and why we consider something beautiful. Kant was also unable to explain this. Kant merely established that an aesthetic judgement is not made by reason, nor does it emanate from an ethical position. Beauty is not an aspect of truth nor of goodness.

Whether we regard something as beautiful depends on personal or cultural tastes. In *On Beauty*, Umberto Eco (b. 1932) ascertained that the principle of beauty 'has never been absolute and immutable but has taken on different aspects depending on the historical period and the country.' He nevertheless formulated several formal characteristics of beauty, but we notice that he did not take them much further than Kant. 'If we reflect upon the detached attitude that allows us to define as beautiful some good that does not arouse our desires, we realise that we talk of Beauty when we enjoy something for what it is, immaterial of whether we possess it or not.'[177]

It remains a mystery why 'something' is appreciated as beautiful in one culture whereas another culture sees it as extremely ugly. The same question can be asked with respect to personal differences in taste. In 1757, Hume (admired by Kant) had already written succinctly about this subjective viewpoint in *On the Standard of Taste*. One needs to realise how revolutionary this viewpoint was in the classic tradition at the time. 'Beauty is no quality in things themselves. It exists merely in

176 Sheppard 1987: 71.
177 Eco 2004:14.8.

the mind which contemplates; and each perceives a different beauty. One person may perceive deformity, where another is sensible of beauty.'[178] This became the outline of the modern classic viewpoint. However, Hume and others did not deny the possibility of objective criteria. But if they do exist, we will never be able to discover them consciously.

Jung's perspective on 'aesthetics'

Jung was entirely dedicated to this subjective viewpoint. In 1912 he plainly wrote in *Transformations and Symbolisms of the Libido*: "Beauty does not indeed lie in things, but in the feeling that we give to them."[179] This is Hume's viewpoint. In the same book he also wrote: "Nature is beautiful only by virtue of the longing and love given her by man. The aesthetic attributes emanating from that has influence primarily on the libido, which alone constitutes the beauty of nature."[180] It is remarkable that in the revised edition of this book, published in 1952, he changed this sentence's structure but not its spirit. "Nature is beautiful because I love her, and good is everything that my feeling regards as good. Values are chiefly created by the quality of one's subjective reaction." This is almost the same as in 1912. But he added: "This is not to deny the existence of so-called 'objective' values; only, their validity depends upon the consensus of opinion."[181] The 'so-called' ('sogenannter' in German) must not escape our attention; when validity depends on 'a consensus of opinion', it implies again that this validity is of a subjective nature.

Jung believed that when a person adopts an aesthetic viewpoint, that is, to value something as beautiful or not, it is mainly intuition and sensation that are activated in him. Not thinking and feeling.[182] As we have seen, Kant had a similar viewpoint. When we call something beautiful, we are not using our reason. Nor our feeling, Jung would add. He saw these as the two judging functions. Thinking is the psychological function which structures contents of awareness into a conceptual coherence. Feeling is a process which relates a certain value to a content. It is a form of judgement that functions to accept or reject this content.[183] An aesthetic viewpoint involves intuition and sensation in particular. During the years 1916–1918, it was a Dutchwoman who exercised an important influence on Jung in this respect. Just as Spielrein influenced his understanding of the 'complex' and 'libido', Moltzer did this with respect to the notion of 'intuition'. It is worthwhile having a closer look at this episode.

178 Hume 1886: Volume 3, 268.
179 Jung 1912/1944: 107.
180 Jung 1912/1944: 107.
181 Jung 1952/1956: 85.
182 See Jung 1921/1990: 145.
183 See Jung 1921/1990: 433, 481. Emotions or affects can accompany thinking and feeling, but according to Jung they are essentially different from feeling.

Moltzer and the birth of intuition

Until 1995, Moltzer (see plate 3) was no more than a footnote in Jung's complete oeuvre. We can read this footnote in *Psychological Types* (1921): "The credit for having discovered the existence of this type belongs to M. Moltzer."[184] The bearing of this simple sentence is huge. It is concerned with the 'intuitive type'. Since 1913, Jung had opted for two types of persons, the thinking and the feeling; but between 1916 and 1919, he saw it necessary to dramatically change this typology. He included intuition and sensation. At the same time he understood that these two functions in particular were central to creative processes. But nobody knew Moltzer. When *Psychological Types* was included in the *Collected Works* in 1971, 'Miss' was added to her name. Her name suddenly came to the fore because Richard Noll (b. 1959), in his notorious books *The Jung Cult* and *The Aryan Christ*, mistakenly attributed a text written by Moltzer to Jung.[185] When Shamdasani gave a counter-plea to Noll in 1998, it was necessary to search through the archives in order to find information about her. Only then did she receive a face and we discovered a woman who had an important influence during the first years of the analytical psychology movement.

Maria Moltzer (1874–1944) was the daughter of the proprietor of the Dutch *Bols* company. Rebelling against her father and protesting against alcohol abuse, she left the Netherlands to become a nurse at the alcohol-free Burghölzli clinic in Zürich. Jung met her there around 1908. They were of almost the same age. He trained her as a psychotherapist and she became his assistant. He felt strongly attracted to her. When he left the Burghölzli in 1909, she became one of his close assistants. She had first-hand experience of the Freud–Jung period and, after the break with Freud, she became closely involved in the origination of the range of thoughts that constitutes analytical psychology. In 1911 she participated in the Weimar Congress organised by the International Psychoanalytical Association and in 1912 she travelled with Jung to New York where he gave his Fordham Lectures. Moltzer spoke perfect English and was responsible for the English version of his lectures.

From 1913, Moltzer was an independent analytical psychologist in Zürich. She replaced Jung during his absence, for instance during his yearly military service, and took over some of his patients.[186] She led a withdrawn and sober life. Those around her were not aware of her extreme wealth. Often she was called 'Schwester Moltzer' (Sister Moltzer). She was serious, very intelligent, spiritual and driven. Jung was fond of her and there can be no doubt that they had a strong intellectual bond.[187]

During those years, Moltzer was one of the central figures in the analytical psychology movement. Jung involved her in all his discussions and questions. And she also joined in without being asked. However, she could be irritating sometimes.

184 Jung 1921/1990: 454, footnote 1.
185 See Noll 1994, 1997.
186 See Bair 2003: 259–260.
187 One can speculate about the question of how intimate the relationship between Moltzer and Jung was. Freud was convinced they had an affair (see Shamdasani 2005a: 51–52).

She complained that it was difficult for a woman to settle as an analyst, even more so because the Swiss did not want to be analysed by a Dutchwoman. She was embittered with many people in Jung's circle. She had a sharp pen and spoke her mind to everyone, but... she was usually right. She was continually in discussion with Jung. She had a high regard for his vision, but always pointed out to him the lack of logic in his theories and his incoherent way of explaining things.[188]

The people around Jung became increasingly irritated. Everywhere Moltzer was excluded and ignored. In 1918 the situation became untenable and she withdrew completely and for ever.[189] She stayed in Switzerland and found a home in Zollikerberg, where she died and was buried in 1944.[190] Moltzer corresponded extensively with Jung, again and again trying to convince him that he should at least consider her views before openly ridiculing or speaking sarcastically about them in lectures or personal conversations. It is unfortunate that these letters are still not released to the public.[191] She knew Jung during the most crucial, turbulent and creative period in his life.

During the summer of 1916, Moltzer gave two critical lectures at the Psychology Club.[192] In these lectures she discussed Jung's typological division. In those years, discussions about typological theories were frequent. Everyone spoke of 'introversion' and 'extraversion'. Moltzer made it clear that she was fed up with these 'typological' discussions. In clear language she confronted the Jungians with their most painful spot, as she compared them with the Freudians. 'Just as the Vienna school reduced practically everything to sexuality, after it discovered its value – so in the last years has the Zürich school reduced everything to types. We must guard against this danger as centralising on two types leads to the reduction to formula of all psychic life which threatens to annihilate the new life born from the introduction of the libido theory.'[193]

For a good understanding of the importance of Moltzer's ideas during the summer of 1916, it is essential to know to what extent Jung had developed his theory at the time. Jung (still) divided people into two types – extravert and introvert – and equated extraverted types with feeling and introverted types

188 See Bair 2003: 259, 734, footnotes 22, 23.

189 On 1 August she wrote to one of her patients, Fanny Katz: 'Yes, I resigned from the Club. I could not live any longer in that atmosphere. I am glad I did. I think that in time, when the Club really shall become something, it shall be thankful I did. My resignation has its silent effects. Silent, for it seems that it belongs to my path that I openly don't get the recognition or the appreciation for what I do for the development of the whole analytic movement. I always work in the dark and alone. That is my fate and must be expected' (quoted in Shamdasani 1998a: 72).

190 See Shamdasani 2005b: 105–106, footnote 339.

191 See Bair 2003: 752, footnote 62.

192 Founded on 26 January 1916 in Zürich, 'The Club' functioned as a sort of society, intended as a place to promote analytical psychology. It was the meeting place of analysed persons and analysts. The Club was accommodated in an impressive three-storey building where one could stay overnight (see Bair 2003: 271–273).

193 Quoted in Shamdasani 1998b: 114.

with thinking. He thought thinking was underdeveloped in a strong feeling type and vice versa in the thinking type. This was the situation in the summer of 1916. Moltzer held the opinion that maintaining a distinction between 'feeling' and 'thinking' types implies a disregard for the most important psychological function of the human person – that of intuition. According to Moltzer, 'feeling' and 'thinking' might be useful for a general typology of people, but they are not sufficient to characterise the concrete, individual person. If someone wants to give a personal character to his life, feeling and thinking are insufficient; he also needs to use a third function: intuition. When a person only thinks and feels, he will never be capable of 'creatively' generating something new. For Moltzer, thinking provides abstractions of reality in a rational way, whereas feeling irrationally loses itself in it. She believed that we need a function which *connects* the irrational and the rational. Intuition has its roots in the unconscious *and* appears in our consciousness; it simultaneously dwells in the instinctive and the rational realms. In the blink of an eye, not as a result of thinking or feeling, a person suddenly receives a bright insight! We need this liberating intuition, particularly in harsh times. During such times, we can think and feel until we faint but without realising any progress. A community awaits a liberating intuition.

Moltzer expressed it thus: 'Intuition is also a collective function and has its roots in the personal and impersonal unconscious, contains elements of feelings as well as of thoughts, and tries to solve a given problem and create an adaptation in bringing together these half conscious and half unconscious elements. (...) This type of individual seems to me to appear in its perfection at times of great cultural evolution – at times when neither the mechanism of feeling nor the mechanism of thought is capable of solving the problem demanding a solution. In these times of human agony [she spoke during the First World War], the saving work can be found through the help of intuition.'[194]

It is characteristic of intuition that it balances the irrational and the rational. Therefore, we don't have to choose one-sidedly in favour of rationalism or irrationality. Especially in 'difficult times' we are often afraid of 'strange' elements which we refuse to *think* about, towards which we have no *feeling* and which we subsequently repress. 'Here however intuition comes to the fore, it registers the impressions received and brings the compensatory tendency over into consciousness.'[195] It could hardly have been expressed in a more Jungian way. Nevertheless, it is Moltzer who relayed this intuitive perspective to Jung. Maybe she sharpened her position a little when she wrote: 'as the introverted attitude reacts with thought and the extraverted attitude with feeling, so the intuitive attitude reacts with understanding.'[196] For Jung, the message was clear. Only through intuition can a person concretely know what he needs to do; only through intuition is a person is creative.

194 Quoted in Shamdasani 1998b: 109–110.
195 Quoted in Shamdasani 1998b: 115.
196 Quoted in Shamdasani 1998b: 116.

How does intuition make itself known? Through the imagination. Moltzer asserted that intuition reveals itself in images, in the same way as thinking expresses itself in concepts and feeling is known through emotions. 'Intuition stands at the threshold of consciousness and introversion of the function leads of itself to the pictures within the unconscious.'[197] In her second lecture, she expounded upon this theme and started to reflect on art. Taking everything into consideration, a creative idea never arises from thinking or feeling but from intuition. When an artist is able to assimilate the unconscious and allow it to fully surface, he is able to achieve this because of intuition.[198]

Moltzer claimed that the function of 'image-making' was already operating in prehistoric cave painters. 'As far as I can see,' she says, 'intuition is the oldest human function and has grown out of instinct. I consider intuition to be the differentiation and the conscious function of instinct. (...) The cave dwellers have left us pictures on their walls which show us that even at that time the function of image-making was developed, and it was through visions that mankind was seeking its further differentiation. It is my opinion that herein lies the origin of consciously directed thought and of religion.'[199]

On the whole, Jung agreed with Moltzer's thoughts. He knew he was indebted to her. The one footnote says it all. Her ideas had a great authority. When, in 1921, he included intuition into his typology, he placed it within a fourfold model: thinking, feeling, intuition and sensation. All four types can have an extraverted or introverted orientation.[200] Subsequently there are eight types. Nothing remained of his idea expressed in 1916. Moltzer was aware of 'sensation', but considered it more or less identical with intuition.[201] Jung also thought they were closely related. In an interview in 1955, he used them almost interchangeably: "So my definition is that intuition is a perception via the unconscious."[202] Likewise, he could have said that sensation it is an intuition via a sensual impulse.

In our daily experience, sensation and intuition never function in their pure form. They are always mingled with thoughts and feelings. However, an intensified sensation, such as an *aesthetic* sensation, creates distinctions within this multitude, it represses some impressions, occasionally prefers one aspect, rejects admixtures and gives a degree of purity and clarity which daily experience can never achieve. The aesthetic view is per definition an abstraction. Jung described it thus: "The concrete sensation of a flower (...) conveys a perception not only of the flower as

197 Quoted in Shamdasani 1998b: 117.
198 See Shamdasani 1998b: 116.
199 Quoted in Shamdasani 1998b: 116–117.
200 According to Jung, a person is mainly determined by extraversion-introversion. These are anchored within our biological constitution and more determining than the four function types: thinking, feeling, intuition and sensation. Extraversion and introversion are in a compensatory relationship. When consciousness is extravert, then the unconscious is introvert and vice versa (see Jacobi 1962: 19–23).
201 See Shamdasani 1998a: 99.
202 Jung 1977/1978: 307.

such, but also of the stem, leaves, habitat, and so on. It is also instantly mingled with feelings of pleasure or dislike which the sight of the flower evokes, or with simultaneous olfactory perceptions, or with thoughts about its botanical classification, etc. But abstract sensation immediately picks up the most salient sensuous attribute of the flower, its brilliant redness, for instance, and makes this the sole or at least the principal content of consciousness, entirely detached from all other admixtures. *Abstract sensation is found chiefly among artists.* Like every abstraction, it is a product of functional *differentiation,* and there is nothing primitive about it."[203]

The aesthetic view, extremely formulated

It is important to understand that intuition and sensation in their pure form *only register and observe.* They have no interest in thinking and feeling; moreover, the latter two should be interested in them. During a seminar held in 1933, Jung said that he would illustrate in an 'extreme' way the 'aesthetic attitude'. He compared it to a 'religious attitude'. A religious person is able to see the 'gods' in a dewdrop, a flower, a falling star, an animal which crosses his path, a sunbeam. When this happens, he has a total experience. But if he adopts an aesthetic attitude towards this flower or this dewdrop, he looks at only one aspect. The aesthetic attitude is a partial attitude. Such an attitude protects against an abundance of other sensations and is therefore per definition one-sided and superficial.

Jung gave an example. "I will give you an example of an extreme aesthetic attitude. It is not an exaggeration. On a snowy street an automobile skids, hits a child, and crushes its skull against the curbstone; you come along and see people standing about, and the blood on the snow, and you hear: 'Awful accident! Child has been killed!' Naturally, you would be impressed. But if you have the gift of the aesthetic attitude, you say: 'What an interesting picture, how beautiful!' You see the beauty of the horror, which means you are shielded from the whole thing, you have experienced only the surface. The characteristic group of people around the place of disaster is very dramatic, and you can make a drawing of it which will be most artistic, most suggestive; and the contrast between the cold snow and the warm blood, the dead white and the bright red colour, is most remarkable, most suggestive and you can paint it."[204]

In this example, Jung emphasised that an aesthetic attitude gives an *incomplete* experience of reality. Of course, he said, one can look aesthetically at everything, but no one would claim that the essence of something is known if one only approaches it aesthetically. To approach something in a purely aesthetic manner means approaching it only in as far as one perceives it. Jung continually repeated that for the individuation process more is needed than an aesthetic attitude. Above all it needs the question whether we regard something as good or true. He described

203 Jung 1921/1990: 462 (italics mine).
204 Jung 1997: 919.

this succinctly in *Psychological Types*: "Just as the world of appearances can never become a moral problem for the man who merely senses it, the world of inner images is never a moral problem for the intuitive. For both of them it is an aesthetic problem, a matter of perception, a 'sensation'."[205]

Nonetheless, intuition and sensation are valuable functions. Jung merely criticised a one-sided emphasis. This same one-sidedness can also be true with respect to a purely thinking and/or feeling attitude. However, to the artist it is essential to have an aesthetic attitude. If he did not posses an aesthetic distance, he would simply not be capable of creating art. In the example of the child's accident, it would have been impossible to portray this scene if the person adopting an aesthetic attitude could not estrange himself from the tragedy. "The aesthetic attitude is a necessity for the artist, for he *must* shield himself against the object or the vision or the experience – whatever it is – in order to be able to reproduce it; if you are absolutely in it you are caught, destroyed, you are not an artist. You begin to howl like a dog perhaps, but that is not artistic. You must be able to remove yourself from it. Therefore the artist must have an aesthetic attitude."[206]

In this context it is significant to note how outspokenly critical Jung was of Franz Riklin (1878–1938), his former colleague and friend, when the latter wanted to follow his artistic aspirations. In 1904, Riklin and Jung initiated the well-known Studies in Word Association at the Burghölzli. It made them famous. However, in the following years, Riklin increasingly followed his vocation as an artist, a painter. His work as a psychoanalyst suffered because of this. Jung thought that Riklin lacked the most important characteristic of an artist: an aesthetic attitude which is detached from reality. According to him, Riklin lost himself in his work. In a conversation with Erika Schlegel (librarian of the Psychological Club at Zürich) on 10 March 1921, Jung spoke his mind about it and left no room for any misunderstanding. The next day, she wrote in her notebook: 'I wore my pearl medallion (the pearl embroidery that Sophie[207] had made for me) at Jung's yesterday. He liked it very much, and it prompted him to talk animatedly about art – for almost an hour. He discussed Riklin, one of Augusto Giacommetti's students, and observed that while his smaller works had a certain aesthetic value, his larger ones simply dissolved. Indeed, he vanished wholly in his art, rendering him utterly intangible. His work was like a wall over which water rippled. He could therefore not analyse, as this required one to be pointed and sharp-edged like a knife. He had fallen into art in a manner of speaking. But art and science were no more than the servants of the creative spirit, which is what must be served.'[208]

205 Jung 1921/1990: 400.

206 Jung 1997: 920.

207 Sophie Taeuber-Arp (1889–1943), the sister of Erika Schlegel, was a member of the Dada movement. She painted, sculpted, and practised applied art and the art of dancing.

208 Quoted in Shamdasani (2009: 204. In *Memories, Dreams, Reflections*, Jung is still critical of Riklin: "He believed that he was a misunderstood artist and this destroyed him. The reason for his failure? He was not rooted in his own sense of self-worth, but depended on the recognition of others. That is dangerous." (Jung 1962/1997: 190).

For an artist an aesthetic attitude is required and sufficient; however, for someone who is mentally ill it is not. In 1928, in one of his most important writings, *The I and the Unconscious*, Jung made a sharp distinction between a 'human' and an 'aesthetic' experience. The artist interprets and understands his fantasies, but does not *experience* them. His patients not only have to observe their fantasies, but also need to *interiorise* them. "For the important thing is not to interpret and understand the fantasies, but primarily to *experience* them."[209]

In 1955, Jung stated in *Mysterium Coniunctionis* that many patients and their psychiatrists, with respect to their active imagination, are not going much further than the sensation of images and the observation of them. This is surely a beginning of an individuation process, but it does not yet involve a confrontation with the unconscious. "As this experience is not uncommon I can only conclude that the transition from a merely perceptive, i.e. *aesthetic,* attitude to one of *judgement* is far from easy."[210]

Above we saw that Kant distinguished two aspects of aesthetic taste: finding-pleasure-in and keeping-distance-from. It is possible to reduce one's whole attitude to life to this double disposition: finding pleasure in something whilst keeping a distance, only being able to find pleasure in something when keeping it at a distance. According to Jung, such a hedonistic view of life is per definition "superficial".[211] However, he realised that a person does not always have a choice in this respect. Just as the painter of the child's deadly accident needs to shield himself from the tragedy of the event in order to create the drawing, in the same way other people, forced by necessity, shield themselves from their dark impulses and superficially keep up good appearances. Jung thought that Nietzsche was an outspoken example of such an aesthetic person.

Nietzsche's aesthetic view of life

Jung thought Nietzsche was mentally disturbed. He was certain that this disturbance had been present much longer than the final 12 years of Nietzsche's life. He also thought that the aesthetic view of life which Nietzsche had developed was related to his disturbance. In his writings, Nietzsche repeatedly emphasised the significance of an 'aesthetic attitude', which, in his view, is the only attitude that can liberate us. Religion and morality have ceased to be normative for the modern person. Hence, the world can only be justified as an aesthetic phenomenon. It is the only sound perspective to sustain us in this mortal life. Nietzsche said: 'The truth is ugly. We have *art* so we are not destroyed by the truth' [212] and 'I repeat my earlier sentence that only as an aesthetic phenomenon do existence and the world appear

209 Jung 1928/1966: 213.
210 Jung 1955–56/1963: 530.
211 In this regard, Jung used the term 'Ästhetismus', meaning 'an aesthetic view of life', rather than the term 'Ästhetizismus', meaning 'doing aesthetics' (see Jung 1921/1990: 121, footnote 94).
212 Nietzsche 1997: 346.

justified; which means that tragic myth in particular must convince us that even the ugly and disharmonious is an artistic game which the Will, in the eternal fullness of its delight, plays with itself.'[213]

Nietzsche constantly adjusted this 'aesthetic' viewpoint. In his doctoral thesis, *The Birth of Tragedy*, he still thought art could alleviate human suffering. In his later writings he no longer thought art was capable of doing this and asserted that our problems are inherent to life itself. Therefore, our own life needs to be a work of art, the 'Übermensch'. Nietzsche's aesthetic experience exists in an increase of the feeling of power and of life, in the 'will to power', in order to acknowledge reality in all its manifestations, even the most absurd and meaningless.[214]

Jung was convinced that Nietzsche had developed this 'artificial' vision of our 'insufferable' life because life was unbearable to him. Subsequently, there was only one option left: to live 'superficially'. If he had descended into the depths of his unconscious, he would have been overwhelmed by it; and in the end this turned out to be his destiny. Nietzsche tried to endure his life by keeping up 'appearances'. Jung said: "Nietzsche once said that the world was merely an aesthetic problem, and that was because, if he had not assumed such an attitude, he would have suffered so much from his world that the problem would have become insupportable. So he covered up the abyss, he was quite satisfied apparently with the polished surface of things."[215]

Jung emphasised that a person needs the courage to confront the *depths* of the unconscious – otherwise it will irrevocably get a hold on him at some point in time. After all, reality itself is not an aesthetic problem lying like a veil over us. Reality has a grip on us. "It goes right under the skin. That is what he [i.e. Nietzsche] was always trying to escape, but he did not escape it, though he tried to deny it. (...) He *was* a great artist, but he was also a philosopher and we expect a philosopher to think. His work ran away with him and that was his weakness. Such a thing would not have happened to Goethe, or Schiller, or Shakespeare. That was his weakness: he was a genius with a big hole in him."[216]

It is generally known how, in his doctoral thesis, Nietzsche tried to reduce the apollinian and dionysian drives to 'artistic drives'. This attempt had such an impact that his terminology still pervades our culture. The apollinian force compels us to look *at* reality from a distance, whereas the dionysian force is inebriated by

213 Nietzsche 1999: 113. 'As an aesthetic phenomenon existence is still *bearable* to us, and art furnishes us with the eye and the hand and above all the good conscience to be *able* to make such a phenomenon of ourselves' (Nietzsche 2001: 104).

214 See also Baumeister 1999: 326, 330.

215 Jung 1997: 929. On many occasions in his writings Nietzsche recommended this superficial life, for instance in the preface of *The Gay Science:* 'Oh, those Greeks! They know how to *live*: what is needed for that is to stop bravely at the surface, the fold, the skin; to worship appearance, to believe in shapes, tones, words – in the whole Olympus of appearance! Those Greeks were superficial – *out of profundity*! (...) Are we not just in this respect – Greeks? Worshippers of shapes, tones, words? And therefore – artists?' (Nietzsche 2001: 8–9).

216 Jung 1988: 1255.

the immersion *in* this reality. In his thesis, he proposed that the Greeks reconciled these two drives in their tragedies and the Europeans of his age in Wagner's operas. In these works of art, or actually in all works of art, the artist knows how to control his dionysian intoxication through his apollinian dream.

Jung response was to bemoan that this perspective on history indicates that we no longer have a clue about the meaning of these primal forces. The Greeks did not consider these drives to be an aesthetic reality but an existential one. Jung thought Nietzsche had forgotten that the philosophers never saw their conflict about Apollo and Dionysius as an aesthetic problem, but as a problem with a *purely religious* nature. The Dionysian cult was a kind of totem festivity with a mystical bent. Greek tragedy originated from religious ceremonies, and this is a similar development to our modern theatre, which goes back to the Medieval passion plays with their religious meaning. Ancient culture never saw the mystery plays in a purely aesthetic light, as we do now. Jung wrote: "With Nietzsche the religious viewpoint is entirely overlooked and is replaced by the aesthetic. These things obviously have their aesthetic side and it should not be neglected. Nevertheless, if medieval Christianity is understood only aesthetically its true character is falsified and trivialised, just as much as if it were viewed exclusively from the historical standpoint. A true understanding is possible only on a common ground – no one would wish to maintain that the nature of a railway bridge is adequately understood from a purely aesthetic angle."[217]

However, Jung's most important criticism towards Nietzsche is that the aesthetic view of life is insufficient because it forgets, denies or represses the ugly. This is inherent to aesthetic reduction. The aesthetic attitude is per definition not based on empathy, but on distance and pleasure. When we take this as our point of departure, we come to see the 'ugly' as beautiful.[218] "Aestheticism is not fitted to solve the exceedingly serious and difficult task of educating man, for it always presupposes the very thing it should create – the capacity to love beauty. It actually hinders a deeper investigation of the problem, because it always averts its face from anything evil, ugly, and difficult, and aims at pleasure, even though it [may] be of an edifying kind. Aestheticism therefore lacks all moral force, because *au fond* it is still only a refined hedonism."[219] The resulting conflict is so confusing that in the best scenario a person comes to repress the untrue and ugly without being liberated from it. An *ethical* attitude is necessary if we want to be liberated from this conflict: virtuous effort, being prepared to bring offers and religious earnestness.[220]

217 Jung 1921/1990: 141.
218 See Jung 1921/1990: 140–141.
219 Jung 1921/1990: 121. "The aesthetic approach immediately converts the problem into a picture which the spectator can contemplate at his ease, admiring both its beauty and its ugliness, merely re-experiencing its passions at a safe distance, with no danger of becoming involved in them" (Jung 1921/1990: 142).
220 See Jung 1921/1990: 121.

Jung and Nietzsche

Jung was convinced that his life, like Nietzsche's, would become unbearable if he allowed himself to be one-sidedly guided by the aesthetic attitude. Nietzsche's life and thoughts had a strong impact on him. The student Jung could not ignore Nietzsche, because he studied in *his* city, Basel. Nietzsche was appointed there in 1869, at the age of 24, as professor of philosophy. He kept this position for ten years. In 1879, he had to give up his professorship for health reasons. He subsequently led a peripatetic existence and became increasingly ill, both psychically and physically, until he collapsed in 1888 and became completely submerged in a world of insanity. This would last for 12 years. He died in 1900. Jung studied in Basel during those 'insane' years. He frequently heard rumours about the 'secret disease' of the great philosopher. His family could not get the name of this blasphemous philosopher over their lips. But from the mouths of others, such as Jacob Burckhardt (1818–1897), Nietzsche's friend and ex-colleague, Jung heard grave messages about his insanity. At a certain point, Jung even became afraid that he himself might suffer from some form of insanity.[221] Like Nietzsche, he was also a vicar's son and he similarly had weird thoughts about religion and morals. Without a doubt, Jung (rightly or wrongly) blamed Nietzsche's fall on his aesthetic view of life.

Like Nietzsche, Jung also had a natural artistic inclination. Someone who is acquainted with Jung's life knows that he was artistically busy in different areas: I express this vaguely on purpose. He painted. He took his brush and went out to paint landscapes, city views and seaviews. Some of his paintings created between 1900 and 1905 still exist.[222] He dedicated *Seine landscape with clouds* to his wife.[223] A river landscape with hills in the background was dedicated to his mother.[224] Jung wrote poems, amongst them the Gnostic poem *Septem Sermones ad Mortuos* (*Seven Sermons to the Dead*)[225]; he was an architect and built his own tower; he was a sculptor and carved ornaments into stone; he painted mandalas and created many etchings.

One can say that Jung was at least a 'Sunday-artist' or someone who made a sort of primitive art. However, he was ambivalent about these activities, possibly because of his caution with regard to aesthetics. His entire life he maintained that whatever he might have done in this respect, it had nothing to do with art. Did he

221 See Jung 1961/1989: 101–102.

222 See Bair 2003: 79–80; Jaffé 1989: 124; Wehr 1989: 6.

223 On the back is written: "for my dearest fiancée at Christmas 1902. Paris. December 1902. Painted by C. G. Jung" (depicted in: Jaffé 1983: 43).

224 In 1902 he wrote on the back: "To my beloved Mother at Christmas 1901, and for her birthday, 1902." In 1955, when his wife died, he gave the painting to his daughter Marianne. He added: "To my dear daughter Marianne, in gratitude, from her father. Painted by C. G. Jung. Christmas 1955" (depicted in Jaffé 1983: 43). Two of his other paintings from this period are known. A view of the lake of Zürich from 1904 and a seascape from 1905. The 'Lake of Zürich' is depicted in Gaillard 1998: 207; the seascape in Wehr 1989: 47.

225 See Jung 1961/1989: 378.

have a blind spot for his own principles or did he express a subtle perspective on art? Nonetheless, he did think that his work had aesthetic qualities. But he did not consider this to be equal to art. He was cautious about aesthetics.

It is fascinating to follow Jung's thoughts on this subject in the next chapter. Sometimes they seem opposed to his formal perspective on art, whereas at other times they deepen it. It is this perspective which is the main subject of this book.

Chapter 6

Jung's ideas about himself as an artist

> Therefore I gave up this estheticising tendency in good time, in favour of a rigorous process of understanding.
>
> (Jung 1961/1989: 188)

> When the stone was finished, I looked at it again and again, wondering about it and asking myself what lay behind my impulse to carve it.
>
> (Jung 1961/1989: 228)

Jung made a sharp distinction between the aesthetic products which he created with his own hands. He was convinced that his mandalas and the pictures in his *Red Book* had nothing to do with art, but rather with aesthetics. With respect to his other works, for example his sculptures and reliefs which are still on display in the garden in Bollingen, he occasionally recognised their artistic value. However, he was cautious to acknowledge this to the outside world. With respect to this subject, he rarely disclosed what was going on in his mind. He did so only once: when his square stone was not artistically appreciated 'künstlerisch'.

Preface

This chapter is not intended to review all the works of art made by Jung nor to judge them artistically, with or without reference to his own ideas (even though that would be interesting). I am still concerned with Jung's own thoughts about art, but this time in relation to his own artistic products. At the end of the previous chapter, I mentioned how he denied any artistic value to his work. I will illustrate this with an example. When the American sculptor Don L. Stacy questioned him about his sculptures, he replied: "I'm no artist. I only try to get things into stone of which I think it is important that they appear in hard matter and stay on for a reasonably long time. Or I try to give form to something that seems to be in the stone and makes me restless. It is nothing for show, it's only to make these troublesome things steady and durable. There is not much of form in it, chiefly inscriptions, and you would learn nothing from it."[226]

We might assume that Jung was hiding his true nature in this conversation, because in the second part of this chapter we will see how much he was *artistically* attached to, for example, the square stone full of inscriptions that he had created two years earlier. We have to guess why he adopted this defensive attitude. Did he want to protect himself? Did he not want to take the risk of being undervalued as an artist? Perhaps he did not want to disclose his inner life at all? Was he afraid that if he was seen as an artist, as a consequence he might no longer be respected as a scientist? Nevertheless, we shall see that later he did start to regard himself an artist.

In the first part of this chapter, we are concerned with those artistic products made by Jung's hands which, in his view, are clearly different – the mandalas and pictures he made during the crisis after his break-up with Freud. With respect to these artistic products, Jung took an exceptionally sharp position: these products have nothing to do with art. Nonetheless, he did consider them to be aesthetic. Against the background of the previous chapter, it will become clear what he meant.

The Red Book

We have already seen that Jung distinguished between art and aesthetics. We can clearly specify this distinction with reference to a remarkable event taken from his life. It is well-known that Jung went through a spiritual crisis in 1913. Sometimes he thought schizophrenia was threatening him. At a certain moment he became aware that it was healing to give the images and voices in his mind a chance to get 'on stage' and for him to have a conversation with them in some way. He wrote as stories many of his dreams, fantasies and hallucinations. He did this in the so called *Black Books*. "As a result of my experiment I learned how helpful it can be, from the therapeutic point of view, to find the particular images which lie behind emotions."[227]

In the summer of 1914, he commenced writing a draft of what became *The Red Book*. He copied most of the fantasies from the *Black Books* and to each of these added a section explaining the significance of each episode, combined with a lyrical elaboration. After completing this handwritten draft (556 pages), he thought he should embellish these texts. He commissioned a large folio volume of over 600 pages, bound in read leather, and subsequently copied them into what later was called *The Red Book*. The work is organised like a medieval illuminated manuscript, with calligraphic writing. Jung then illustrated the text with paintings, historiated initials, ornamental borders, and margins. Initially, the paintings refer directly to the text. At a later point the paintings become independent from the text.[228]

226 Jung 1990: 83 (letter dated 1 September 1952).
227 Jung 1961/1989: 177.
228 See Shamdasani 2009: 202–203.

According to Jung, he painted his first mandala on 16 January 1916 (see plate 4). He wrote on the back of it in English: "This is the first mandala I constructed in the year 1916, wholly unconscious of what it meant."[229] Many other mandalas followed. Each morning during the years 1918–1919, he sketched a small circular drawing in his notebook, which, in his own words, "seemed to correspond to my inner situation at that time. With the help of these drawings I could observe my psychic transformations from day to day."[230]

Jung had no intention of publishing the book. He thought the book revealed too clearly that he had lost his grip on life during those years, even though he also called this period "the vessel of my oeuvre".[231] When, at the age of 70, he entrusted the book's content to his English translator Richard Hull (1913–1974), the latter was astounded; but his admiration for the man whose texts he had been translating for more than 20 years increased. Referring to what he had read in *The Red Book*, Hull disclosed in 1961: 'Jung was a walking asylum in himself, as well as its head physician. (...) He went through everything an insane person goes through (...) had it not been for his astounding capacity to stand off from those experiences, to observe and to understand what was happening, he would have been overwhelmed by the psychotic material that came through the 'dividing-wall'. His achievement lay in hammering that material into a system of psychotherapy that worked.'[232]

Jung continued to work at *The Red Book* until 1930. Then he locked it away in a cupboard in Küsnacht, where it more or less remained until 1984, when Jung's family transferred it to a Zürich bank vault. In 1997 Sonu Shamdasani approached the family with the idea of publishing a complete scholarly edition. They eventually agreed. *The Red Book* was published in 2009. Shamdasani's achievement is unquestioned. He practically lived with the book for nearly a decade. His extensive introduction and more than 1,000 footnotes place Jung's work in its historical and cultural context.[233]

"No, it is not art! On the contrary, it is nature"

In *Memories, Dreams, Reflections*, Jung revealed how on a certain day a female inner voice seduced him into seeing his creations as art. He absolutely refused this. It is clarifying to closely study Jung's reasoning in this respect. He immediately recognised this voice as Moltzer's, the Dutchwoman we encountered in the previous chapter who showed him the importance of intuition.[234] I will quote the crucial passages in their exchange of thoughts, which continued for several years:

229 Quoted in Shamdasani 2009: 206. Depicted in Jung 2009: 364.
230 Jung 1961/1989: 195.
231 See Bair 2003: 295, 500.
232 Quoted in Bair 2003: 292–293.
233 See Jung 2009.
234 See Bair 2003: 745, footnote 6; Shamdasani 1999: 43.

When I was writing down these fantasies, I once asked myself, 'What am I really doing? Certainly this has nothing to do with science. But then what is it?' Whereupon a voice within me said, 'It is art.' I was astonished. It never entered into my head that what I was writing had any connection with art. Then I thought, 'Perhaps my unconscious is forming a personality that is not me, but which insists on bringing its own insights to expression.' (...) Obviously what I was doing wasn't science. What then could it be but art? It was as though these were the only alternatives in the world. (...) I said very emphatically to this voice that my fantasies had nothing to do with art, and I felt a great inner resistance. No voice came through, however, and I kept on writing. Then came the next assault, and again the same assertion: 'That is art.' This time I caught her and said, 'No, it is not art! On the contrary, it is nature.' (...)

If I had taken these fantasies of the unconscious as art, they would have carried no more conviction than visual perceptions, as if I were watching a movie. I would have felt no ethical obligation toward them. (...)

It was only toward the end of the First World War that I gradually began to emerge from the darkness (...) I began to understand my mandala drawings. (...) One day, for example, I received a letter from that aesthetic lady in which she again stubbornly maintained that the fantasies arising from my unconscious had artistic value and should be considered art. The letter got on my nerves. It was far from stupid, and therefore dangerously persuasive. The modern artist, after all, seeks to create art out of the unconscious. The utilitarianism and self-importance concealed behind this thesis touched a doubt in myself, namely, my uncertainty as to whether the fantasies I was producing were really spontaneous and natural, and not ultimately my own arbitrary inventions. (...) Out of this irritation and disharmony within myself there proceeded, the following day, a changed mandala: part of the periphery had burst open and the symmetry was destroyed.

Only gradually did I discover what the mandala really is: 'Formation, Transformation, Eternal Mind's eternal recreation.' And that is the self, the wholeness of the personality, which if all goes well is harmonious, but which cannot tolerate self-deceptions. My mandalas were cryptograms concerning the state of the self which were presented to me anew each day.[235]

235 Jung 1961/1989: 185–186, 187, 195–196. Fanny Bowditch Katz, Moltzer's patient, wrote in her diary entry of 31 July 1916 that Moltzer herself kept a similar book with texts and pictures, 'her Bible'. But Moltzer saw little artistic value in her own products. Fanny noted that Moltzer regarded her paintings as 'purely subjective, not works of art' (quoted in Shamdasini 2009: 204). This obviously shows that she did not appreciate herself as an artist, which makes it all the more convincing that she really appreciated Jung's pictures as art. In all kinds of ways, Moltzer tried to promote art amongst the Jungians in Zürich. Her great example was her friend Franz Riklin.

Against the background of what we know at this point about Jung's perspective on art, we can pursue his adamant, eccentric flow of thoughts as it was expressed in this elaborate quote. We remember from Chapter 4 Jung's claim that art per definition does not belong to nature but to culture. He knew what he intended when he asserted that mandalas are not cultural but natural products. But what was the reason for this opinion?

To begin with, the above quotation has several parenthetic clauses wherein Jung clearly described what he considered art. He asked himself: "*Perhaps my unconscious is forming a personality that is not me, but which insists on bringing its own insights to expression.*" We know what he was saying here: maybe my unconscious has formed an autonomous complex. Because this is exactly what happens to an artist. In art the I does not express a meaning, because the creative process is impersonal; it emerges unconsciously, separate from the conscious I. Art emanates from the separate partial-psyche and enforces itself with its own force from the unconscious upon the artist's consciousness.

The artist observes it, Jung stated above, like watching a film, as if looking at something which is going on outside of him: "*They would have carried no more conviction than visual perceptions, as if I were watching a movie. I would have felt no ethical obligation toward them.*" We have already encountered this line of thought. Only the functions of perception, that is intuition and sensation, are involved in the origination of art. Not thinking and feeling. The artist is not primarily concerned with ethics. He relentlessly observes reality. One only has to remember the example of the child's accident.

Jung was convinced that none of this was happening in his own situation. Therefore *The Red Book* was not art. He knew about the possibility of being submerged in a complex and becoming a puppet of the unconscious. This frightened him during his crisis. He tried to safeguard his conscious I and subsequently employed all kinds of active imagination (mandalas, drawings, reflections and so forth) in order to prevent his partial-psyche from taking over his conscious I and to protect himself against losing the ground beneath his feet. For this reason he used his *natural* regressive forces. The above quotation also conveys Jung's uncertainty.

Jung wrote that he was uncertain as to "w*hether the fantasies I was producing were really spontaneous and natural, and not ultimately my own arbitrary inventions.*" Once more we read the word 'natural'. Since we are inclined to think that it is the artist who works in a 'spontaneous and natural' way, we need to realise that in this case 'arbitrary inventions' refers to art. 'Spontaneous and natural'; this was the process when he drew his mandala. He saw the mandala as a natural product. The form of the mandala is *not* arbitrary, no, it is archetypal. For centuries, Tibetan monks, Aboriginals and Indians have created them, and schizophrenic patients draw them *inadvertently*. It is important not to disturb this natural process. With irritation, Jung realised that he was seduced by the anima-voice[236] to make curves in the mandala at his own volition and as such he began

236 The archetype 'anima' in the psychology of Jung is 'the symbolic figure of the female soul-powers in the man' (Timmer 2001: 36).

to imitate the artist. This caused a loss of symmetry and subsequently the loss of the curative wholeness he needed.

Jung repeatedly underlined this aspect of mandalas: they originate *naturally*. In 1955 he wrote about the 'spontaneous origination' of mandalas: "As a rule a mandala occurs in conditions of psychic dissociation or disorientation."[237] He gave examples of children whose parents are divorcing, adults who suffer from a neurosis and schizophrenic patients: "This is evidently *an attempt at self-healing* on the part of Nature, which does not spring from conscious reflection but from an instinctive impulse."[238] Jung experienced this personally during his own crisis. It had nothing to do with art, but (again) with regressively finding his way in the course of nature.

Jung was ill, he was trying to control *symptoms*, he was rebalancing his (instinctual) nature. He was therapeutically, not artistically, engaged. Jung was afraid that, if the artistic spirit were to possess him, he would become a puppet of the unconscious. He did not want to lose the grip of his conscious I. He wanted to offer this I the river bed of nature, he had no intention of creating culture.

We know that Jung encouraged his patients to depict their inner fantasies in all kinds of ways, for example in drawings. But he was always watchful that they did not consider their work 'art'. In 1929 he wrote: "Although my patients occasionally produce artistically beautiful things that might very well be shown in modern 'art' exhibitions, I nevertheless treat them as completely worthless when judged by the canons of real art."[239] As a matter of fact, it is essential that they should be considered worthless, otherwise my patients might imagine themselves to be artists, and the whole point of the exercise would be missed. It is not a question of art at all – or, rather, it should not be a question of art – but of something more and other than mere art, namely the living effect upon the patient himself. The meaning of individual life, whose importance from the social standpoint is negligible, stands here at his highest, and for its sake the patient struggles to give form, however crude and childish, to the inexpressible. (...) A patient needs only to have seen once or twice how much he is freed from a wretched state of mind by working at a symbolical picture, and he will always turn to this means of release whenever things go badly with him."[240]

However, the final word about *The Red Book* has not yet been spoken. Although it is not a work of art, Jung did regard it as an aesthetic product. And as such it was a blessing to him. In the above quotation, Hull was already implying this when he wrote: 'had it not been for his astounding capacity *to stand off from those experiences, to observe and to understand* what was happening, he would have

237 Jung 1955/1959: 387.

238 Jung 1955/1959: 388.

239 Shamdasani wrote: 'Jung could easily have exhibited some of his works in such a setting [during the First World War there were several contacts between the Zürich School and the avant-garde movements of art in Zürich], had he so liked. Thus his refusal to consider his work as art occurs in a context where there were quite real possibilities for him, to have taken this route' (Shamdasani 2009: 204).

240 Jung 1929/1966: 48, 49.

been overwhelmed by the psychotic material.' The sentence I italicised in fact states the core of the aesthetic way of beholding: to observe something from a distance. By adopting this attitude, Jung made sure that he would not succumb. The aesthetic attitude was his safeguard.

In the 'epilogue' to *The Red Book*, Jung wrote that this work "will appear as completely insane to a superficial judge. It would have become an insane work *if I had been unable to work through the overwhelming power of the original experiences*. I always knew that these experiences carry within them something valuable, and therefore I did not know what else to do than to write them down in a 'valuable', that is to say expensive, book and to draw the images that emerged whilst re-experiencing them as well as possible."[241] Here he is saying that he can process the overwhelming power of his experiences through such an abstract intervention. Aesthetics props up the drama of life. This was Nietzsche's message.

But Jung realised that in the end this is insufficient. Precisely because he was able to keep life at a distance *for a short time*, he knew what to do and felt an ethical and existential obligation. This became clear when Jung, at the end of his life, explicitly discussed the 'aesthetic side' of *The Red Book* one last time in a conversation with his secretary, Aniela Jaffé (1901–1991): "In *The Red Book* I tried an aesthetic elaboration of my fantasies, but never finished it. I became aware that I had not yet found the right language, that I still had to translate it into something else. Therefore I gave up this aestheticising tendency in good time, in favour of a rigorous process of *understanding*. I saw that so much fantasy needed a firm ground underfoot, and that I must first return wholly to reality."[242] (...) "*The aesthetic editing in* The Red Book *was necessary* – even though I was irritated and annoyed about it – because through this I received insight into the ethical obligation in the face of the images of the unconscious. This had a decisive influence on my way of life."[243]

Jung affirmed his aesthetic editing of existentially experienced material. And even though an artist will *also* choose an aesthetic perspective with respect to symbols, an aesthetic perspective does not necessarily lead to a work of art. Very different laws were involved in the creation of aesthetic products of the active imagination which Jung and his patients practised during their crises. In those situations an aesthetic attitude can be *a phase* in a curative process.

241 Jung 1962/1997: 387.

242 Jung 1961/1989: 188.

243 Jung 1962/1997: 387 (italics mine). When, during his conversations with Jaffé in 1959, Jung re-experienced the period of crisis in his life, he again took up *The Red Book* 'to finish the last incomplete drawing'. But he was unable to do it. "It is because of death," he said. He did write a fairly long 'fantasy conversation' that took place between him, Elias, Salome and the snake. For they were his partners in conversation in *The Red Book*. Furthermore, he wrote a short 'epilogue'. It stops in the middle of a sentence. The sentence is: "I know how tremendously insufficient this whole undertaking has been, but despite much work and distraction I stayed faithful to it, even though another option..." (Jung 1962/1997: 387).

'Mythological creative fantasy' is a necessary matrix for the insane, and the ill, and the religious, and the artist, and the scientist. But how differently this matrix works for each of them. An aesthetic view can help a relaxed person to uphold his conscious I, whereas for the artist it is a means to bypass his ego via the numinous autonomous complex. Jung did *not* want to run away from his unconscious, animal nature. He wanted to confront it not only with his intuition and sensation, but also with feeling and thinking. He would not allow himself to get lost in the 'lovely appearance' of an aesthetic perspective. He did not want to "shed a deceptive aesthetic veil over the problem [of his life]."[244] It was, however, worthwhile to look from a distance at the objects which his 'insane' mind produced. Depicting them in a 'lovely' way enabled him to do this, for it brought into the spotlight what he needed to confront.

The stone

We can now understand why Jung stubbornly refused to consider his mandalas and paintings in *The Red Book* as art. We must now turn to the question of whether he was equally convinced about this opinion in regard to his other works, for instance the sculptures and reliefs which he made at Bollingen. This certainly will have included work which he would not deem worthy of the name art, but in principle he most likely would not consider them therapeutic products. Jung always spoke reluctantly about the artistic value of his works, but the question is whether he truly meant this. Certainly on one occasion, towards the end of his life, he demonstrated how sensitive he was about their artistic value. In Jung's correspondence with the American ethnologist, author and painter Maud Oakes (1903–1990), we unexpectedly read that the *künstlerische* value of one of his creations was close to his heart. The letters concentrate on one of his works of art, the square stone, but there is no reason to conclude that his sensitivity was only directed to this specific work. After a visit to Bollingen, Oakes planned to closely study the stone and write an essay on it. Jung was honoured by her plan. In a letter he let her know: "All the volumes I have written are 'in nuce' contained in it [i.e. the stone]."

It is exciting to read how Jung told 'the story of the stone' in his own words. It is not a story of how he worked with the stone, but rather how the stone worked with him (see plate 5).[245] In 1950, he wanted to build a wall around the 'garden' of Bollingen. One day, the stones were delivered by boat. But one of the stones was 'a wrong one'. Instead of a triangular cornerstone they had brought a square stone about twenty inches thick. The bricklayer wanted to return the stone, but Jung prevented this. To him, it looked as if the stone was 'called for':

> But when I saw the stone, I said: "No, that is my stone. I must have it!" For I had seen at once that it suited me perfectly and that I wanted to do something with it. Only I did not yet know what.

244 Jung 1921/1990: 139.
245 Depicted in Gaillard 1998: 229 and Jaffé 1983: 192, 204.

The first thing that occurred to me was a Latin verse by the alchemist Arnaldus de Villanova (d. 1313). I chiselled this into the Stone; in translation it goes:

> Here stands the mean, uncomely stone,
> 'Tis very cheap in price!
> The more it is despised by fools,
> The more loved by the wise.

This verse refers to the alchemist's stone, the *lapis*, which is despised and rejected.

Soon something else emerged. I began to see on the front face, in the natural structure of the stone, a small circle, a sort of eye, which looked at me. I chiselled it into stone, and in the centre I made a tiny homunculus. This corresponds to the "little doll" (pupilla) – yourself – which you see in the pupil of another's eye; a kind of Kabir, or the Telesphoros of Asklepios.[246] Ancient statues show him wearing a hooded cloak and carrying a lantern. At the same time he is a pointer of the way. I dedicated a few words to him which came into my mind while I was working. The inscription is in Greek; the translation goes:

> Time is a child – playing like a child – playing a board game – the kingdom of the child. This is Telesphoros, who roams through the dark regions of this cosmos and glows like a star out of the depths. He points the way to the gates of the sun and to the land of dreams.

These words came to me – one after the other – while I worked on the stone (see plate 6).

On the third face, the one facing the lake, I let the stone itself speak, as it were, in a Latin inscription. These sayings are more or less quotations from alchemy. This is the translation:

> I am an orphan, alone, nevertheless I am found everywhere. I am one, but opposed to myself. I am youth and old man at one and the same time. I have known neither father nor mother, because I have had to be fetched out of the deep like a fish, or fell like a white stone from heaven. In woods and mountains I roam, but I am hidden in the innermost soul of man. I am mortal for everyone, yet I am not touched by the cycle of aeons.

246 Kabirs are dwarf gods, guardians on the threshold between the unconscious and the conscious. They have a transforming influence on the dark geologic levels of existence and work on the 'metals'. They are creative forces which provide consciousness with useful intuitions and ideas. Telesphoros [who brings fulfilment and perfection] is the name of the kabir of Asklepios, the Greek God of healing powers (see Timmer 2001: 386–387, 733).

> In conclusion, under the saying of Arnaldus de Villanova, I set down in Latin the words "In remembrance of his seventy-fifth birthday C. G. Jung made and placed this here as a thanks offering, in the year 1950."
>
> When the stone was finished, I looked at it again and again, wondering about it and asking myself what lay behind my impulse to carve it."[247]

Jung left the back of the stone pristine and uncarved. "Do you know what I wanted to chisel into the back face of the stone? *'Le cri de Merlin!'* For what the stone expressed reminded me of Merlin's life in the forest, after he had vanished from the world. Men still hear his cries, so the legend runs, but they cannot understand or interpret him."[248]

The Stone Speaks

Oakes saw the stone for the first time in 1951, when she and Jerome Hill visited Jung in Bollingen. Hill had taken up the idea to make a film about Jung and wanted to speak with him. His cousin Maud accompanied him. She saw the stone, which was just finished, and was very impressed. At the foot of a 'lone tree' she thought she was seeing something like 'a gravestone'. However, she did not speak about it with Jung. Back in New York, the stone did not leave her mind and she started to make notes about it. After a while, Hill suggested to her that he would include her thoughts about the stone in his film. They decided to visit Jung once more to tell him about their idea. They visited him in the autumn of 1953, this time in his house in Küsnacht.

Jung, who was 78 at the time, initially responded in such a way that Oakes lost all courage: "My friends, how can I help you? I realise how difficult your task is. The Stone is nothing. I am not an artist; I did it to amuse myself. It is a holiday thing – as if I sang a song." Oakes tried to secure her idea, saying: 'But the Stone is very powerful.' However, Jung pretended not to hear her and repeated: "How can I help you? I don't know who I am. I am the last person to tell you who I am. I am invisible. I am nothing; I am an old man."

But as Oakes was leaving, Jung mentioned something that enkindled her hope: "I need not have written any books; it is all on the Stone." He advised her to visit his friend in America, a psychoanalyst, and to discuss the stone with him. As Oakes was descending the stairs, he opened the door once more and shouted: "Now be sure and let me know what happens. Let me know what you do. I am very curious. I am anxious to know."[249]

We encounter here the typically reserved Jung who expressed himself ambiguously. On the one side the stone is 'nothing', on the other hand it is 'all'. We get the impression that Jung made an estimation of his partner in conversation

247 Jung 1961/1989: 226–228.
248 Jung 1961/1989: 228.
249 Oakes 1987: 15, 16.

and weighted whether his words were 'pearls thrown before swine'. Those who don't have 'ears to hear' simply do not get anything to hear. I think that he was not convinced by Oakes and thus advised her to see his friend, the analyst in America, first.

Nevertheless, Oakes was encouraged by Jung's final words and started to write a new text. The manuscript was finished in December 1955. On 7 January 1956 she wrote a letter to Jung, in which she told him that she had thought a lot about the case after their last meeting in Küsnacht and had decided to write an essay about the stone, which was now finished. She wrote: 'There was only one way for me to approach the Stone and that was to experience it in myself.' She also wrote that she had sent him a separate package containing the essay, entitled *The Stone Speaks*. She asked him to be so kind as to read it and possibly give her some suggestions.

Jung immediately responded to her letter, before receiving the package, and told her how honoured he was by her essay. He also thought that she looked at the stone with the right attitude. "Your method to realise its content through your *subjective experience* is unexceptionable, as a matter of fact the only correct way of reading its message. That is just the virtue of symbolic expression, that it can be read in many different ways by many different individuals. And if they are honest, the reading will be correct. Thus, as you see, I am prepared for the shock of getting the manuscript about a thing most emphatically belonging to my innermost self."[250]

Several days later, after having received and read the manuscript, he wrote another letter. He expressed his satisfaction about the content, but considered it appropriate to make some warning remarks. He emphasised two points. First, he pointed out to her that thought-images are different from sensual-images, that a concept is not a symbol. "You understand the Stone as a statement about a more or less limitless world of thought-images. I quite agree with your view. One can read the symbols like that. When I hewed the Stone *I did not think*, however. I just brought into shape what I saw on its face. Sometimes you express yourself (in the manuscript), as if my symbols and my text were a sort of confession of belief. Thus it looks as if I were moving in the vicinity of Theosophy. In America, especially, one blames me for my so-called mysticism. Since I don't claim at all to be the happy proprietor of metaphysical truths, I should prefer that you attribute to my symbols the same tentativeness which characterises your explanatory attempts. You see, I have no religious or otherwise convictions about my symbols. They can change tomorrow. They are mere allusions, they hint at something, they stammer and often lose their way. They try only to point in a certain direction, viz. to those dim horizons beyond which lies the secret of existence. (...) They are nothing but humble attempts to formulate, to define, to shape the inexpressible. '*Wo fasz ich Dich, unendliche Natur*' *(Where shall I, endless Nature, seize on thee)*

250 Quoted in Oakes 1987: 17–18.

(*Faust*). It is not a doctrine, but a mere expression of and a reaction to the experience of an ineffable mystery."[251]

The stone is an artistic, symbolic reality

There is little doubt about Jung's convictions here. The stone is a symbolic reality, which, like every symbol, reflects what will remain an ineffable mystery pertaining to our reason. I also refer to the words I italicised; that he *did not think* whilst hewing the stone. This is also an essential point in regard to creative processes. They are not the result of thinking and feeling. In his description of the origination of the stone, he also continually spoke about things 'coming to him'. He went about working without thinking and beautiful ancient quotes came to his mind. And he was surprised by the result.

Apart from the remark that it is not about thought-images but about sensual-images, Jung made a second remark in his letter. And later, in his third letter, he would confirm how important this issue was to him: "There is one point more I want to mention: the stone is not a product only of thought-images, but just as much of feeling and local atmosphere, i.e. of the specific *ambiente* of the place. The stone belongs to its secluded place between the lake and the hill. Where it expresses the *beata solitudo* and the *genius loci*, [252] the spell of the chosen and walled-in spot. It could be nowhere else and cannot be thought of or properly understood without the secret web of threads that relate to its surroundings. Only there in its solitude it can say: *Orphanus sum* and only there does it make sense. It is there for its own sake and only seen by a few. Under such conditions only, the stone will whisper its misty lore of ancient roots and ancestral lives."[253]

Jung returned Oakes' manuscript with his personal corrections. He obviously considered it valuable. Oakes edited her manuscript and posted it back to him in 1957. Because she had to be in Switzerland, she proposed to visit him in Bollingen in order to discuss the essay together. In 1957 she visited Bollingen, which had changed since 1951. In 1955, the final rebuilding had taken place. The top floor was built and the whole area was walled in. Oakes wrote: 'There was a striking contrast between the walled-in house and garden and the open aspect toward the lake – one side was enclosed, protected, and the other side was completely open to the living lake. Between the two sides – the enclosed and the open, the hills and the lake – stood the Stone. How different it was from the first time I had seen it six years before, when it had been newly set in the garden! Moss now grew on the inscriptions, and the lone tree was only one of many trees and shrubs.'[254]

251 Oakes 1987: 18 (italics mine).

252 'Blessed solitude' and 'local guardian spirit'. In Ascona, on the grounds where the yearly Eranos conferences were held (of which Jung was the inspiring centre) there stood an altar with the inscription: *Genio loci ignoto* [To the unknown spirit of this place] (see Timmer 2001: 263).

253 Quoted in Oakes 1987: 18–19.

254 Oakes 1987: 22.

Whilst she was looking at the stone for some time, Oakes suddenly heard a piercing voice behind her from someone loudly greeting a passing shipper. It was Jung. He welcomed her and they took a seat in the two chairs standing next to the stone. "Yes, you have done it," he said, referring to the essay. Oakes asked if she could publish it. "Yes, in America," he said, "but not in Europe until after my death." He did not explain this further. He also told her that back in 1953 he had recommended her to his friend, the analyst.

'When it was time for me to leave,' Oakes wrote, 'Dr. Jung and I stood silently gazing at the Stone. He then conducted me to the gate. His last words [Oakes would never see Jung again] were a suggestion that I visit the prehistoric caves at Lascaux in France.'[255] She did this one month later. It was an overwhelming experience. She thanked Jung in a letter for his suggestion. But she also wrote that she would very much appreciate it if he would tell her what he thought about the manuscript, because this was left unsaid during her pleasant stay at Bollingen. When she arrived back in America, there was Jung's third letter, written on 3 October 1957.

Jung was very honest. What he was afraid would happen had actually happened. In his view it had become too much of a theoretical narrative. And he emphasised that she had overlooked the *artistic value* of the stone. The artist in Jung was responding. It is a fine letter: "Since you want to hear my opinion about your essay on the stone, I should say that I find it a bit intellectual inasmuch as it considers the thought-images only, but as I have already called your attention to its *ambiente*, I miss the all important feeling tone of phenomena. *This is of exclusively artistic consideration*, but if you want to do justice to the stone, you have to pay particular attention to the way in which it is embedded in its surroundings: the water, the hills, the view, the peculiar atmosphere of the buildings, the nights and the days, the seasons, sun, wind and rain and man living close to the earth, and yet remaining conscious in daily meditation of everything being just so. The air round the stone is filled with harmonies and disharmonies, with memories of times long ago, of vistas into the dim future with reverberations of a world far away, yet the so called real world, into which the stone has fallen out of nowhere. A strange revelation and admonition. Try and dwell in this wholeness for a while and see what happens to you (see plate 7)."[256]

I have of course italicised the sentence in which Jung pointed to the artistic value of his creation. It is particularly exciting to read that the following part of the letter is a description of the ambience of the garden. Isn't Jung making it tangible that the essence of the stone can only become clear from the ambience? The place where the stone stands is a transition between nature and culture, between 'the lake' and 'the tower', between 'the wilderness' and 'the garden'. It is a transitional object, a product of culture; for Jung this meant a product of nature that is worked upon. The uncut stone navigated out of nowhere into his garden,

255 Oakes 1987: 23.
256 Quoted in Oakes 1987: 25 (italics mine).

but it underwent a transformation, its forces were cultivated and transmuted. It is not a coincidence that Jung also carved alchemical texts into the stone. On the one side the stone was totally impregnated by *participation mystique*, on the other side it was completely withdrawn from this and began to speak in words. An ancient alchemist said: 'For those who possess the symbol, the transition is effortless' (*In habentibus symbolum facilis est transitus*) (Mylius). In the terms of the psychoanalyst Donald Winnicott (1896–1971), we are here dealing with a transitional object par excellence. We are dealing with a work of art. And surprisingly, for the most part it is an abstract work of art. Jung was afraid that Oakes overlooked the *participation mystique*. All art is rooted in this. The fear of every artist is that the beholder will explain what is inexplicable. Jung thought that an autonomous process had taken place within him on the basis of intuition and sensation, resulting in an ancient symbol: the philosopher's stone. How can one explain that one's whole life and work is *in nuce* contained in it?

After reading this letter, Oakes realised that she had not been capable of doing what Jung asked of her at the end of the letter. 'I knew that I must put away all my notes and books and rid myself of my preconceived ideas. This emptying would open the way to what the Stone had to say directly to me (...), perhaps leading to an inner experience of healing and growing into wholeness.'[257] This process took 30 years and in 1987 a completely new book by her hand was published. Only the title stayed the same: *The Stone Speaks*. In the second chapter she talked about her personal experiences with Jung in the Fifties. The book is a beautiful example of what Jung called 'amplification'. Around the stone she narrated her process of individuation throughout the years. All great stone-images, concrete stones and symbolic stones, cornerstones and capstones, they are all passing by. It is not only a description of the hermetic, mysterious stone in Bollingen, it is at the same time a parable of human life searching for the 'philosopher's stone'. One is inclined to thinks that such a thing can only result in a work of art.

When, in the following chapter, we look at the outlines of a psychology of art according to Jung, we shall see that an artist's opinion about his work is certainly not crucial in deciding whether something is art or not. It is of greater importance whether his work becomes a symbol to us (whether Jung appreciated this or not). The fact that the work becomes independent from its maker has a more decisive influence on its artistic value. This is of course also true of the mandalas in *The Red Book*.

Jung's line of thought on art is getting clearer to us. In his discussion with Moltzer, he concretely-existentially sharpened the differences between aesthetics and art, and between aesthetics and ethics; and via 'his' stone he beautifully showed the work of art as a symbol originating from *participation mystique* between the human and reality. Probably a little too definite in both cases, but to us it is clarifying as we want to discover his vision.

257 Oakes 1987: 26.

Chapter 7

A psychology of art

> It makes no difference whether the artist knows that his work is generated, grows and matures within him, or whether he imagines that it is his own invention. In reality it grows out of him as a child from its mother. The creative process has a feminine quality, and the creative work arises from unconscious depths – we might truly say from the realm of the Mothers.
>
> (Jung 1930/1978: 103)

Even though it is relevant that the artist experiences the creative process in an extraverted or introverted way, this is not a decisive artistic criterion. It is more important that the work of art grows within the artist as a numinous complex, structured by his perceptions and intuitions. He expresses his artistic matter, springing from *participation mystique*, in an aesthetic form. His creative eye only ruthlessly observes, chasing all the possibilities in the creative womb of his unconscious. Without bringing himself into play.

Extraversion and introversion

In the previous chapters, we studied Jung's thoughts on art from different perspectives. These perspectives (cryptomnesia, the complex, *participation mystique*, the symbol, aesthetics) do not have an inherent artistic nature, but each of them takes us to the heart of art. I will now try to capture all these thoughts on art scattered through the different chapters, and add some of Jung's other thoughts about the theme, in order to place them in a more structured whole and to focus on what might possibly be a psychological theory of art by Jung. In the preface, I quoted Jung's conviction that no scientific approach is able to approach the true essence of art. "But for the purpose of cognitive understanding we must detach ourselves from the creative process and look at it from the outside."[258] This is what we are going to do in this chapter.

258 Jung 1922/1978: 78.

"From the outside," Jung would in the first instance consider the creative process from the perspective of extraversion-introversion. He had been looking at it in this way since 1921. He placed all psychological processes within this model, hence also the creative. Extraversion and introversion are the basic psychological attitudes of the human person. A certain person prefers to be extravert, whereas another prefers to be introvert. This *conscious* preference is anchored in our biological constitution. We are, so to speak, born with it and have little control over it. It indicates the direction psychological energy is primarily inclined to take.[259] "Everyone whose attitude is introverted," Jung wrote, "thinks, feels, and acts in a way that clearly demonstrates that the subject is the prime motivating factor and that the object is of secondary importance."[260] The opposite is true in regard to the extraverted attitude as the object powerfully determines the subject, sometimes even against his intention.[261]

For Jung, this primary typological distinction between people became almost an a priori. He did not think he was speculative, as he based it on an overwhelming amount of factual material, present throughout history, in all areas of the human psyche. Therefore also in art. "So when we discuss the psychology of art, we must bear in mind these two entirely different modes of creation, for much that is of the greatest importance in judging a work of art depends on this distinction."[262]

There are introverted works of art "that spring wholly from the author's intention to produce a particular result. He submits its material to a definite treatment with a definite aim in view (...) His material is entirely subordinated to his artistic purpose; he wants to express this and nothing else."[263] In regard to extraverted art, "these works positively force themselves upon the author (...) he is overwhelmed by a flood of thoughts and images which he never intended to create and which his own will could never have brought into being. (...) He is aware that he is subordinate to his work or stands outside it, as though he were a second person; or as though a person other than himself had fallen within the magic circle of an alien will."[264]

It is now important to realise that we are here concerned with a process as it exists *within the consciousness* of the artist. He *thinks* he has control over it or he *thinks* he is not in control. "For in the one case it is a conscious product shaped and designed to have the effect intended. But in the other we are dealing with an event originating in unconscious nature; with something that achieves its aim

259 See Jung 1921/1990: 427, 452.

260 Jung 1921/1990: 452–453.

261 Jung considered it of great importance that a person realises what his prime response is, extravert or introvert, and at the same time realises that, *unconsciously*, the other pole is present as well – usually very powerfully. Psychological adulthood means not staring oneself blind on that one conscious drive but also integrating the unconscious opposite pole, which incidentally, is not easy.

262 Jung 1922/1978: 73.

263 Jung 1922/1978: 72.

264 Jung 1922/1978: 73.

without the assistance of human consciousness, and often defies it by wilfully insisting on its own form and effect."[265]

Again and again, Jung employed this distinction. When he encountered dichotomies in the works of others, he tried to show that they can be integrated in *his* extraversion/introversion theory. The renowned dichotomy by Nietzsche, 'dionysian' and 'apollinian'; the classic distinction made by Schiller between 'naive art' and 'sentimental art'; and Worringer's classification of art as 'empathy' and 'abstraction', Jung classified them all as extraverted or introverted art respectively. In his 1930 article, he introduced a new dichotomy: 'psychological' and 'visionary' art. The first is introverted in nature, the second extraverted.

Jung gave many examples of works of art and of artists belonging to either the psychological or the visionary type. He repeatedly referred to Goethe's *Faust*. He considered *Faust I* a significant example of introverted (psychological) art, but *Faust II* as an explicitly extraverted (visionary) work of art. "Two extremes," he said.[266] Both of them are accomplished works of art. It did not come to his mind not to qualify *Faust I* as a work of art, even though we can deduce from many instances that he was personally attracted by visionary art. *Faust I* moves within the confines of human consciousness. All its experiences are transparent. "The love-tragedy of Gretchen is self-explanatory. (...) There is no work left for the psychologist to do – unless perhaps we expect him to explain why Faust fell in love with Gretchen, or why Gretchen was driven to murder her child. Such themes constitute the lot of humankind; they are repeated millions of times and account for the hideous monotony of the police court and the penal code."[267] He wrote that a "gulf" separates *Faust I* from *Faust II*. "Here everything is reversed. (...) The material for artistic expression is no longer familiar. It is something strange that derives its expression from the hinterland of man's mind, as if it had emerged from the abyss of pre-human ages, or from a superhuman world of contrasting light and darkness. It is a primordial experience which surpasses man's understanding and to which in his weakness he may easily succumb."[268]

265 Jung 1922/1978: 75.
266 Jung 1930/1978: 89.
267 Jung 1930/1978: 88–89.
268 Jung 1930/1978: 90. Two remarks on the side. First, we need to ascertain that Jung had a very unlucky intuition when he called the first form of art 'psychological' and the second 'visionary'. As if visionary art is not psychological! Of course we understand what he meant, but he easily could have picked another name for psychological art, for example 'realistic art'. In general, Jung's terminology is also close to literary and plastic art. His terminology is sometimes hard to transpose to other arts. What is the difference between a psychological and a visionary sonata? A psychological poem is clear, but a psychological cathedral is more complicated. Second, there is a common misunderstanding regarding the terms extraversion and introversion. People sometimes think that extraversion means: to be directed outward and introversion to be directed to the personal inner world. This is wrong. If it was true, one should be very surprised that, according to Jung, *Faust II*, which mainly sprouted from the fantasies and images of Goethe's inner world, is an extraverted work of art (see Jung 1922/1978: 73). Therefore, extraversion does not deal per se with objects in the outer world; it is about the awareness of the conscious I that an 'object',

However, if a work of art can originate from either an extraverted or an introverted attitude, then *extraversion or introversion are not within themselves determining criteria of art*. Jung considered it of decisive importance (we studied this extensively in Chapter 3) that *both types* of artists descend into the *participation mystique* of their existence and that works of art manifest themselves as symbols.

Both types of artist, therefore, are only partially aware of what happens within them. Even though he doesn't realise this, the introverted artist has only a partial control over his work. And whereas the extraverted artist may think that he was completely possessed, this is only partially true. Even though Goethe might not have *realised* it whilst writing *Faust I*, he was also partially unconsciously motivated at the time. You might think you have been working autonomously, but in reality there was also a heteronomous power. And the extraverted artist might think that he was possessed by a demon, but in fact he was also strongly in control of his own creative process. Jung wrote: "It might well be that the poet, while apparently creating out of himself and producing what he consciously intends, is nevertheless so carried away by the creative impulse that he is no longer aware of an 'alien' will, just as the other type of poet is no longer aware of his own will speaking to him in the apparently 'alien' inspiration, although this is manifestly the voice of its own self. The poet's conviction that he is creating in absolute freedom would then be an illusion: he fancies he is swimming, but in reality an unseen current sweeps him along."[269] Therefore, it is too simple to presuppose that Goethe, whilst writing the visions of *Faust II*, was not in control of his work. Control would have been important precisely during such moments.

Jung emphasised that extraversion and introversion are superficial appearances through which works of art become visible to us. They really are illusionary appearances. Extraversion and introversion are conscious attitudes; the work of art is of unknown origin. He phrased this beautifully in 1930: "It makes no difference whether the artist knows that his work is generated, grows and matures within him, or whether he imagines that it is his own invention. In reality it grows out of him as a child from its mother. The creative process has a feminine quality, and the creative work arises from unconscious depths – we might truly say from the realm of the Mothers."[270]

This is the core of Jung's theory of art. A creative process works like an unconscious autonomous process. It is important for both types of artist to realise

whether inside or outside, captures you and forces itself upon you. A mystical experience in which the object 'God' numinously captures you from within, is an extraverted experience. And a scientific researcher who, through his measuring apparatus, enforces his will upon the object of a 'star' is occupied in an introverted way. Therefore, it is of importance how the artist experiences himself *as subject* during the creative process. The introverted artist has the idea that he controls the object, the extraverted artist thinks that he is controlled by it.

269 Jung 1922/1978: 74.
270 Jung 1930/1978: 103.

that they are both standing under an unconscious 'sacred obligation' even though in a different way.[271]

'A high, standing clock made of black varnished wood'

Jung was convinced that a subtle analysis of 'psychological' work would show that it has the same unconscious background as the 'visionary'. When you watch attentively, you will see that the so called consciously working artist is also *seized by* his work. You will notice that such a "writer in what he thinks he is saying, clearly says more than he thinks. He just does not realise this. With respect to these types of artists, you will perceive that unconscious motives have to play a role because sometimes there will occur severe psychological complications when the creative work must be abandoned at some arbitrary moment. Moreover, to what extent does cryptomnesia influence the introverted artist? What comes up in him with clarity turns out to have dark sources."[272]

I have found a striking example of such a depth analysis of a 'psychological' work in the Dutch author Harry Mulisch (1927–2010). In *Portret met Tulband* (*Portrait with Turban*) (1961) he relates that he was asked to write something about the background of his novel *Het Zwarte Licht* (*The Black Light*) (1956). In the conviction that every book should contain indisputable key sentences next to many indifferent sentences, he was inspired by the idea to search for one such sentence that would capture the whole novel. After some searching, he did not hesitate. He instinctively chose: 'Against the wall stood a high, standing clock made of black varnished wood.' In Jung's terminology this is a perfectly clear, consciously composed sentence. Understandable for everyone. Mulish began to wonder why he considered this exact sentence of such crucial importance. And in his exploration he noticed that this novel originated from him as an unconscious force.

Mulish was aware that this sentence was placed at the awful nucleus of the story (the girlfriend of the main character is in an adulterous relationship with a Negro and this leads to her death), but he still hardly understood why he had written this sentence. 'It was possible that the black colour referred to the Negro – but why a clock? Why not a mirror, or a vase, or a barometer? But I clearly saw a standing clock, and I was experienced enough to allow it to stand there: a writer has the difficult task to take himself seriously sometimes. But later on I became aware that it was the same clock as the one which occurs in a scene at the beginning of the story; a scene which I had written down with the same sense of estrangement.'[273]

271 "Accordingly, the poet who identifies with the creative process would be one who acquiesces from the start when the unconscious imperative begins to function. But the other poet, who feels the creative force as something alien, is one who for various reasons cannot acquiesce and is thus caught unawares" (Jung 1922/1978: 75).

272 Jung 1922/1978: 74–75.

273 Mulisch 2001: 116.

In this scene, the main character visits his doctor and sees a clock standing in a dark hallway. 'Halfway through the hallway, he stopped in front of a high, standing clock made of black varnished wood. A copper pendulum slowly swayed behind the glass. Silence everywhere, except for the slow ticking... Click. Clack... With wide opened eyes he looked at the shiny pendulum, which, hidden in a hallway and holding its breath, rowed through time in silent ecstasy... Slowly he approached, staring at the shiny movement. Captured, he sank on his knees, lay his hands on the wood and pressed his nose against the glass.'[274]

Pondering over this estranging text, five years later, a memory suddenly came to Mulisch's mind. He suddenly remembered an event from his childhood, to which he had not given any thought whilst writing. It surfaced out of the mist of the past. Harry was nine years old. He sat in the gallery of their house on the first floor. The gallery surrounded a void. Behind one of the doors he heard his parents having a conversation, sometimes loud, sometimes soft. Instinctively, he knew that they were speaking about their divorce. After several hours, his mother came out of the room. She didn't say anything. He slowly stood up.

> "Are you leaving?" I ask.
>
> She says: "Yes."
>
> A few flakes of face powder twirl down from her face unto the ground. She turns around and walks through the door of her own room. At that moment, I see nothing but the high, standing clock made of black varnished wood standing between the closed doors. Behind glass the slow copper swaying of the pendulum in the dark hall.[275]

This is pure cryptomnesia. In Jung's terminology, the 'black varnished, high' clock relates to the personal unconscious of the author. It was a 'hidden memory'. Mulisch was not at all aware of this connection, even though he composed everything very thoughtfully. Moreover, Mulisch noticed that throughout his entire book there are many archetypal images of Time which are related to the collective unconscious. He had not been aware of this.[276] 'Luckily, I was unaware of these connections whilst writing; for it would have become a bad story, and now is it not so bad. The sentence proved to be the key to the story, and hence made me doubt its arbitrariness. But, of course, that is what I had wanted to prove: that there is no arbitrary sentence. Each sentence is a key to the oeuvre.'[277]

In Jung's typology, Mulisch is an introverted writer who created a 'psychological' work whilst staying fully conscious of his composition. He composed in a clear, lucid, recognisable manner. No psychologist is needed, one could say. It is very simple, this 'black clock'. Everyone can see it standing in the hallway.

274 Mulisch 2001: 117.
275 See Mulisch 2001: 114.
276 Mulisch 2001: 116.
277 Mulisch 2001: 117.

But the visionary artist also needs to realise that he stayed lucid under the bombardment of his overwhelming experiences. He must know how to control what happens to him. Extraversion and introversion, they are both needed in the creation of a work of art. "For artistic creation," Jung wrote, "both functions are needed. Both are always present in every individual, though in most cases they are unequally differentiated."[278]

In his book *Istanbul*, Orhan Pamuk (b. 1952) beautifully describes how 'drawing' happened in him. For some time he thought he would become a visual artist. He masterfully describes how extraverted drivenness and introverted mastership work together, and *need* to work together, in a creative process: 'After a time, my hand had become as skilled as my eyes. So if I was drawing a very fine tree, it felt as if my hand was moving without my directing it. As I watched the pencil race across the page, I would look on it with amazement, as if the drawing was the proof of another presence, as if someone else had taken up residence in my body. As I marvelled at his work, aspiring to become his equal, another part of my brain was busy inspecting the curves of the branches, the placement of the mountains, the composition as a whole, reflecting that I had created this scene on a blank piece of paper. My mind was at the tip of my pen, acting before I could think; at the same time I could survey what I had already done. This second line of perception, this ability to analyse my progress, was the pleasure this small artist felt when he looked at the discovery of his courage and his freedom. To step outside myself, to know the second person who had taken up residence in me, as to retrace the dividing line that appeared as my pencil slipped across the paper, like a boy sledding in the snow.'[279]

In Chapter 3 we saw the importance of the co-operation between extraversion and introversion. The artist descends into *participation mystique*, but does not succumb. Partially he unites himself with it in an *extraverted* way, partially he *introvertedly* distances himself from it, and in a sense releases the (artistic) object from a primitive fusion. Not *Auflösung* but *Erlösung*.

To the extent that the artist works in an introverted manner, he contests the original *participation mystique* and he clearly and precisely creates the 'standing, black varnished clock'. To the extent that he works in an extraverted manner he gives magical power from *participation mystique* to the clock. A work of art always carries a double weight. It derives this weight from the extraverted *participation mystique* of the ancient unconscious root system, as well as from the introverted *participation artistique* of the artist. Because the artist has given a form to the extraverted nature in an introverted manner – an aesthetic form.

The artist does not have a personal message

A person is never introverted or extraverted just like that. These attitudes always appear in a certain form. It is the same with fruit: you cannot buy just fruit in

278 Jung 1921/1990: 296.
279 Pamuk 2006: 135.

shops. You buy it in the form of apples, pears, etc. Jung thought that extraversion and introversion appear in four ways: in thoughts, feelings, sensations and intuitions. In the previous chapter, we were able to get closer to the core of artistic processes because of the realisation that it is not thinking and feeling that are determining functions, but sensation and intuition. Jung even called these last two functions the 'aesthetic functions'.

First, I will summarise what we have already discussed about these functions. Intuition and sensation have something in common: we use them to observe and register. The creative eye of the artist *perceives*. This is not a daily perception, mixed with other functions, no, the artist abstracts his perceptions. He sees a complete event from one single perspective which is so eye catching that it fascinates us. He does this intuitively. The artist does not judge, he is not led by any moral principle. It is an instinctive, immediate 'seeing'. For this reason Jung also called intuition and sensation 'irrational functions'. With respect to intuitive seeing this mainly happens from within (it is the more introverted function of the two), whereas with sensation it happens more from the outside.[280]

According to Jung, an aesthetic experience is *not a complete human experience*. We know that he emphasised this again and again. If his patients only *perceived* their images, without thinking and feeling and knowing themselves to be ethically obligated, they would *only* be aesthetically engaged. However, for the artist this is unimportant. For him, intuition and sensation are exclusive vehicles. If he started to think and feel (the two other, judging, functions), the creative process would stagnate. He does not reason or moralise, he aestheticises.[281]

Because of its irrational and unconscious character, it cannot be traced how intuition, still the most important antenna of the artist, operates and knows how to penetrate into *participation mystique*. Jung thought that intuition can best be compared to the *daimon* of Socrates.[282] What significance do these concisely summarised ideas have with respect to the place of art and the artist in society?

Exactly because of its intuitiveness such an artistic creative process has a strong estranging character. For this reason, the artists often situates himself outside society and even outside his own self. He positions himself amongst the dreamers, the seers and the fantasists. He doesn't ask questions such as: "What does this mean for me and the world? What emerges from this vision in the way of a duty or a task?" No, Jung says, "the pure intuitive who represses his judgement, or whose judgement is held in thrall by his perceptive faculties, never faces this question squarely, since his only problem is the 'know-how' of perception. He finds the moral problem unintelligible or even absurd, and as far as possible forbids his thoughts to dwell on the disconcerting vision."[283]

280 See Jung 1921/1990: 367.

281 See Jung 1928/1966: 213.

282 See Jung 1921/1990: 145–146. Socrates saw his *daimon* (guardian spirit) as a warning, inspiring interior voice with which he had conversations (see Timmer 2001: 168).

283 Jung 1921/1990: 402.

As an individual, the artist can occupy himself with moral questions and might take a clear standpoint. But essentially this has nothing to do with creating art. Looking at the personal views of artists, we find among them utterly abject and elevated, conservative and progressive standpoints. One's view on life is seemingly not influential in the creation of art as art.[284] Mozart did not necessarily have to be a womaniser in order to compose *Don Giovanni*, nor a mystic to create his *Requiem*.

In *Manifesten* (*Manifests*) (1961) Mulisch wrote about artistry: 'Who writes about the "message" of an artist is talking either about someone who is not a writer, or, when he does refer to a writer, doesn't understand what literature is. A writer is not allowed to declare anything. No writer ever had a "message" – except that of the paper: creation, reality, a scent of eternity. What was Tolstoi's "message"? Or Shakespeare's? Joyce's? We are not your messengers!'[285]

Mulisch brilliantly described how ruthlessly intuition functions in an artist, without any reflection, empathy or compassion. Jung would have fully agreed with the following quotation: 'The writer is present in his writing by means of an enigmatic organ, which did not turn him into a fantasising hallucinator but into a writer. (...) That organ (...) is an unrelentingly cold mechanism, which flawlessly executes indefinable laws. It reveals itself within his body as a cool clarity, a high space, wherein nothing is unseen and mercilessness reigns. It is an interrogation of the third degree, with ruthless spotlights burning straight into the face of the arrested, with beatings, screws, amputations, and twenty-four hours of questioning, deceptions and tricks, according to an unknown system which always leads to confession.'[286]

Jung spoke about the "awkward indifference" of artists in the face of reality. "Pressing on quite heedless of human considerations (...) [they] move from image to image, chasing after every possibility in the teeming womb of the unconscious, without establishing any connection between them and *himself*. Just as the world of appearances can never become a moral problem for the man who merely senses it, the world of inner images is never a moral problem for the intuitive. For both of them it is an aesthetic problem, a matter of perception, a 'sensation'."[287]

The artist is the mouthpiece of his epoch

Intuition detects contents, but is itself without content. It is a sounding lead. By now, we know that with respect to great art Jung let this sounding lead down into the archetypes of the collective unconscious. Intuition detects the images which

284 Jung thought, furthermore, that artists in particular hardly realise what kind of processes are involved. "Poets are human too, and what they say about their work is often far from being the best words on the subject. It seems as if we have to defend the seriousness of the visionary experience against the personal resistance of the poet himself" (Jung 1930/1978: 94).

285 Mulisch 2001: 86.

286 Mulisch 2001: 87, 88.

287 Jung 1921/1990: 400.

stem from the archetypes. Its deepest essence is beyond the reach of our daily experience.[288] Exactly these forces which are impersonal and estranging to the artist can influence society and culture in a remarkably meaningful way and open new perspectives. Artistic images turn out to have a prophetic force. What seems to be unfruitful at first sight can subsequently lead a culture onto new pathways. Jung wrote: "The artist is not just a *reproducer* of appearances but a *creator* and *educator*, for his works have the values of symbols that adumbrate lines of future development. Whether the symbols have a limited or general social validity depends on the viability of the creative individual."[289]

They are indispensable to our society, these intuitive minds that behold in the unconscious images with a creative force. These images are possibilities of ideas which might be able to give a new flow to the energy stream. This type, Jung wrote "is indispensable to the psychic life of a people. Had this type not existed, there would have been no prophets in Israel."[290]

Once more we encounter what Jung considered to be of eminent importance in great art: its compensatory character. Art interacts with the spirit of the age which has become imbalanced. Two quotations will suffice to convey Jung's thoughts:

> Therein lies the social significance of art: it is constantly at work educating the spirit of the age, conjuring up the forms in which the age is most lacking. The unsatisfied yearning of the artist reaches back to the primordial image in the unconscious which is best fitted to compensate the inadequacy and one-sidedness of the present. The artist seizes on this image, and in raising it from the deepest unconscious he brings it into relation with conscious values, thereby transforming it until it can be accepted by the minds of contemporaries according to their powers.[291]

> Like every true prophet, the artist is the unwitting mouthpiece of the psychic secrets of his time, and is often as unconscious as a sleepwalker. He supposes that it is he who speaks, but the spirit of the age is his prompter, and whatever this spirit says is proved true by its effects.[292]

The nature of art allows us to draw conclusions about the character of the epoch in which it originated. The arts indicate what the spirit of that age needed most.[293]

288 "Introverted intuition apprehends the images arising from the *a priori* inherited foundations of the unconscious" (Jung 1921/1990: 400). These are the archetypes.

289 Jung 1921/1990: 432. "We cannot, therefore, afford to be indifferent to the poets, since in their principal works and deepest inspirations they create from the very depths of the collective unconscious, voicing aloud what others only dream" (Jung 1921/1990: 191).

290 Jung 1921/1990: 400.

291 Jung 1922/1978: 82–83.

292 Jung 1932/1978b: 122–123.

293 See Jung 1922/1995: 95. "Every period has its bias, its particular prejudice, and its psychic malaise. An epoch is like an individual; it has its own limitations of conscious outlook, and

Materia and forma

So far we have mainly considered the creative *process* leading to art. Now we have reached the point were we are ready to study its *product*: the work of art. One usually speaks about a work of art when some or other *materia* has received its aesthetic composition by means of a certain *forma*. When there is nothing more than (archetypal) material lacking aesthetic form (which often happens, for example in our dreams), one cannot speak of a work of art. When a vulgar material gives us aesthetic pleasure because of its form, Jung certainly would not consider this art. *Materia* and *forma* are inseparable in a work of art. This is not a coincidental relationship like, for instance, water taking the shape of the bucket wherein it is poured, because that same water can subsequently take the shape of a vase. No, in art the *forma* has made such an *im*-pression upon the *materia* that henceforth it cannot be *ex*-pressed differently than *in* this *forma*. As such, every form of art 'formats' a specific material in its own way. The formless marble, the chunk of clay, sounds, they are transformed into an autonomous new product with its own nature. Creation has taken place.

Before discussing Jung's ideas about the form and content of a work of art, I will give an example to illustrate the merging of content and form through intuition. The example is taken from the art of photography. In Jung's view every artist is an intuitive observer. The photographer is an observer par excellence: through his lens he selects a part of reality, chooses a perspective and presses the shutter.

Arturo Pérez-Reverte (b. 1951) magnificently described this intuitive moment in his novel *The Painter of Battles*. During the recent Balkan War, the successful war photographer Faulques is in the proximity of retreating, defeated Croatian troops. He sees an approaching group of soldiers. 'Faces bathed in sweat, mouths open, eyes crazed with fatigue, weapons hanging from their straps or being dragged along the ground. They had just run four kilometres with enemy tanks right at their heels; now, under the reverberating sun, they were moving along the road at a lethargic, nearly ghostly pace, and the only sound was the muffled rumble of distant explosions and the scraping of their feet over the ground. (...) He put the camera to his face, and while he fiddled with the focus, f-stops and composition he let a couple of faces go by, then captured the third in his viewfinder, almost randomly: bright, extremely vacant eyes, features distorted by weariness, skin covered with drops of the same sweat that plastered his dirty, tangled hair to his forehead. He had an old AK-47 carelessly slung over his right shoulder and held by a hand wrapped in a dark, stained bandage. After the shutter clicked, Faulques had gone on his way, and that was all there was to it. The photograph was published

therefore requires a compensatory adjustment. This is effected by the collective unconscious when a poet or seer lends expression to the unspoken desire of his times and shows the way, by word and deed, to its fulfilment – regardless whether this blind collective needs results in good or evil, in the salvation of an epoch or its destruction" (Jung 1930/1978: 98).

four weeks later, coinciding with the fall of Vukovar and the extermination of all its defenders, and the image became a symbol of the war. Or, as the professional jury that awarded him the prestigious Europe Focus for that year concluded, the symbol of all soldiers of all wars.'[294]

This vividly narrates how an artist approaches his work. Pérez-Reverte describes only sensations and perceptions and the intuitive search for *the* image. In principle, every work of art is created in this way. Faulques was very pleased about the picture. 'Cold, objective. Perfect. (...) The invisible geometrical lines that supported it as if on a coarse canvas: foreground, the exhausted soldier, the lost gaze that seemed to form part of the lines of that road that led nowhere, the nearly polyhedral walls of the ruined house peppered with the pox of shrapnel, the distant smoke of the fire, vertical as a black, baroque column, without a breath of a breeze. All of that, framed through a viewfinder and imprinted on a 24 x 36 mm negative was more the fruit of instinct than of calculation.'[295]

Jung would have said that this is the essence: '*more the fruit of instinct than of calculation*', more the result of intuition and sensation than of thinking and feeling. He operates in an impersonal way, but 'something' in him was moved, 'something' in him saw 'the' tragedy. And this 'collective something' subsequently moves us. Suddenly, we also see *the* soldier, *the* war.

The story continues in a captivating and dramatic way. The soldier in the picture is, of course, in reality a concrete man, not *the* soldier, but *this* soldier, with this name, someone who has a home with a wife and children. When the crowned picture is published and people recognise the soldier, they take an awful revenge and murder his entire family. The man succumbs to despair and anger, his whole life is ruined and he starts searching for the photographer in order to kill him. When they are standing eye to eye, the artist realises that the other does not know what a work of art is, that he was not concerned about *him* when taking the picture (but that only increases the man's fury) and that for this reason he does not feel guilty. Pushing the shutter was an aesthetic act, not an ethical one. At the time he did not feel compassion. If he had felt compassion, if he had thought about it, he most likely would be unable to take any picture at all. These are all the more reason for the soldier to kill this man.

We will not further elaborate upon this example. Let us return to the subject under discussion.

Both form and content originate from unconscious drives

It is not undisputed amongst researchers how Jung treated the theme of the 'form and content of a work of art'. Some think that Jung valued the second above the first. This is, for example, the opinion of David Maclagan in his recent study,

294 Pérez-Reverte 2008: 22–23.
295 Pérez-Reverte 2008: 28.

Psychological Aesthetics, published in 2001. He elaborates upon a fascinating theme, that is, that the aesthetic qualities of art (and not only its content) are *by nature* (psychologically) relevant and that they are essential in valuing works of art. He argues that Jung undervalued this aspect and for this reason he associates him with Freud. He writes: 'Both treat aesthetic appeal as a purely formal, surface phenomenon that is indeed seductive and misleading, has little or nothing to do with a work's underlying psychological significance (...) Aesthetic qualities that once had an other-worldly aura are now brought brutally down to earth: their disinterested character is shown to be merely a cover for frankly instinctual impulses and unconscious infantile wishes.'[296] I will not further discuss Maclagan's lack of differentiation between Jung and Freud (as this has been adequately discussed in the preceding pages). I will, however, vehemently argue against his other assertion in which he claims that Jung appreciated the aesthetic composition as superficial.

In *The Transcendental Function*, written in 1916 (a key text for understanding his oeuvre), Jung convincingly emphasised the inseparable and equal relation between the form and content of an artistic product.[297] In this text he discussed the image material which was acquired by means of active imagination during a therapeutic session. For instance, drawings created by a patient. The question is: how do we interpret such material? Jung remarked that there are often 'two different tendencies'. The first is inclined to look at the form, the other is inclined to consider the meaningful content.[298] When the *principle of form* prevails, one is interested in the operation of aesthetic motives. However, when the *principle of understanding* prevails, the aesthetic aspect receives little attention and is even regarded as a hindrance. At this point Jung wrote: "Whereas the aesthetic expression tends to concentrate on the formal aspect of the motif, an intuitive understanding often tries to catch the meaning from barely adequate hints in the material, without considering those elements which would come to light in a more careful design."[299] In other words, according to Jung, one can never detect the content separate from the form. Jung certainly did not devalue the aesthetic form, as if the form is merely a superficial, seductively conscious embellishment of the content. Nor is it the case that only the content has an unconscious source and that its design is a conscious work. Both form and content flow forth from unconscious drives.

"With regard to content and form the lead must be left as far as possible to the chance ideas and associations thrown up by the unconscious. This is naturally something of a setback for the conscious standpoint and is often felt as painful."[300] Once more Jung is cautious about a one-sided tendency; he has known this caution

296 Maclagan 2001: 22, 25.
297 See Jung 1957/1960.
298 See Jung 1957/1960: 84.
299 Jung 1957/1960: 84.
300 Jung 1957/1960: 85–86.

throughout his entire life and with respect to each theme. "Both [tendencies] have their typical dangers and may lead one astray. The danger of the aesthetic tendency is over-evaluation of the formal or 'artistic' worth of the fantasy-productions. (...) The danger of wanting to understand the meaning is over-evaluation of the content, which is subjected to intellectual analysis and interpretation, so that the essentially symbolic character of the product is lost."[301]

To me, this comes across as a very clear viewpoint. The content of a work of art cannot reveal itself other than *in* its aesthetic form, and the latter is completely empty without the first. In short, and it is Jung who italicised: "*One tendency seems to be the regulating principle of the other*; both are bound together in a compensatory relationship. (...) We could say that aesthetic formulation needs understanding of the meaning, and understanding needs aesthetic formulation."[302]

In some respects he even gave precedence to the form: "It has better prospects of success if it [the dream-material] begins only with the [aesthetic] formulated product. The less the initial material is shaped and developed, the greater the danger that understanding will be governed not by the empirical facts but by theoretical and moral considerations."[303] Jung never revised this viewpoint. At age 70, in the middle of his lecture at an Eranos meeting, he diverted his thoughts towards art and beautifully emphasised the unavoidable bond between aesthetic formulation and content: "And so it is with the hand that guides the crayon or brush, the foot that executes the dance step, with the eye and the ear, with the word and the thought: a dark impulse is the ultimate arbiter of the pattern, an unconscious a priori precipitates itself into plastic form. (...) Over the whole procedure there seems to reign a dim foreknowledge not only of the pattern but of its meaning. *Image and meaning are identical; and as the first takes shape, so the latter becomes clear. Actually, the pattern needs no interpretation: it portrays its own meaning.*"[304]

For the person who ponders these sentences (Pamuk could have read them), especially the sentences I italicised, it will be difficult to claim that Jung considered the aesthetic form as a *purely formal surface phenomenon.*

The primacy of the work of art

The way we have demarcated each subject so far might on first glance seem to correspond to the course of the creative process; nevertheless, we have now reached the point where we are asked to make an almost Copernican change in our approach. Until now it has seemed that the artist descends into the collective unconscious in order to unearth a beautiful gem, a work of art, in an extraverted/introverted manner and through intuition/sensation; but according to Jung, the

301 Jung 1957/1960: 84–85.
302 Jung 1957/1960: 85.
303 Jung 1957/1960: 87.
304 Jung 1954/1960: 204 (italics mine).

reverse is true. First there is the archetypal appearance of the gem; subsequently intuition 'sees' it; subsequently one searches for the adequate formulation, etc. We already know that the work of art presents itself as an autonomous complex, and when activated it compulsorily finds its way and includes all kinds of associations along the way. The primacy of the work of art is the core of Jung's perspective on art. In this regard, his texts are without compromise.

At this point, I have to make an important remark. Of course, a work of art does not *only* consist of unconscious factors and even less of only *collectively unconscious* factors. This is where the deepest impulse of a great work of art resides, but once released, this autonomous complex attracts different elements. It works like a magnet. It also includes material from the artist's personal unconscious, themes from his conscious memory, what he has learned from his education, what he has seen in other artists' works, preferences he has had during a certain period, perhaps what he saw on the street the day before, what he 'remembers' through cryptomnesia, etc. But the *autonomous* complex clusters all of this; it forms the heart of the whole process. And consequently, in *this* respect the artist is in second place. Two beautiful quotations:

> Art is a kind of innate drive that seizes a human being and makes him its instrument. The artist is not a person endowed with free will who seeks his own ends, but one who allows art to realise its purposes through him. As a human being he may have moods and a will and personal aims, but as an artist he is 'man' in a higher sense – he is 'collective man', a vehicle and moulder of the unconscious psychic life of mankind. That is his office, and it is sometimes so heavy a burden that he is faced with sacrificing happiness and everything that makes life worth living for ordinary human being.[305]

> The unborn work in the psyche of the artist is a force of nature that achieves its end either with tyrannical might or with the subtle cunning of nature herself, quite regardless of the personal fate of the man who is his vehicle.[306]

One does not know what constitutes the autonomous creative complex nor what it looks like. "Of this we can know next to nothing so long as the artist's work affords us no insight into its foundations."[307] We have seen this before: in the unconscious there are no images nor representations. It is a world of potentials. First there was a vision, which subsequently wishes to incarnate itself with unyielding force, wants to become a symbol, without any concern for the person of the artist.

We have looked at this extensively. The symbol pulls a person towards a higher mental order. "But works that are openly symbolic do not require a subtle approach;

305 Jung 1930/1978: 101.
306 Jung 1922/1978: 75.
307 Jung 1922/1978: 79.

their pregnant language cries out at us that they mean more than they say (*ich 'meine' über mich hinaus*). We can put our finger on the symbol at once, even though we may not be able to unriddle its meaning to our entire satisfaction."[308]

All of this happens at the expense of the artist. He needs to 'disappear'. Certainly, he is the womb of a work of art. But eventually, at the birth of the 'child', he is purified and, as it were, depersonalised. The artist remains hidden behind the work of art. The mystery of creation results in an autonomous object: a work of art.

In the following chapter we will illustrate, apply and test Jung's perspective on art, as we distilled it in this chapter, from one specific viewpoint: his attitude to "modern art". This will give us a more concrete idea of his perspective.

308 Jung 1922/1978: 77.

Chapter 8

Jung's perspective on "modern art"

> I am including "modern art"– and passionately – though I see you indulgently smiling.
>
> (Jung 1990: 589)

> "Modern art" is "cubistic" in the deepest sense of the word because it resolves the picture of reality into an immensely complex painting. (...) Cubism is not a disease but a tendency to represent reality in a certain way – and that way may be grotesquely realistic or grotesquely abstract.
>
> (Jung 1932/1978b: 117)

From an artistic viewpoint Jung knew how to appreciate "modern art", from a psychological viewpoint he had great difficulty with it. It portrays the immense destruction of the classic forms; of religion, politics and ethics, and shows us the ruins. "But no one speaks about what it does to your soul! The nature of 'modern art' is morbid. Am I allowed to say this?" He also did not think of most "modern art" as 'great art'. It remains stuck. It shows us our dreadful situation, but it no longer gives us a perspective. This does not apply to the great artists. He wrote beautifully about, for instance, Joyce, Picasso and Tanguy. They had the courage to listen to the unconscious "subjective factor" in themselves that per definition longs for wholeness.

Preface

From the start of his career, Jung realised that there could exist a completely different type of art than classical art. By 1913, as we saw in Chapter 3, he had already learned from the art philosopher Worringer that there are two types of art: one originating from 'empathy' and one from 'abstraction'.[309] And in 1921, in *Psychological Types*, he showed his ability to characterise "modern art" from the viewpoint of this dichotomy. He wrote: "Since antiquity, our general attitude to

309 See Jung 1913/1990: 505.

art has always been empathetic, and for this reason we designate as beautiful only those things we can empathise with. (...) We can empathise only with organic form – form that is true to nature and has the will to live. And yet another art principle undoubtedly exists, a style that is opposed to life, that denies the will to live, but nevertheless lays a claim to beauty."[310]

Jung never kept it a secret that he found it difficult to 'empathise' with this art; he despised any form of art which represses life. In principle this art could claim beauty; in practice he mostly thought about it as unmistakably ugly. As a reminder, we are here dealing with those types of art which became known from the beginning of the twentieth century as Cubism, Surrealism, Abstract art and Dadaism. In all these types of art the organic reality dissolves into non-organic forms. This type of art did not resonate with Jung's personal taste; he preferred classical art.[311]

As we shall see, Jung's attitude towards "modern art" was complicated. On the one hand he understood it, but on the other he despised it. His own theories formed a key to this art, but he sometimes used this key with aversion or simply not at all. Even though at the start of his career he could have some appreciation for its products, his dislike increased throughout the years. In this chapter, I try to analyse his view.

Jung's dislike of "modern art"

Since he was outspoken about his dislike of "modern art", Jung was often astonished that artists wanted to discuss their work with him and that they sometimes travelled far to meet him. When his famous pupil, Esther Harding (1881–1971), decided to bring the work of the poet Thomas Stearns Eliot

310 Jung 1921/1990: 291.

311 For instance, in the art of painting, this gives the following picture. Jung was deeply moved by the classical Dutch, German and Italian masters. He appreciated them so much that he built up his own collection of etchings. Aniela Jaffé, his secretary, who knew him from 1937 until his death, wrote about his lifelong love and care for this collection of etchings which he collected in his youth (see Jaffé 1989: 124). Jung had no difficulties with contemporary art as such. He was, for example, captivated by *Jugendstil*. Also *Symbolism* had a strong impact on him. In those years these were movements which represented an outspoken counterculture, movements which were resisting a technological, pragmatic culture and used a transcendental experience of space and time. For Jung, 'contemporary art' is not the same as abstract, cubist, surrealist "modern art". When Ernest Jones, the later biographer of Freud, once asked Jung whether the fashionable *Dadaïsme* has a 'psychological principle', he replied: "It is too foolish to be able to be insane in some or other decent way" (quoted in Zuch 2004: 92).

A painter who was much admired by Jung was the Swiss Arnold Böcklin (1827–1901) (see Bair 2003: 79). Böcklin was a true Symbolist. Most of his paintings show allegorical, mythological or dream motives. Jung thought of Böcklin as someone who prepared the way to a new time, who made the rational person conscious of his irrational drives and his individuality. During a seminar in 1937 he spoke agreeably about what is perhaps Böcklin's most important painting, *Die Toteninsel* (see Jung 1988: 1191–1192). Mostly, Jung had the same classic interest with respect to other forms of art.

(1888–1965) to his attention and wrote that she wanted to send him *Murder in the Cathedral* and *The Waste Land*, he answered on 8 July 1947: "I don't know T. S. Eliot. If you think that this book is worthwhile, then I don't mind even poetry. I am only prejudiced against all forms of modern art. It is mostly morbid and evil on top of that."[312] This is quite unequivocal language. On 12 August 1940, at the beginning of the Second World War, Jung wrote to his good friend Helton Godwin Baynes (1882–1943): "It is difficult to be old in these days. One is helpless. (…) In autumn I resume my lectures at the E. T. H.[313] about the individuation process in the Middle Ages! That's the only thing with me one could call up to date. I loathe the new style, the new Art, the new Music, Literature, Politics, and above all the new Man. It's the old beast that has not changed since the troglodytes."[314]

Once more, undisguised language. But it is important to read meticulously what Jung was saying. We could conclude from this quotation that Jung did not think of "modern art" as art. However, that is not what he is saying. Jung disliked *new* art; he disliked the *new* person, and subsequently everything this person stands for. He did think about it as art, but he loathed it. He had no doubts about the artistic ability of the – in his view – great "modern" artists, he only ascertained that he is hurt by their art. Occasionally, its nature is even morbid. Nonetheless, he also thought that classical art could be morbid. In *Memories, Dreams, Reflections* he wrote about Nietzsche's *Also Sprach Zarathustra*: "And *Zarathustra* – there could be no doubt about that – was morbid. (…) Just as *Faust* had opened a door for me, *Zarathustra* slammed one shut, and it remained shut for a long time to come."[315]

Jung continually tried to explain why he considered this type of art repulsive. But when he expressed his thoughts, he encountered strong resistance in his audiences and readers. Not only did he feel misunderstood, but also abandoned. His most important psychological notes were not understood. It also disturbed him tremendously that the artists and their admirers could not be open to criticism. On 13 November 1932 he expressed his irritation to Walter Mertens: "I am only against artists getting away with it like the theologians, about whom one may not say anything critical. I don't see why artists should not have exactly the same human psychology as everybody else. To claim to be the infallible mouthpiece of god is as odious to me in art as in theology. *From the artistic standpoint I can well appreciate the achievement of modern art, but from the standpoint of the psychologist I have to say what the nature of these achievements is.* (…) Yet psychology seems to be as hateful to artists as it is to theologians, and as I say I find this extremely repugnant."[316]

As he got older, Jung became increasingly disappointed, even embittered. We can see this clearly in his letters. On 2 September 1960, the 85-year-old Jung

312 Jung 1973: 469.
313 Eidgenossische Technische Hochschule in Zürich.
314 Jung 1973: 286. The troglodytes were cavemen in Southeast Egypt around 500 BC.
315 Jung 1961/1989: 102, 103.
316 Jung 1973: 107–108 (italics mine).

complained about his distress to his friend Herbert Read (1893–1968). Read had given him his latest book, *The Form of Things Unknown*, a collection of essays about art in which Jung's thoughts take a prominent place.[317] Read considered Jung's ideas appropriate for an understanding of the phenomenon of art, in particular "modern art". Jung's negligence with regard to "modern art" is a pity, he wrote. Jung took this remark badly. He stayed friendly towards his friend, but thought he should correct him on this point. He emphasised that he was intensely occupied with "modern art", but... no one would listen to him. "I am including 'modern art' – and passionately – though I see you indulgently smiling. I have regretted very much not to have had the opportunity of a real talk with you about your book, which has brought back to me all my thoughts about art. I have never been explicit about them because I was hampered by my increasing awareness of the universal misunderstanding I encountered. As the problem is subtle, its solution demands subtlety of mind and real experience of the mind's functioning. After sixty solid years of field work I may be supposed to know at least something about my job. But even the most incompetent ass knew better and I received no encouragement. On the contrary I was misunderstood or completely ignored. Under those circumstances I even grew afraid to increase the chaos of opinion by adding considerations which could not be understood."[318]

The letter continues in much the same vein. Read answered him in a long letter. Later, I will return to both letters, but for now it is clear: Jung felt underappreciated. He thought he had appropriately characterised "modern art", but his opponents had no idea what he meant by, for instance, "real experience of the mind's functioning" and "psychic reality". Art flows forth from the soul of the artist and touches the soul of the beholder. He wrote to Read: "In *Ulysses* [the novel by James Joyce (1882–1941)], a world comes down in an almost endless, breathless stream of debris, a "catholic" world, i.e. a universe with moanings and outcries unheard and tears unshed, because suffering had extinguished itself, and an immense field of shards began to reveal its aesthetic 'values'. But no tongue will tell you what has happened in his soul."[319] This last sentence mirrors the cry of Jung's own soul. Is one allowed to consider it appalling and morbid what sufferings these artists cause to the soul?

Jung's dislike of "modern art" was strongest between 1938 and 1955. Before these years, there was a time when he occupied himself extensively and constructively with it. Moreover, after these years some kind of appreciation is also noticeable. For instance, in 1958, he published a probing review on a painting by the surrealist Tanguy. This discussion is central to the final chapter of this book. During and after the Second World War, his dislike was strongest. Most likely, he made a direct connection between the terrible ruins of that time and the debris he considered characteristic of "modern art". In 1945 he wrote in *After the*

317 See Read 1960.
318 Jung 1990: 589.
319 Jung 1990: 589.

Catastrophe that the post-war mental condition of the "whole of Europe" is painstakingly portrayed by "our art, that most delicate of all instruments for reflecting the national psyche. How are we to explain the blatantly pathological element in modern painting? Atonal music? The far-reaching influence of Joyce's fathomless *Ulysses?* Here we already have the germ of what was to become a political reality in Germany."[320] These words reflect what went on in Jung's heart.

"Modern art" is not schizophrenic but schizoid

Sometimes it seems as if Jung thought of "modern art" as a product of mental illness. On 17 June 1952 he said to the British art critic Joseph Paul Hodin (1905–1995): "No, I cannot occupy myself with modern art any more. It is too awful. That is why I do not want to know more about it. At one time I took a great interest in art. I painted myself, sculpted and did wood carving. I have a certain sense of colour. When modern art came on the scene, it presented a great psychological problem for me. Then I wrote about Picasso and Joyce. I recognised there something which is very unpopular, namely the very thing which confronts me in my patients. These people are either schizophrenics or neurotics. Neurotics smart under the problem of our age. Art derives its life from and expresses the conditions of our time. In that sense art is prophetic. It speaks as the plant speaks of nature and of the earth, of ground and background. My patients make similar pictures. When they are in a chaotic state, all forms dissolve. Then panic grips them. Everything threatens to fall to pieces and we are in a state of panic – though it is an unadmitted panic. What does this art say? This art is a flight from the perceptible world, from the visible reality. What does it mean, to turn one's eye inward? The first thing people see there is the debris of destruction, and the infantilism of their own souls."[321]

In Chapter 1, we saw that Jung asserted that art *never* emanates from an abnormal, sick mind. And with respect to an artist who clearly has a psychological disturbance, we cannot establish a causal relationship between this illness and the art he produces. It is impossible for someone to create art during an outbreak of psychosis. This does not imply that there is not a lot of mentally disturbed work. Jung thought "that a great deal of modern art, painting as well as poetry, is simply neurotic", but that it "is little short of grotesque" to reduce truly great art to neurosis.[322]

But what he said to Hodin in the quote above could make us suspicious that he did think that great artists like Joyce and Picasso created mentally ill work. Does it not say in few words that Picasso and Joyce respectively were schizophrenic and neurotic? Most likely, Hodin understood these words as such. But this is not at all what Jung wanted to say. We know this for sure, because 20 years earlier Jung also used the terms 'schizophrenic' and 'neurotic' in the same context. At the time his

320 Jung 1945/1964: 210.
321 Jung 1977/1978: 221–222.
322 Jung 1932/1977: 766.

remarks encountered much resistance. In an infamous article about Picasso in the *Neue Zürcher Zeitung*, published on 13 November 1932, he claimed that Picasso belonged to a group of schizophrenics. It caused an unrelenting outbreak of criticism. When, in 1934, he included this article in one of his books, hence republished it, he felt obligated to explain in a footnote what he meant by 'schizophrenic'. Picasso produced images, he said, which show him to be so torn that we can speak of a certain schizophrenia. I use this term, he said, because I see in the drawings of my schizophrenic patients the same kind of 'fractured lines' and 'shifting crevices'. Hence, he clearly saw an *analogy*. In daily conversation, Jung could simply say about someone that he or she was schizophrenic or hysteric whilst he was aware that they are not so in any clinical sense. In the footnote he wrote: "In the case under discussion [i.e. Picasso], the designation 'schizophrenic' does not, therefore, signify a diagnosis of the mental illness schizophrenia, but merely refers to a disposition or *habitus* on the basis of which a serious psychological disturbance could produce schizophrenia. Hence I regard neither Picasso nor Joyce as psychotics, but count them among a large number of people whose *habitus* is to react to a profound psychic disturbance not with an ordinary psychoneurosis but with a *schizoid*[323] syndrome."[324]

Of importance here is "a large number of people". According to Jung, many of us belong to this group. A great part of society is 'neurotic', that is to say, they experience how profoundly torn society is and they react to it in a 'schizoid' way. That is, with an attitude which is *similar to* schizophrenia. The artist who is sensitive by nature, in particular, is susceptible to these signals and by implication is psychologically 'disturbed'. He is a gifted disruptor of the status quo, he depicts this 'tornness' in the same way as do schizophrenic patients. The psychiatrist in particular can value this, but he can also appreciate the differences between both products. Jung continually emphasised the differences. A great work of art cannot be compared to material which is created by someone in psychologically disturbed circumstances. The nature of such material is stereotyped and monotonous. Jung pointed to this whilst discussing *Ulysses*, which, in his eyes, is a 'terrible' work. "*Ulysses* may be anything, but it is certainly not monotonous in the sense of being repetitious. (...) The presentation is consistent and flowing, everything is in motion and nothing is fixed. The whole book is borne along on a subterranean current of life that shows singleness of aim and rigorous selectivity, both these being unmistakable proof of the existence of a unified personal will and directed intention. The mental functions are under severe control. (...) These are traits not ordinarily found in the insane. (...) It would never occur to me to class *Ulysses* as a product of schizophrenia. (...) *Ulysses is no more a pathological product than modern art as a whole.*"[325]

323 'Schizophrenic' refers to the affliction of a split consciousness. 'Schizoid' literally means '*similar* to being split'.

324 Jung 1932/1978a: 137, footnote 3 (italics mine).

325 Jung 1932/1978b: 116–117 (italics mine).

It is a typical 'cubist' product, Jung said further on, and he used that term as a characterisation of all "modern art". "It is 'cubistic' in the deepest sense because it resolves the picture of reality into an immensely complex painting whose dominant note is the melancholy of abstract objectivity. Cubism is not a disease but a tendency to represent reality in a certain way – and that way may be grotesquely realistic or grotesquely abstract."[326]

Product of the unconscious *Zeitgeist*

But what is the reason that "modern art", whilst being authentic art, manifests itself as such? According to Jung, the reason is that it gives expression to an analogous unconscious *Zeitgeist*. "In the modern artist it is not produced by any disease in the individual but is a collective *manifestation of our time*. The artist does not follow an individual impulse, but rather a current of collective life which arises not directly from consciousness but from the collective unconscious of the modern psyche. Just because it is a collective phenomenon it bears identical fruit in the most widely separated realms, in painting as well as literature, in sculpture as well as architecture."[327]

In Jung's view, as we have seen, this is an essential characteristic of all great art. It reacts compensatorily to the *Zeitgeist*. Hence it is the *Zeitgeist* in which the work of art comes into being that has malevolent traits. In the letter to Read cited earlier, Jung wrote about the huge problem that our age does not understand what is happening in the world. Darkness and unfamiliar impulses originate from the unconscious. "It hollows out and hacks up the shapes of our culture and its historical dominants. We have no dominants any more, they are in the future. Our values are shifting, every thing loses its certainty, even *sanctissima causalitas* [the empirical law of cause and effect] has descended from the throne of the axiom and has become a mere field of probability. (…) Our hitherto believed values decay accordingly and our only certainty is that the new world will be something different from what we were used to. *If any of his urges show some inclination to incarnate in a known shape, the creative artist will not trust it. He will say: 'Thou art not what thou sayest', and he will hollow them out and hack them up. That is where we are now.*"[328]

Art reacts and presents forms which for some or other reason are needed by the spirit of the age in order to find its balance. And when seeing or hearing this art, we suddenly realise what is going on unconsciously. Art functions like a mirror to the *Zeitgeist*: "Though seeming to deal with aesthetic problems, it is really performing a work of psychological education on the public by breaking down and destroying their previous and aesthetic views of what is beautiful in form and meaningful in content. The pleasingness of the artistic product is replaced by chill

326 Jung 1932/1978b: 117.
327 Jung 1932/1978: 117 (italics mine).
328 Jung 1990: 590 (italics mine).

abstractions of the most subjective nature which brusquely slam the door on the naïve and romantic delight in the senses and on the obligatory love for the object."[329]

During the Second World War, the artist and journalist Arnold Kübler (1890–1983) asked Jung why can we no longer paint like the Romantics? Jung answered with a significant question: how can the artist be romantic at *this time*? "If one is sitting on a volcano and can be contemplative, this is a superhuman heroism which is itself a contradiction in terms. Nowadays it is no longer any use appealing to any certainties. Deep down we know that everything is tottering. (…) Therefore it is much better for modern art to paint the thousand-hued debris of the shattered crockery than to try to spread a deceptive quietness over the bottomless disquiet."[330]

Summarised, for now, the function of this art is to make visible the strongest motives of its time (which it has in common with all art); to sweep away all classical, totalitarian ideologies, to show the debris we have reached, and to provide us with air.[331]

Dissolution of objective reality

Hence, according to Jung, the core aspect of "modern art" is the systematic breaking down and dissolution of tangible reality. He thought that this is grounded in a historical process which started with the disintegration of the medieval world into different faiths. For this reason the inner unity and quiet had to make way for the materialistic urge to conquer the outside world. In the appearing sciences this material reality was emphasised, researched and conquered. Modern art began to resist this enlightened modern spirit by dissolving objective reality and starting to search for what is basic, that is, our inner spiritual reality.[332]

During a seminar in 1925, Jung said that he once closely studied this dissolution process. That was in 1913, at an exhibition of "modern art" in New York. He looked meticulously at each of Picasso's paintings. Jung told his students: "I once followed very carefully the course of Picasso's painting. All of a sudden he was struck by the triangular shadow thrown by the nose on the cheek. Later on the

329 Jung 1957/1964: 303.

330 Jung 1973: 316. In 1958, three years before his death, Jung still expressed the same opinion: "It is, indeed, a law of painting to give visible shape to the dominant trends of the age, and for some time now painters have taken as their subject the disintegration of forms and the 'breaking of tables'. (…) Just as women's fashions find every innovation, however absurd and repellent, 'beautiful', so too does modern art of this kind. It is the 'beauty' of chaos. (…) One can well imagine that in an epoch of the 'great destroyers' it is a particular satisfaction to be at least the broom that sweeps the rubbish into the corner" (Jung 1958/1964: 383). "But it is only modern man who has succeeded in creating an art in reverse, a backside of art that makes no attempt to be ingratiating, that tells us just where we got off" (Jung 1932/1978b: 119).

331 "These episodic or regular disruptions of the accustomed order should be regarded as psychohygienic measures since they give vent from time to time to the suppressed forces of chaos" (Jung 1990: 81).

332 See Jung 1926/1989: 56.

cheek itself became a four-sided shadow, and so it went. These triangles and squares became nuclei with independent values of their own, and the human figure gradually disappeared or became dissolved in space."

Jung also talked about his confrontation with a cubist painting by Marcel Duchamp (1887–1968), *Nude Descending a Staircase* (see plate 8). "There was exhibited (...) a painting called the *Nude Descending the Stairs* [sic]. This might be said a double dissolution of the object, that is in time and space, for not only have the figure and the stairs gone over into the triangles and squares, but the figure is up and down the stairs at the same time, and it is only by moving the picture that one can get the figure to come out as it would in an ordinary painting where the artist preserved the integrity of the figure in space and time. The essence of this process is the depreciation of the object. (...) The artist takes the object away from our eyes, and substitutes a partial derivative. (...) This process inevitably drives the interest away from the object to the subject, and instead of the real object, the internal object becomes the carrier of the values."[333] He told this in 1925. Nothing, yet, showed his dislike of this kind of art. His words are very different from the letter he wrote to Read in 1960 wherein he described "modern art" as a kind of devastating fragmentation bomb.

A journey through Hades, the Nekyia

Until midway through the Thirties, Jung seriously tried to understand and analyse "modern art". He was not all that impressed by the processes of dissolution he saw at work in this art. It belongs to the essence of all art, he thought, because it must first go into the melting pot of *participation mystique* in order to reappear from it as a symbol. In what Jung considered the biggest work of art, *Faust*, the main character undergoes the dissolving, hellish powers in all sorts of ways and at a certain time he descends into the underworld, Hades. There he needs to find a key to rebirth. These scenes (the Walpurgnis Night and the Witches' Sabbath) have a dissolving character. It is a central theme in *Faust II*: descending into the Realm of Mothers. Like no other, Goethe saw the pale, manly one-sidedness of the modern Faustian person. In order to release the creative powers of this colourless *animus*, the craters of the unconscious female *anima* need to be uncovered.[334]

We are here dealing with an archetypal mythical fact. We know many examples. Little Red Cap and the wolf, Persephone in Hades, Osiris in the Nile, Jonah in the

333 Jung 1926/1989: 54.

334 When Faust, shivering, descends into the underworld to compel the divine pair Paris and Helena to resurrect, and thus to perform (again) the holy marriage of the oppositions, he receives a key to take with him. 'This key will show you where and how, follow it, it leads you to the Mothers' (*Faust II:* 6263–6264). With it Faust will touch the holy tripod in the realm of the witches. Because he has 'the key' to this *conjunctio*-secret, he will not disappear into the witches' cooking pot but return enriched.

whale, Jesus in the grave; all of them experience this phase in order to resurrect in full power. For Jung, this is more like descending into the unconscious and parting with the conscious upper world.

Jung thought he had encountered in Picasso this subterranean journey into Hades, this Nekyia, in an almost literal way. He saw it at the exhibition in Zürich in 1932. "Thus Picasso starts with the still objective pictures of the Blue Period – the blue of night, of moonlight and water, the *tuat*-blue of the Egyptian underworld. He dies, and his soul rides on horseback into the beyond (see plate 9). The day-life clings to him, and a woman with a child steps up to him, warningly (see plate 10). As the day is woman to him, so the night and the dark soul (anima). The dark one sits waiting, expecting him in the blue twilight, and stirring up morbid presentiments. With the change of colour, we enter the underworld. The world of objects is death-struck, as the horrifying masterpiece of the syphilitic, tubercular, adolescent prostitute makes plain. The motif of the prostitute begins with the entry into the beyond, where he, as a departed soul, encounters a number of others of his kind. When I say 'he', I mean that personality in Picasso which suffers the underworld fate – the man in him who does not turn towards the day-world, but is fatefully drowned in the dark; who follows not the accepted ideals of goodness and beauty, but the demonical attraction of ugliness and evil. It is these antichristian and Luciferian forces that well up in modern man and engender an all-pervading sense of doom, veiling the bright world of day with the mists of Hades, infecting it with deadly decay, and finally, like an earthquake, dissolving it into fragments, fractures, discarded remnants, debris, shreds, and disorganised units. Picasso and his exhibition are a sign of the times, just as much as the twenty-eight thousand people who came to look at his pictures."[335]

Hence, the journey is necessary: "The Nekyia is no aimless and purely destructive fall into the abyss, but a meaningful *katabasis eis antron*, a descent into the cave of initiation and secret knowledge. The journey through the psychic history of mankind has as its object *the restoration of the whole man.*"[336] In *Faust*, the purpose of the descent into the Realm of the Mothers is the resurrection of the whole person. Of this whole person, encompassing both Paris and Helena, the modern person is no longer aware. This underground, unconscious whole person (also called the archetype of the Self by Jung) always affects the upper-world in uncertain times. This means, Jung wrote, that "the *katabasis* and *katalysis* are followed by a recognition of the bipolarity of human nature and of the necessity of the conflicting pairs of opposites. After the symbols of madness experienced during the period of disintegration there follow images which represent the coming together of opposites: light/dark, above/below, white/black, male/female, etc."[337]

In 1932, Jung thought he saw the beginning of a *peripeteia*, a turning point, in Picasso. In any case, he saw the opposites standing eye to eye in his paintings. "In

335 Jung 1932/1978a: 138–139.
336 Jung 1932/1978a: 139–140 (italics mine).
337 Jung 1932/1978a: 400 (italics mine).

Picasso's latest paintings, the motif of the union of opposites is seen very clearly in their direct juxtaposition. One painting (although traversed by numerous lines of fracture) even contains the conjunction of the light and dark *anima*. (...) As to the future Picasso, I would rather not try my hand at prophecy, for this inner adventure is a hazardous affair and can lead at any moment to a standstill or to a catastrophic bursting asunder of the conjoined opposites."[338]

Jung must have felt that he had done his utmost to look positively at Picasso. Hence, it must have disappointed and irritated him that his article was received so negatively. In fact, since that year he never published anything substantial about "modern art", except again in 1958, three years before his death. In letters and interviews he mostly expressed his aversion.

Where Jung's questions begin

What was bothering Jung so much in this type of art? Not the fact that it meant a breach with the past. In his view it was not the first time in history that a form of art radically broke with the previous era and presented itself seemingly formless, ugly, without any recognisable beauty. He gave several examples: the 'perverse change in style' in ancient Egypt under pharaoh Amenophis IV (Echnaton, 1372–1354 BC); the foolish lamb-symbolism of the first Christians; the 'poor human figures' of the Pre-Raphaelite primitives; and the 'suffocating curls' of the late baroque. They are dislocating tendencies at certain moments in human history, opening the door for new great eras. Such relatively short 'perverse changes' in style only have meaning when they anticipate something new.[339] Subsequently there is an incubation period, which per definition gives birth to something new. It may be necessary and important to dwell in Hades for a while, but we need to resurface. Jung encountered in "modern art" the problem that it stayed in Hades, that it showed little of a renaissance. With some exceptions. Perhaps nothing was bred and thus it was pure destruction. Jung spoke in his letter to Read about the fact that the "modern" artist hollows out and demolishes what comes into his hands. Then he wrote: "That is where we are now." Jung seemed to be thinking: illusionary worlds are destroyed, but which world do I see being built? He could not see anything like a 'turning point', even less a 'return'. He predominantly saw *katabasis* and *katalysis*, only descent and dissolution. This work shows us our

338 Jung 1932/1978a: 140.

339 "Such manifestations of the collective psyche disclose their meaning only when they are considered teleologically as anticipations of something new. The epoch of Ikhnaton was the cradle of the first monotheism, which has been preserved for the world in Jewish tradition. The crude infantilism of the early Christian era portended nothing less than the transformation of the Roman Empire into a City of God. The rejection of the art and science of this time was not an impoverishment for the early Christian, but a great spiritual gain. The Pre-Raphaelite primitives were the heralds of an ideal of bodily beauty that had been lost to the world since classical times. The Baroque was the last of the ecclesiastical styles, and its self-destruction anticipates the triumph of the spirit of science over the spirit of medieval dogmatism" (Jung 1932/1978b: 118).

dreadful situation, but does not give us any new perspective. It works like black magic. It elevates its annihilating impulses to the level of undisputed truths. The means which are used are primitive, fascinating, anxious images, statements which are incomprehensible to our normal reason, strange words and forms, primitive rhythms, etc.

Jung longed for white magic. On 1 September 1952 he wrote in a letter: "There can be no doubt that the unconscious comes to the surface in modern art and with its dynamism destroys the orderliness that is characteristic of consciousness. (…) I myself am inclined to view what rushes up as the opposite of art, since it very evidently lacks order and form. The uprushing chaos seeks new symbolic ideas which will embrace and express not only the previous order but also the essential content of the disorder. Such ideas would have a magical effect by holding the destructive forces of disorder spellbound, as has been the case in Christianity and in all other religions. In ancient traditions this magic is called white magic."[340]

In the letter to Hodin on 17 June 1952 he again mentioned this subject: "I am pessimistic about the pile of wreckage. A new revelation from within, one that will enable us to see behind the shattered fragments of infantilism, one in which the true image appears, one that is constructive – that is what I am waiting for."[341] However, he did not think that art is solely responsible for this wreckage: "Everything that should represent the irrational and fails to do so is responsible. (…) Theology is one of the causes of soullessness. Science, because it claims exclusiveness; the priest, when he subordinated himself to the intellect; art, which has all of a sudden lost its belief in beauty and looks only inwardly where there is nothing to be found but ruins, the mirror of our world: they all want to descend into the Realm of the Mothers without possessing Faust's key. In my own way I try to get hold of a key and to open closed doors with it."[342]

We may be surprised about Jung's sharp criticism of "modern art". Because, according to his own perspective (!), it is not up to us to call upon the responsibility of art or the artist for the misery they show us. According to his own view, it is not the case that art has caused this dissolution, but the unconscious *Zeitgeist*. The artist only detects it. *Eventually*, the symbolising forces of *participation mystique* will set in motion a reversal. In due course, the artist will project these uniting forces outward. But he has to await his time. Art is also delivered to the unconscious *Zeitgeist*. Of course it is a subtle indicator, but it is nothing more than a messenger. An artist is equally responsible for his works of art as we are for our dreams. Therefore, we have to call the unconscious *Zeitgeist* malevolent instead of art or the artist. Jung knows this very well. It is the unconscious *Zeitgeist* which eventually anticipates future changes, not art. "The striving for self-knowledge is altogether not without prospects of success, since there exists a factor which, completely disregarded, meets our expectations halfway. That is the *unconscious*

340 Jung 1990: 81.
341 Jung 1977/1978: 223.
342 Jung 1977/1978: 223, 224. For an explanation of the key, see footnote 334.

Zeitgeist. It compensates the attitude of the conscious mind and anticipates changes to come. An excellent example of this is modern art."[343]

Above, I quoted Jung's letter wherein he said that the "modern" artist is unable to paint romantically and may not pretend a false quiet above an abyss of disquiet. At the end of his letter he knew very well how impotent art itself is: "And if a new certainty does not start up somewhere, art will continue to express disquiet and inhumanity."[344] Therefore, art has to do what it needs to do, even though it is not by far what one wishes it to be. To Mertens, who responded to the Picasso article Jung wrote on 24 November 1932, "[Art] fails entirely in its educative purpose if people don't see that it depicts the sickness of our time. That is why this art is neither enjoyable nor elevating, but as you rightly say a 'scream'. But a scream is always just that – a noise and not music. (...) Naturally I don't want to discourage modern art; it must continue its attempts and I wish it luck. The creative spirit cannot be discouraged anyway, otherwise it would not be creative."[345]

Hence, there is not much else to do than to 'scream'. The *Zeitgeist* does not allow much else. One cannot reproach "modern art". Even less the "modern" artist, one would think. And yet, Jung continued to do this.

Jung remains headstrong

From the Second World War until the end of his life, Jung kept reproaching the "modern" artist. Even the fact that the unconscious *Zeitgeist* is at the basis of art is, for him, not enough to excuse the artist. This can only imply one thing, and Jung acknowledged this in few words: that many "modern" artists know only how to listen one-sidedly to this *Zeitgeist*. Because in the collective unconscious the message of the whole person sounds... but one does not know how to listen. In this respect his criticism becomes most fierce. He thought that the average "modern" artist does not have anything like the stature of the classical artist. The "modern" artist has little understanding of the objective unconscious spirit within him, and is mainly occupied with his conscious I. This is the cardinal point in his letter to Read. The "modern" artist no longer trusts his dreams, does not suspect that what is truly creative within him is his unconscious mind. He thinks that everything comes forth from his conscious I.

"They [the modern artists] have not yet learned to discriminate between their wilful mind and *the objective manifestation of the psyche*. They have not yet learned to be objective with their own psyche, i.e. [to discriminate] between the thing which you do and the thing that happens to you. (...) If the artist of today could only see what the psyche is spontaneously producing and what he, as a consciousness, is inventing, he would notice that the dream, for instance, or the object is pronouncing (through his psyche) a reality from which he will never

343 Jung 1957/1964: 303.
344 Jung 1973: 316.
345 Jung 1973: 108.

escape, because nobody will ever transcend the structure of the psyche. We have simply got to listen to what the psyche spontaneously says to us. What the dream, which is not manufactured by us, says is *just* so. Say it again as well as you can. *Quod Natura relinquit imperfectum, Ars perfecit* [What nature left imperfectly, (alchemical) art perfects]. It is the great dream which has always spoken through the artist as a mouthpiece. (…) We only know what we know, but there is plenty more of which we might know if only we could give up insisting upon what we do know. But the Dream would tell us more, therefore we despise the Dream and we are going on to dissolve *ad infinitum*. (…) We cannot know better than the unconscious and its intimations. There is a fair chance of finding what we seek in vain in our conscious world. Where else could it be? I am afraid I never find the language which would convey such simple arguments to my contemporaries."[346]

This is of course a key quotation. Jung is right. His idea, "the objective manifestation of the psyche", was and still is not understood. Among other things, the unconscious psyche exists and works via dreams and intuitions. This is an objective fact, even though it is not empirically verifiable. There exists an unconscious knowing which encompasses and influences my conscious knowing. Awkwardly, Jung called this objective, unconscious knowing the 'subjective factor'. He meant to say that there exists an 'objective factor' within 'subjective experience'. This particularly influences art.

In the letter above, we read: if only the modern artist could see "what the psyche is spontaneously producing" and knew how to distinguish it from "what he, as a consciousness, is inventing". Jung thought that in "modern art" one has little or no eye for the objective psyche; again, very awkwardly called by him the 'subjective factor'.[347]

In 1925, in his seminars on analytical psychology, Jung revealed his thoughts on this subject, particularly in relation to "modern art". And he was beginning to notice that his public does not understand his formulations. When one of his students remarked that it is characteristic for "modern art" to be 'subjective', Jung immediately presupposed that she attached a different meaning to the term than he did: "If you say that, you must be very careful to define what you mean by subjective. Very often it is assumed that an experience is subjective because it takes place within the mind of the subject, but it is not then necessarily in opposition to objective, because the images of the collective unconscious, from their collective character, are just as truly objects as things outside the psyche. Now, I think modern art tends to be subjective in the sense that the artist is concerned with his individual connection with the object, rather than with the object *per se*."[348]

The final sentence is cryptically formulated, but Jung is expressing in it his fundamental objection to "modern art". He said that the "modern artist" is not

346 Jung 1990: 590–592 (italics mine).

347 He was of course playing with the word 'factor', which contains 'fact'. He wanted to express that the subjective also has it hard facts.

348 Jung 1926/1989: 52.

sufficiently open to objective impulses which spontaneously, *per se*, occur to him. He is only engaged with his 'individual response', that is, occupied subjectively in the ordinary sense of the word.

The group did not understand much of it and one seminar later Jung needed to explain once more what he meant by the 'subjective factor'. And Jung again explained it: "I call the subjective factor these pre-existing mental images with which the stream of our personal experience comes into contact. (…) The subjective factor is held to be made up of objective material, namely ancestral views. He leaves the outer object and returns to the object as seen by his mind rather than as seen by his senses."[349] Of course, that year he had already discussed archetypes.

It is certain that Jung was not referring to the whole of "modern art". He was convinced that also in this sector 'great art' exists, but sparingly. The utmost part of "modern art" did not arise from that collective, *objective* unconscious. But with artists like Joyce and Picasso, Jung is not hesitant. They draw from *participation mystique*. And it was these artists he had in mind when in 1933 he said in Cologne: "But when we compare the *psychology of modern art* with the findings of psychological research, and this again with the products of mythology and philosophy, *we shall discover irrefutable proofs* of the existence of this collective, unconscious factor."[350]

Jung's attitude to "modern art" is a mixture of different motives which influence and enhance each other, cleave to each other and sometimes impair each other. Jung made an effort to understand at least psychologically a style of art which did not appeal to him. He saw clearly that it depicted the *Zeitgeist*, but thought it did so one-sidedly. He meant to provide a constructive theoretical contribution to the 'modern' debate, but became more or less embittered because of misunderstanding and lack of appreciation. Without a doubt he had worked through his negative attitude regarding everything 'modern' in his attitude towards "modern art".

We always need to remember that Jung was concerned with a *psychology* of art. When he judged this art in general as 'morbid', this is not an aesthetic qualification. In the following and final chapter, I want to show concretely how Jung analysed what, in his view, is a great work of art. It is a painting of the French surrealist Tanguy. All the important ideas of his perspective are included in this analysis. Of course it would also have been possible to choose a classical work of art, for instance Goethe's *Faust,* about which Jung wrote extensively. This work appealed to him a thousand times more than a surrealistic painting. But Jung knew that art can be art without *Einfühlung*. An analysis of *Faust* would have been too 'easy'. It is so obvious that it is 'great art', that it is almost unnecessary to search why that is the case. This question is still relevant when it pertains a "modern" painting. It is fascinating to see how Jung analysed an abstract work, a work which did not naturally appeal to him and which belongs to a movement with which he had great difficulty.

349 Jung 1926/1989: 59.
350 Jung 1934/1964: 146 (italics mine).

Chapter 9

Jung analyses a Surrealist painting

> Since even the boldest fantasy of the creative artist, however much it may exceed the bounds of intelligibility, is always bounded by the limits of the psyche itself, there may easily appear in his pictures unknown forms which indicate certain limiting and predetermined factors.
>
> (Jung 1958/1964: 398–399)

In 1958, Jung analysed a painting by the French Surrealist Yves Tanguy (1900–1955) which had been in his personal possession since 1929. In this analysis we can see how Jung concretely applied his perspective on art to what he saw as a 'great' work of "modern art". He worked in a completely non-conformist way, judging the abstract image as if it was a Rorschach test. It is fascinating to see how he remarked that the painter unconsciously used the most archaic archetypes, those of form and number. Tanguy abstracted new primal forms out of chaos. A new beginning, a new creation. Hopeful signs in the sky.

A remarkable acquisition

At the exhibition Abstract and Surrealistic Paining and Plastic Art at the Kunsthaus in Zürich, which took place from 6 October until 3 November 1929, Jung bought an exhibited painting by Tanguy that was made in the same year.[351] The catalogue registered it with the title 'Noyé indifférent' ('indifferent drowned person') (see plate 11). Its size is 92 x 73 cm. There were three paintings from this artist. At the time, Tanguy was a fairly unknown painter and this was his first exhibition abroad. Jung merely trusted his intuition when buying this painting. It probably moved him. The catalogue did not mention anything about Tanguy's work, it did not even include an introduction to Surrealism.[352] At the time, this

351 Jung made a mistake when he discussed the painting in 1958. He wrote: "This painting by Yves Tanguy dates from 1927." Tanguy clearly signed with 'Yves Tanguy 29', even though in tiny handwriting. The eyes of the 83-year-old man could probably no longer distinguish a 9 from a 7.

352 On 17 August 2006, I received by email the following message from Mrs. Brüngger, librarian

movement had only existed a few years. The *Surrealist Manifesto* was published in 1924 and was written by André Breton (1896–1966), the undisputed charismatic ideologist of this movement. Even if Jung had read something about Surrealism, which can be doubted, it would have made little impression on him. He used the term only once throughout his work; in his article *Ulysses*, published in 1932, about James Joyce's novel. He wrote that it did not immediately occur to him to discuss such a morbid novel. "Ordinarily, I would no more be doing this than writing about any other form of Surrealism (what is surrealism?) that passes my understanding."[353] We know what Jung was saying here. Every time he suspected that he was dealing with 'metaphysics' – when one thinks it possible to speak about a reality which is 'above reality' – something theologians have been good at, he rebelled against it. However, if he had only read three sentences by Breton, he would have known that the movement was not concerned with anything supernatural. Almost 30 years later, in 1958, Jung would elaborately describe and discuss this painting by Tanguy. After his death, his daughter Marianne inherited the painting.[354]

Jung thought that the painting did not have a title. He made a note: "Painting by Yves Tanguy (title unknown)."[355] This is remarkable, because, in 1929, the painting was recorded in the catalogue with the title 'Noyé indifférent'. Thirty years later Jung had apparently forgotten this and was no longer in possession of the little catalogue. When, in 2000, a curator looked carefully at the painting because it was going to be displayed at an exhibition in Stuttgart, he saw a title written on the back. It was not written in Tanguy's handwriting, but in that of the Paris art dealer with whom Tanguy exchanged his paintings for painting material since he was penniless at the time. On the back was a different title than the one in the catalogue: 'Noyer indifférent'. This can literally mean 'indifferent walnut tree'. But if 'noyer' is a verb, it can also mean 'drowning'. The title would then be 'the indifferent drowning'. If Tanguy said the title aloud (for he did not write it down), he could have meant a number of things, including 'noyé', as it was registered in the catalogue of the Kunsthaus. As such it means 'indifferent drowned person'. Did the Kunsthaus ask Tanguy to classify the spelling; and this time did he give the correct spelling of the title? I think this must have been the case.[356]

at the Kunsthaus Zürich: 'In our library we are in possession of the catalogue which you mention. The catalogue contains only 12 pages without pictures and text. Of Yves Tanguy there are only three pictures with a title without any text.' On 1 September 2006, I received from her the titles of the three paintings by Tanguy: Nr. 135 'C'est lui qui brûle les maisons' (It is him who sets the houses on fire); Nr. 136 'Noyé indifférent' (Indifferent drowned person); Nr. 137 'La main est dans ma poche' (The hand is in my pocket).

353 Jung 1932/1978b: 115.

354 In 2000 Jung's daughter made the painting available to the Tanguy Exhibition in Stuttgart. In 2001 it was auctioned at Christie's in London. Currently it belongs to the collection of Galerie Krugier in Geneva (see Zuch 2004: 97–98; Maur 2000: 58–60, 233).

355 Jung 1958: 85, Figure IV.

356 If, in 1929 at the Kunsthaus, one looked at the back of the painting, one would have seen written 'Noyer indifférent'. Normally one would maintain this title. But that did not happen. Hence, we must assume that the title was incorrect. We should not forget that the title was not by Tanguy's

Jung never turned the painting around. Someone like him would never disregard the title if he had known it. He assumed the painting had no title. Nonetheless, he painstakingly studied the painting. In a picture taken in 1960, the painting stood in a prominent place in his library at Küsnacht. It was an improvised place, on the seats of two chairs placed against each other.[357] He probably took it from the wall in order to study it and it subsequently stayed on the chairs for several years.

In the painting, we see a monochrome black underground which is broken by three clear, porous lines. Between them and on top of them we see four standing yellowish, blue-greyish creatures; three of them have small ear-shaped horns. They stand on top of a white, vegetable, fan-like figure that seems to be free from the ground. Above the horizontal lines, we see the vague outlines of round and outstretched forms.

"Something is seen, but one doesn't know what"

The 83-year-old Jung discussed the painting in his book *Flying Saucers: A Modern Myth of Things Seen in the Skies*. In those days, the subject of this book was seen as an exceptionally exciting phenomenon: flying saucers, usually called UFOs. Jung was not interested in the question of whether UFOs really exist (in his book he repeatedly wrote "I have not seen them"), but in the overwhelming psychological fact of the massive excitement surrounding them. "*Something is seen, but one doesn't know what.*" He described it as "a *visionary rumour*".[358]

Jung assumed that this kind of massive rumour is always based on a collective affective tension, which is caused by an urgent situation or by a vital need of the soul. It was not difficult to sense such a tension in the Fifties. The catastrophe of the Second World War still had an all-encompassing influence. There was an increasing secularisation and technicalisation of society. The threat of a new 'cold' war was tangible, the disastrous H-bomb was a fact. Too much tension and despondency. "In just these cases the unconscious has to resort to particularly drastic measures in order to make its contents perceived. It does this most vividly by projection, by extrapolating its contents into an object, which then reflects back what had previously lain hidden in the unconscious. (...) In the threatening situation of the world today, when people begin to see that everything is at stake,

hand. It is also possible that at the Kunsthaus no one looked at the back and instead inquired (probably with Tanguy) about the correct title. In both cases, this advocates the title in the catalogue. How unreal and absurd Surrealist titles may be, it seems to me to be very difficult to see a walnut tree on the canvas, unless it is the finely twigged 'plant' in the middle of the *quincunx*. But even then, because there is such a clear evocation of the atmosphere of water and sea in the painting, the connotation of 'drowning' is more plausible than 'walnut tree'. Therefore, I think that since 2000 (because only then was the title discovered on the back) the painting has been wrongly registered as 'Noyer indifférent'.

357 Jaffé 1983: 146–147.

358 Jung 1958/1964: 312, 314.

the projection-creating fantasy soars beyond the realm of earthly organisations and powers into the heavens, into interstellar space, where the rulers of human fate, the gods, once had their abode in the planets."[359]

The unconscious can never be directly perceived, but only indirectly via 'its' projections into our consciousness. Jung deliberately did not want to write an erudite book; he wanted to initiate the reader as straightforwardly as possible into the 'origination' of this 'modern myth'. Applying his own famous amplification method, he showed that UFOs are merely a symptom of a broader psychic reality. Jung placed these flying saucers against the background of similar projections throughout history – for instance in art. On the cover of the first edition is written: "Description and interpretation of a current phenomenon, using psychological material as comparison; dreams, *modern paintings* and historic parallels."[360] This is typical of Jung's method. His method is not reductive, like Freud's. Of course, Jung also saw UFOs in the shape of a cigar, and he would, as usual, acknowledge that the sexual drive has its phallic projections, but there are more 'signs in the sky' than the Freudian or Adlerian.

Jung noticed in particular the big, 'round' archetype of wholeness, which signifies a union between opposites, and illustrated how the archetype of the 'round object' has influenced our and other cultures in the past and continues to do so in the present. Many of these examples of *rotondas* – discs, circles, saucers, platters and mandalas – are convincing since they are universally present. In Plato's philosophy, in our dreams, in alchemistic and astrological symbolism, in brochures from Basel and Nuremberg from the sixteenth century, in myths and visions of saints, the circular shape is mentioned continually – as symbol of the soul, of wholeness, of the Self, of benediction. In this sequence, he devoted a separate chapter of his book to 'UFOs in modern painting'. Consciously or unconsciously (modern) painters project *unidentified flying objects* upon their skies, as we can see for instance in Tanguy's painting.

This method seamlessly connects to Jung's perspective on art. In art, the vital needs of the soul are projected. In other words, via the artist, collective unconscious drives are projected like (warning) 'signs in the sky', always in a figurative way of speaking but with respect to this particular theme also literally speaking. Jung wrote: "It is, indeed, a law of painting to give visible shape to the dominant trends of the age."[361] This is one of the first sentences in the chapter. And he continued with a reflection upon "modern art" in general. I elaborated upon this in the previous chapter. We considered the components of his reflection and we saw his hope for new bridge-builders among "modern" artists. It cannot be their objective that the debris, the fragments and distortions will *remain* our share. "It must counter the fragmentariness of our world by a striving to be healed and made whole. But since this apparently cannot be found in the present, we cannot even

359 Jung 1958/1964: 320.
360 Jung 1958 (italics mine).
361 Jung 1958/1964: 383.

conceive what would make us whole."[362] In Jung's view the archetypes in the painting by Tanguy are hopeful. It is a start, and yet...

A Rorschach test

What was Jung's approach in interpreting such a painting? He took as his point of departure that we do not know what it depicts. The painter does not understand it either. In his view this is true for most "modern art". It is certainly true for Tanguy, as we will see. According to Jung, this could only imply one thing: employing a purely intuitive approach to the painting: "As a contemporary painting is usually rather difficult to interpret, because the whole aim is to abolish meaning and form and to replace them by something strange and disconcerting, I have followed the method of showing it to as many different people as possible, in this way conducting a kind of Rorschach test."[363]

This test is well-known.[364] The client is shown symmetrical inkblots, an image which emerges purely coincidentally and without any conscious moulding; its interpretation appeals only to the irrational forces of fantasy. The unconscious is forced to play a part. Nothing can be ascertained with objectivity. As Jung would say: we can only rely on the 'subjective factor'. Jung furthermore referred to the association experiments he employed at the beginning of his career: "The isolated stimulus word uttered by the experimenter bewilders and embarrasses the subject because it may have more than one meaning. He does not quite know what to answer, and this accounts for the extraordinary variety of answers in these tests – and what is more important – for the large number of disturbed reactions which are caused by the intrusion of unconscious contents."[365]

Jung thought that "modern art" has the same effect. "We can therefore attribute to it a conscious or unconscious intention to turn the beholder's eyes away from the intelligible and enjoyable world of the senses and to enforce a revelation of the unconscious as a kind of substitute for the loss of human surroundings."[366]

Whereas this attitude is true for the whole field of "modern art" – in fact for all art – it is particularly applicable to Surrealism. Its adherents wanted to *consciously* force the unconscious to reveal itself. For decades they did not tire from passionately delivering the message that a work of art originates in the artist separately from his conscious intentions. Essentially, an artist does not do anything more than mould irrational impulses, images, hallucinations and visions which surface into the imagination. In Breton's definitions of Surrealism, we read that the artist needs to be guided by the inner voice, inner dream images, and if need be by hallucinations, without any aesthetic or ethical interference. Breton, who had worked on a

362 Jung 1958/1964: 384.
363 Jung 1958/1964: 395.
364 The test was developed by the Swiss psychiatrist Hermann Rorschach (1884–1924).
365 Jung 1958/1964: 397–398.
366 Jung 1958/1964: 398.

neurological hospital ward during the war, had become interested in the dreams and free associations of mentally ill people. He became fascinated by the paranormal (surreal) functioning of the psyche in its countless forms. The circumstances during and after the First World War hugely influenced the movement. Surrealism was a strong accusation against the bourgeois materialistic society which in their view had caused the war. Surrealism thought it could only resist its achievements (materialistic, militaristic, technical and in the field of natural science), which are based on cold rationalism, with a pure anti-attitude; in this case anti-art. It drew its inspiration from those dimensions of the psyche which were officially abhorred and regarded as sick; the irrational. Among other things, this implied that the Surrealistic artist consciously employed coincidence and gave it a decisive function; whereas conventional society wanted to eliminate coincidence. From the previous chapters we are aware how Jungian this approach is. Zuch wrote a fine book about the effect of Jung's ideas on Surrealist artists such as Max Ernst (1891–1976), Victor Brauer (1884–1945) and Hans Arp (1887–1966).[367]

Yves Tanguy

Tanguy was an outspoken Surrealist throughout his entire life. Together with Salvador Dali (1904–1989) and Magritte, he belonged to the core of this movement. He started to paint in 1923 as an autodidact. Straight after the First World War, he sailed the world's seas in the service of the marine trade for one and a half years, following in the footsteps of his father. After his military service, in 1922, he left this trade behind, went to live in Paris and made his livelihood doing all kinds of jobs. One day, in 1923, standing on an open platform of a bus, he saw in a shop window a painting by Giorgio de Chirico (1888–1978), a Surrealist painter *avant la date*. Tanguy was turned upside down. Being totally astonished, during that moment he knew one thing for sure: he would become a painter. It is a classic conversion story. Without any education, he practised different styles and techniques. In the meantime, he was submerged in the alluring cultural life of the capital city. Several years later, in 1925, when he visited the first exhibition of Surrealist painters, he was again so profoundly moved that, arriving back home, he destroyed all his works out of sheer discontent. A few paintings which he had given to his friends are preserved. He started anew and immediately found his own style and also almost immediately mastered it perfectly. In 1927, about 30 paintings were exhibited at an exposition which was completely dedicated to him. His first exhibition abroad was in 1929, in Zürich.

Tanguy's non-conformist work is exemplary of Surrealism, using free association and moving around in a landscape of dream images. Whereas during the first years his work showed only figurative elements, in the course of 1927 all his images progressively dissolved into phantom-like objects. Before he started, he really did not know what he was doing and only afterwards did he search for a title.

367 See Zuch 2004.

Somewhere he said: 'The painting comes into being before my eyes, it reveals its surprises during its development and exactly this gives me the sense of complete freedom.'[368] He allowed coincidence to play a strong part in the choice of his titles. On the occasion of his first exhibition in 1927, Breton and Tanguy spent a whole afternoon thinking about titles for the canvasses which were going to be displayed. In a psychiatric book, they searched for all kinds of statements from psychiatric patients (those statements certainly stem from the unconscious), until a quote 'suddenly' gave them the idea: 'this is it!' In this way titles were found, such as 'I came as I have promised. Adieu.' or 'Mama, papa is wounded!' Tanguy was convinced that 'underneath' this process there must have been a meaningful line (why else the ah-ha feeling), but he did not *understand* the title. He will have followed this course of action to find the title 'Noyé indifférent'. Tanguy took 'psychic automatism' seriously. In the above mentioned psychiatric book, written by the doctor Charles Richet (1856–1935), an author who was also quoted by Jung, Tanguy read elaborate protocols about 'ectoplasmic materialisation' in the hallucinations of patients. Ectoplasm is the non-granulated outer coating of cytoplasm, a protein-like matter of animal and plant cells which is seen as the prime matter. It looks as if the biomorphic, organic, flexible figures in his paintings are made of the same matter – as are the four figures in Jung's painting. Furthermore, he regularly depicted 'empty' landscapes, seascapes, and moon panoramas wherein the horizons are either very sharp or completely absent. These smooth horizons are often characterised by an indefinable, magic, cool light.

Tanguy combined the most 'crazy' things; in particular, he arbitrarily inserted numbers, words and geometrical figures into his paintings, which evoke a sequence of different associations in the beholder, which are subsequently brutalised. Tanguy came from Brittany. He was raised with and fascinated by the world of menhirs and dolmens, kabbalistic symbols and Celtic mythology. More than once, the beholder senses some traces of this fascination and certainly tastes its magical atmosphere. Tanguy did not desire anything else. He never explained his paintings nor did he even try to. He realised that this was impossible and rejected any rational interpretation. Tanguy expert Karin von Maur spoke of an 'image-strategy whose objective is deregulation, and in this way results in a meta-logic, a meta-language and a meta-reality with their own rules.'[369]

Most likely Jung was unaware of all this, but he had a remarkable intuitive understanding of it. "He [Tanguy] has undoubtedly succeeded in expressing the bleakness, coldness, lifelessness, the cosmic 'inhumanness' and infinite desolation of the horizontal, despite the association 'city'. He thus confirms the tendency of this kind of modern art to make the object unrecognisable and to cut off the sympathy and understanding of the beholder, who, rebuffed and confused, feels thrown back on himself."[370]

368 Quoted in Klingöhr-Leroy 2005: 94.
369 Maur 2000: 40.
370 Jung 1958/1964: 397.

If the painter does not understand what he is doing, we should not consider ourselves to be more prudent than him. Therefore, we have to restrain our reason in pursuing its interests and be as 'ascetic' as Tanguy. We have to call upon our own irrational impulses. Jung was also convinced that there was more of a guarantee of finding a common theme if he asked different people about their spontaneous impressions. We need to be aware that for Jung this method was not an emergency measure. It was his fundamental conviction that all great art *is* rooted in the collective unconscious (via the person of the artist), and through this method he would be in touch with the same collective unconscious as the artist.

It will be clear from Jung's discussion of Tanguy's painting that, completely faithful to his view on art, he is not at all interested in the life or the person of Yves Tanguy. The personal causality of a work of art, as we have already seen, is as important for him as is the soil for the flower which grows in it. The artist's personality is rather an obstacle for a good understanding of the impersonal unconscious roots of the work of art. Gaillard was right in his observation that Jung always analysed in this way. Even in his extensive reviews of the works of Joyce and Picasso, he did not say a word about them as individuals. 'We could search in vain for the slightest reference to Joyce's life in Jung's text on *Ulysses*. Jung has no use for it. (…) Neither in this text nor, more generally, in another advancement he makes in the psychoanalysis of art. (…) [Concerning Picasso] he does not at any time in this text make the smallest allusion to the artist's life, to his childhood trials and tribulations, or his adventures of the moment. (…) On the contrary, what attracts and maintains his attention is the dynamics of the work as seen through its manifest and actual expressions, especially the figures presented and represented. He knows the virtue of images when one finds oneself in such a universe, so dark, cold, lugubrious and primitive as to risk a mortal decomposition.'[371] In the following analysis we will see the same minimal attention for the person of Yves Tanguy.

Amplification

Jung first described the different reactions he had gathered and only then did he add his own response. "Most of them took the black and white background, which combines a minimum of intelligibility with a maximum of abstraction, to be a plane surface. This is supported by the fact that the light causes the five central forms to cast shadows. It can be seen that these shadows fall on a plane. The interpretation of this varies considerably; some thought it was a sea covered with drift ice in the Polar night, others a sea of fog at night time, others the bleak surface of a distant planet like Uranus or Neptune, and others a great city illuminated at night, situated along the edge of bays, like San Francisco or New York. The strange *quincunx*[372] suspended over the 'city' left most of them puzzled. Some interpreted it at once as

371 Gaillard 2008: 332, 343, 344.

372 A *quincunx* is a pattern of five unities which are arranged like the five eyes on a dice.

falling bombs and explosions. The form in the middle was taken to be a sea-creature (sea-anemone, octopus, etc.) or a flower, or else a demonic face with tangled hair (looking down to the left); others saw it as the swirling smoke of a great fire. The four figures surrounding it were understood as sea animals, puffs of smoke, fungi, or, because of the horns, as devils. The one at the top left, whose vivid yellow-green contrasts with the dull, indeterminate tones of the others, was interpreted as poisonous smoke, a water-plant, flame, a house on fire, etc.

"I must admit that for me the comparison with a city at night by the sea, viewed from a considerable height as from an aeroplane, was the most convincing. The artist is said to have been a sailor originally, and would thus have had plenty of opportunities for such impressions."[373]

Jung made some remarks about the importance of this procedure with respect to all "modern art": "Modern art is less concerned with the pictures it produces than with the observer and his involuntary reactions. He peers at the colours on the canvas, his interest is aroused, but all he can discover is a product that defies human understanding. He feels disappointed, and already he is thrown back on a subjective reaction which vents itself in all sorts of exclamations. Anyone who knows how to interpret these will learn a lot about the subjective disposition of the observer but next to nothing about the painting as such. For him it is no more than a psychological test."[374]

If the person who reads this does not know anything about Jung, he could easily conclude that this Rorschach manoeuvre is entirely arbitrary and subjective and therefore meaningless. There are as many thoughts as there are minds. And nothing is said objectively about the painting. Moreover, the artist himself does not even know. It is all about nothing. But that is a huge misconception of Jung's perspective. Whoever supposes that he thought this was a weak bid is wrong. For Jung, such a method was particularly relevant and, taking everything into consideration, it was the only right approach. He continued: "This may sound disparaging, but only for those who regard the subjective factor merely as a source of discomfort. But if they are interested in their own psyches, they will try to submit their constellated complexes to closer scrutiny."[375]

The "subjective factor": Forms and numbers

We remember what Jung meant by the 'subjective factor'. He saw it as something outstandingly objective; it is the material that has been stored in the human psyche for millions of years, we inherit it with our birth and it operates autonomously. Our conscious I is in continuous contact with this material. The artist draws from it, and we also draw from it when experiencing paintings.

373 Jung 1958/1964: 395. Jung probably heard something about Tanguy's life as a sailor from one of the guests at the exhibition.
374 Jung 1958/1964: 398.
375 Jung 1958/1964: 398.

The sentence quoted above states that we encounter our "constellated complexes" in the objective psyche. I have devoted a whole chapter (Chapter 2) to Jung's complex theory. Actually, each complex is a constellation, an assembled cluster. In the same way as the planets and the stars in the sky stand in a certain constellation at a certain moment, so can the psychic forces in the unconscious stand in a certain constellation. The soul of the *Zeitgeist* can be subdued to a certain constellation of forces. This constellated complex of the *Zeitgeist* inspires the artist, appears in his work and moves us as its beholders: "In its attempt to leave the world of visible and intelligible appearances and to float in the boundlessness of chaos, modern art, to a still greater degree than the psychological tests, evokes complexes which have sloughed off their usual personal aspect and appear as what they originally were, namely primordial forms of the instincts. They are of a suprapersonal, collective unconscious nature."[376]

On this painting of Tanguy's Jung sees "primordial forms of the instincts". That is, archetypes. In order to grasp the true worth of his view, I first have to mention another aspect of his archetype theory. What are, according to Jung, the most archaic 'pre-existent mental images' in our psyche? They are the arithmetical and geometrical images, those images which are based on number and form. Throughout his work, Jung referred to the primaeval meaning of numbers and geometric forms in dreams and visions. They appear spontaneously. During his crisis, he noticed that he spontaneously expressed his soul stirrings in circles, quadrangles, and triangles.

The circle, the form by which for millions of years the sun and the moon have appeared to humanity, is instinctively experienced as a symbol of wholeness and perfection. The circle has no beginning or end, nor does it give direction or orientation. The symbolic counterpart of the circle is the quadrangle, signifying the earth and matter. Four is a cosmological *orienting* archetype. Since ancient times, we distinguish four seasons, wind directions, lunar phases, quarters, temperaments, rivers in paradise, evangelists, sons of Horus, etc. Gradually, the number four became an independent autonomous archetype, which stands for being grounded solidly on the earth. A square gives us the number four. For instance, when we find ourselves in the middle of a courtyard during a dream, it makes a huge difference whether we are dreaming about a round or a square shape.

As an archetype, the number three gives us a very different experience. Time plays a role in the background. The One between people is experienced as a disintegration into Two, the male and the female, which together become fruitful in the Third, the child. The three moves through time (all good things happen in threes, in three phases) and this number is thus often identified with the energetic process. In the Bible and in fairy tales, the decisive moment is usually unfolded on the 'third day'. Jung wrote extensively about primal forms, for instance in his study on synchronicity: "The method best adapted to the nature of chance is the

376 Jung 1958/1964: 399.

numerical method. Since the remotest times men have used numbers to establish meaningful coincidences, that is, coincidences that can be interpreted. There is something peculiar, one might even say mysterious, about numbers. They have never been entirely robbed of their numinous aura. If, so a text book of mathematics tells us, a group of objects is deprived of every single one of his properties or characteristics, there still remains, at the end, its *number,* which seems to indicate that the number is something irreducible. (...) The most elementary quality of an object is whether it is one or many. The number helps more than anything else to bring order into the chaos of appearances. It is the predestined instrument for creating order, or for apprehending an already existing, but still unknown, regular arrangement or 'orderedness'. It may well be the most primitive element of order in the human mind, seeing that the numbers one to four occur with the greatest frequency and have the widest incidence. In other words, primitive patterns of order are mostly triads or tetrads. That numbers have an archetypal foundation is not, by the way, a conjecture of mine. (...) Hence it is not so much an audacious conclusion after all if we define number psychologically as *an archetype of order* which has become conscious. Remarkably enough, the psychic images of wholeness which are spontaneously produced by the unconscious, the symbols of the self in mandala form, also have a mathematical structure. They are as a rule quaternities (or their multiples). These structures not only express order, they also create it. That is why they generally appear in times of psychic disorientation in order to compensate a chaotic state or as formulations of numinous experiences. It must be emphasised yet again that they are not inventions of the conscious mind but are spontaneous products of the unconscious, as has been sufficiently shown by experience."[377]

Symbols of unity in Tanguy's painting

Against the background of these thoughts, we are no longer surprised that art falls back upon these basic structuring archetypes in times of need. We have seen at length that during these times abstract art rather than empathic art (e.g. Worringer) comes into existence. All references to an organic world is banned in this art. It tries to control reality through geometric forms.

Jung saw this type of primaeval form in Tanguy's painting. Tanguy was not just doing something at random. Moreover, he did not have the freedom to do whatever he wanted. He allowed the 'subjective factor' to do its work and it fell back on the most archetypal principles of order in this desolate modern time. "Since even the boldest fantasy of the creative artist – however much it may exceed the bounds of intelligibility – is always bounded by the limits of the psyche itself, there may easily appear in his pictures unknown forms which indicate certain limiting and predetermined factors. In Tanguy's picture, these are the *quincunx*, the quaternity

377 Jung 1950/1960: 456–457.

with the 3 + 1 structure, and the 'signs of heaven', the circles and the cigar-form – in a word, the archetypes."[378]

Jung saw hopeful symbols in this painting. His incredibly broad cultural view on these symbols, and not to forget his own experience with them, allowed him to *see* 'signs in the sky'. I do not have the space to describe here his profundity and erudition in this area. I will only list the symbols and give a short interpretation of them.

There is the crucial *quincunx*. Worldwide it is the symbol wherein the fifth element, the *quinta essentia* (the quintessence) is depicted. It rises from the sea, it soars above the whole, it descends from heaven, or in whatever way one wishes to see it. It is irrefutable that Tanguy wrested this symbol from his collective unconscious. One of the most beautiful examples of art involving the *quincunx* is the Borobudur on Java. The *quincunx* is a symbol of the Self.

When Jung looked attentively at the four figures surrounding the 'indifferent drowning person', he noticed the 3 + 1 structure. It is a pattern wherein one figure is clearly different from the three comparable others, whereas together they unmistakably form a foursome. Jung wrote extensively about this type of quaternity. It is an essential theme in alchemy in particular. Jung always attested that the Christian trinity needs a fourth figure; the dark unconscious function which Christianity repressed as devilish. In his view, the Christian trinity is perfect, but not complete. The fourth function is lacking, that is, the unconscious. Christian theology repressed the instinctive, dark factor. In Tanguy's painting, Jung saw this fourth function in the shape of a flame. He figured that Tanguy painted a "developed symbol of totality", stemming from the ancient Gnostic quarter-unity of the godhead Barbelo.[379] Exactly this perfect quaternity produces the fivesome, the *quincunx*! One may assume that Jung was moved by this *quincunx* when he bought the painting. Tanguy probably had no awareness of this background when painting it. If he had been aware of it, then it was probably only in hindsight.

But Jung saw more. In the upper part of the painting he saw, painted in concentric lines, two round forms rising above the horizon, rising from the water. Are they a sun and a moon? Above them, to the left, we see an elongated and round body. It unmistakably looks like a flying saucer. Jung was aware of its phallic shape and in relation to the two female *rotundas* underneath it, it reminded him of a 'cohabitation'.

Jung saw all these symbols as symbols of unity. Hence, we are seeing a hopeful constellation in the sky. Of course, in 1929, Tanguy had no knowledge of UFOs and probably would never have believed in them. But it is exactly for this reason that Jung considered these images so important. These images are of all times, or, more appropriately, in *certain dark times* they always appear in the sky, they are

378 Jung 1958/1964: 398–399.

379 The term Barbelo probably stems from the Hebrew Barbe Eloha, meaning 'in the four is God'. From a psychological perspective, Barbelo is an anima-symbol. In the Gnostic manuscript *Actis Joannis* it is the female aspect of the father godhead (see Timmer 2001: 89).

projected. As a visionary loner, usually an artist is the first to project these symbols above a desolate modern society and thus gives us a 'sign' of what is going on. Jung saw Tanguy's painting as 'great art' because this painter did not depict only disorder, but at the same time archetypes which "express order". He wrote: "As though by chance there appears in the chaos of possibilities unexpected ordering principles which have the closest affinities with the timeless psychic dominants. But at the same time they have conjured up a collective fantasy typical of our technological age and painted it in the skies."[380]

He continued: "Pictures of this kind are rather rare but not undiscoverable."[381] Hence, Jung stayed sceptical with respect to the character of wholeness in most modern works of art. When he bought the painting in 1929, he must have seen immediately that the painter not only descended into Hades, because this is of course what Tanguy did on the horizontal level, but also started a vertical movement, towards heaven, even though still from an ectoplasmic primal beginning.

In her elaborate article in the Stuttgart catalogue, the above mentioned Tanguy expert von Maur referred to Jung's thoughts on this painting. She praised him. In her view, Jung distilled excellently the characteristics of Surrealism, even though he probably knew very little about the movement – 'What Jung describes is completely in line with the programme of Surrealism' – even though she had to admit that she could not always understand the cabalistic, alchemical and Gnostic 'high flights of his interpretation'.[382] Von Maur was even more explicit than Jung: there is a spirit soaring above the chaos. And at the horizon the light of a new creation is glowing.

Jung is hardly known in the field of art critics. They do not know how to deal with his views, or, as Jung assumed, do not know them at all. Hence, it is remarkable how this art critic is inspired by him and even more so because it concerns a modern work of art. Jung would have smiled.

380 Jung 1958/1964: 399.
381 Jung 1958/1964: 399.
382 Maur 2000: 60, 61.

Epilogue

> It seems to me synchronicity represents a direct act of creation which manifests itself as chance.
>
> (Jung 1977: 504)

Reflecting on the important themes from the previous chapters, if we want to summarise in a few words what art is according to Jung, we could say that it is *a synchronistic phenomenon*. In the previous chapters I consciously, albeit artificially, left Jung's well-known hypothesis about synchronicity out of my considerations, because I knew I would centralise it as a closing paradigm in the epilogue. Nevertheless, it came up several times.

Synchronicity is still a controversial subject. Yet, in our time there is a broader agreement. It is no longer contested that Jung raises here important issues. No one realised better than Jung himself that his hypothesis was a first feeble attempt to provide clarity. In its elaboration he mainly paid attention to the fields of science and religion. I think art provides an equally strong if not stronger breeding ground. I will first summarise what Jung meant by synchronicity, then I will illustrate it with his perspective on art.

Synchronicity

Jung spoke of synchronicity when spontaneous inner experiences (dreams, visions or premonitions) have a *similarity* with more or less *simultaneous* events in the outer world. This is a concurrence of two processes – one is of a psychic nature and the other of a non-psychic nature – which definitely did not cause each other. Nevertheless, we experience that concurrence as meaningful. Hence, a 'meaningful coincidence'.

One dreams that a plane crashes, and in the morning one hears on the radio that a plane actually crashed that night. Jung told a story about a patient with whom he was walking on a path through the woods: "She tells me about the first dream in her life that had made an everlasting impression upon her. She had seen a spectral fox coming down the stairs in the parental home. At this moment a real fox comes out of the trees not 40 yards away and walks quietly on the path ahead of us for several minutes. The animal behaves as if it were a partner in the human situation. (One fact is no fact, but when you have seen many, you begin to sit up.)"[383] It is obvious that there is no causal relation between this dream and what is going on in the outside world. Nevertheless, this kind of concurrence of events is experienced as meaningful.

Jung's hypothesis means that this type of coincidence points to an ordering force lying at the basis of both the psychic and the physical, and which causes an interaction between them. If they do not cause each other, there must be an acausal relationship. In Jung's terminology: "The meaningful coincidence or equivalence of a psychic and a physical state that have no causal relationship to one another means, *in general terms, that it is a modality without a cause, an 'acausal orderedness'*."[384]

One speaks of synchronicity when there is an equivalent and simultaneous occurrence of psychic and non-psychic phenomena. The simultaneity is captured by the term 'synchronicity', whereas the equivalence is not. Each is an equally strong aspect of this phenomenon. Jung was aware of this, as well as of the fact that simultaneity is a flexible notion. It did not necessarily imply *at the same moment*; but rather *in the same time span*. Research further showed that synchronistic phenomena are dependent on a strong psychic sensitivity to emotional stimuli. It was also ascertained that they occur more strongly when the psyche operates on a less conscious level, like in a dream or a daydream – in general, when the threshold of consciousness is lowered. The core of this hypothesis is that it "requires a psyche that touches matter at some point, and, conversely, a matter with a latent psyche."[385] The psyche does not exist only in the interior of the person, isolated from the cosmos. Psyche and non-psyche are in some way entwined with each other.

One of the most remarkable facets of synchronicity is, of course, that everyday categories of cause and effect, time and space have become irrelevant. This causes the strongest resistance in many people. But exactly at this point, Jung was the least surprised. The revolution in the natural sciences at the beginning of the previous century was of such a nature that the hypothesis of synchronicity was not as audacious as one would think at first glance. Jung was in the centre of this Copernican revolution. At home, he had deep conversations about the idea of relativity with Albert Einstein (1879–1955) during the exact period when Einstein was creating his important theories. Furthermore, Jung was exchanging letters with the quantum physicist and Nobel Prize winner Wolfgang Pauli (1900–1958) about the fascinating subatomic reality. Jung was profoundly impressed by the fact that the hitherto rock-hard reality principle had been dethroned. This principle implies that there is a materialistic reality in time and space existing separate from the observer, and that this reality behaves according to the principle of space and

383 Jung 1973: 395. Jung wrote this in a letter (November 1945) to J. B. Rhine (1895–1980). Rhine was a botanist who later developed an interest in parapsychology and psychology.

384 Jung 1950/1960: 516 (italics mine).

385 Jung 1954/1960: 234.

time. This all became fundamentally unsettling. In physics, processes were discovered which behave without a cause, but which nevertheless occur. Looking at the decay of radioactive elements, there is no explanation for why one element perishes whereas the other does not. The discovery of an acausal process was a strong blow for causal thinking. Why does something happen without a cause? Who or what is responsible for their occurrence? It was discovered that nothing occurs *in* space or time, but that time and space are psychic categories. Jung had already read about this in Kant: space and time are *a priori* categories of our mind. They are only seemingly properties of moving bodies.[386]

Jung did not think his hypothesis was exceptional. He wrote: "Synchronicity is no more baffling or mysterious than the discontinuities of physics. It is only the ingrained belief in the sovereign power of causality that creates intellectual difficulties and makes it appear unthinkable that acausal events exist or could ever occur."[387] He drew an important conclusion from this discovery of the discontinuous character of reality. He assigned great value to the fact that the chain of causality is broken. And he stated that exactly on the basis of the principle of *discontinuity* reality renews itself, evolves and changes. In other words, when people only follow causal pathways *there will never be creativity*. The contingent, coincidental character of reality guarantees the creation of something new.

In a letter to the professor of theoretical physics Markus Fierz (1912–2006), written on 2 March 1950, Jung said: "It seems to me synchronicity represents a *direct act of creation* which manifests itself as chance. The statistical proof of natural conformity to law is therefore only a very limited way of describing nature, since it grasps only uniform events. But nature is essentially discontinuous, i.e., subject to chance. To describe it we need a principle of discontinuity."[388]

"Act of creation"! It does not need clarification that such a characterisation of synchronistic phenomena is relevant to a creative act par excellence – art. Several times Jung pointed out that synchronicity and creativity reciprocally call each other into existence: "But if they do exist [acausal events], then we must regard them as *creative acts*, as the continuous creation of a pattern that exists from all eternity, repeats itself sporadically, and is not derivable from any known antecedents."[389] In other words, on the one side reality is continually created and sustained (a very old patristic thought which Jung knew well),[390] and on the other side reality is characterised by creations scattered through time and

386 See Jung 1950/1960: 436.
387 Jung 1950/1960: 518.
388 Jung 1977: 504.
389 Jung 1950/1960: 518.
390 On this subject, Jung extensively quoted the Fathers. He introduced their texts: "Continuous creation is to be thought of not only as a series of successive acts of creation, but also as the eternal presence of the *one* creative act. (…) What happens successively in time is simultaneous in the mind of God. (…) 'There was no time before time, but time was created together with the world' (Anonymous)" (Jung 1950/1960): 518, footnote 17. What the Fathers expressed in theological terms turn out to be scientific and psychological 'facts'.

space. This is demonstrated by the artistic products scattered through history and prehistory.

Jung thought he could indicate 'the place' where psyche and matter are intertwined: *the archetype*. In his view, the archetype has its roots in the non-psychic, the biological, but stretches its trunk and branches into the psyche. We have seen that Jung does not consider archetypes as purely psychic phenomena. They are rooted in the cosmic matrix.[391] The archetype has, as he described it, a *transgressive* character. In other words, its nature is synchronistic. Occasionally, we *realise* that representations in the psyche correspond with patterns outside the psyche. But apart from these exceptional events, an archetype *is* already synchronistic by nature, whether we are conscious of this or not. Therefore, in the archetype, synchronicity is structured, made possible. One could say that the archetype synchronises by nature, thus creating a connection between matter and psyche.

An archetypal experience will always overwhelm a person. Time, space and cause fall away. Following Otto, Jung spoke of a 'numinous' experience. This means that a complex takes possession of a person. The freedom of the I ends. In an interview with Mircea Eliade (1907–1986) in August 1952, Jung made a direct connection between a numinous experience and synchronicity. He said: "Religious experience is *numinous*, as Rudolf Otto calls it, and for me, as a psychologist, this experience differs from all others in the way it transcends the ordinary categories of space, time, and causality. Recently I have put a great deal of study into synchronicity (briefly, the 'rupture of time') and I have established that it closely resembles numinous experiences where space, time, and causality are abolished."[392]

This passage is remarkable for at least two reasons. First, there is the succinct characterisation of synchronicity as a *rupture dans le temps*. During a numinous/synchronistic experience time stands still, space dissolves, and during an 'eternal moment' one is free from the chain of cause and effect. Furthermore, in Jung's remark to Eliade he employed a wider understanding of synchronicity. Jung expert Murray Stein correctly wrote that Jung employed two descriptions of synchronicity. The first, more *concise* description, refers to the consciously observed meaningful concurrence of a psychic and a non-psychic phenomenon. Like the examples of the crashed plane and the fox. The second, *broader* description, refers to the underlying ordering principle that manifests itself as numinous, acausal, timeless and spaceless in the archetype without a specific reference to the human psyche.[393] When a person experiences this principle of order, he experiences a breach in time, he experiences the numinous. It is a Tao experience, Stein wrote, straight through

391 See Stein 2006: 201–202.

392 Jung 1977/1978: 230.

393 See Stein 2006: 219–220. Jung wrote about this wider conception: "The question now arises whether our definition of synchronicity with reference to the equivalence of psychic and physical processes is capable of expansion, or rather, requires expansion. This requirement seems to force itself on us when we consider the above, wider conception of synchronicity as an 'acausal orderedness'. Into this category come all 'acts of creation', a priori factors such as the properties of natural numbers, the discontinuities of modern physics, etc." (Jung 1950/1960: 516).

the Yin and Yang of everyday life. Psyche and objective world fall together; there is the consciousness of an *unus mundus*. I and reality are one all encompassing, meaningful coincidence. 'And what becomes available to consciousness through such experiences is foundational, a vision into as much of ultimate reality as humans are capable of realising.'[394] Jung had this kind of synchronicity in mind during the interview with Mircea Eliade.

Art as a synchronistic phenomenon

I do not think it is complicated to show that the most important facets of synchronicity can be applied to art, especially to the work of art.[395] First, there is Jung's conviction that an authentic work of art never originates according to the chains of cause and effect. A causal explanation always fails. I bring only one of his many quotes to your attention. "Personal causes have as much or as little to do with a work of art as the soil with the plant that springs from it. We can certainly learn to understand some of the plant's peculiarities by getting to know its habitat. (…) A work of art is not a human being, but is something supra-personal. It is a thing and not a personality; hence it cannot be judged by personal criteria. Indeed the special significance of a true work of art resides in the fact that it has escaped from the limitations of the personal and has soared beyond the personal concerns of its creator."[396]

Art is the result of an autonomous complex. It comes to light from an unconscious, instinctive depth: "Art is a kind of innate drive that seizes a human being and makes him its instrument. The artist is not a person endowed with free will who seeks his own ends, but one who allows art to realise its purposes through him."[397]

Jung regarded the acausal origination of art as so decisive, that it provides a Jungian criterion to distinguish authentic art from non-authentic art. Aesthetic products which can be reduced to causal processes, psychological, social, or otherwise, are *not* art. In his discussion with Freud, Jung emphasised this aspect. A second facet is *participation mystique*. This partial identity between subject and object is a synchronistic ground par excellence. "This identity results from an *a priori oneness* of subject and object."[398] Jung wrote this in 1921. Not until 1950

394 Stein 2006: 219.

395 It is surprising that until now this relationship has been neglected. To my knowledge, only one author has looked explicitly at the aesthetic character of synchronicity, the professor of Jungian Studies Susan Rowland. She wrote: '[Synchronicity] is a way of reading reality non-rationally and symbolically, in ways traditionally assigned to the making of art. So synchronicity treats time and space as aesthetic components of momentary artistic wholes. It is possible therefore, to argue that synchronicity is reality in aesthetic (non-rational) mode, or that it represents the human mind 'reading' or 'composing' acausal events into art without being entirely aware of so doing' (Rowland 2005: 147).

396 Jung 1922/1978: 71.

397 Jung 1930/1978: 101.

398 Jung 1921/1990: 456 (italics mine).

did he unfold his hypothesis about synchronicity. *Participation mystique* can just as well be called *participation synchronistique*. We know to what extent Jung related the creation of art to *participation mystique*. "This re-immersion in the state of participation mystique is the secret of artistic creation."[399]

Whereas the above mentioned factors of art fit into the *wider* definition of synchronicity (that is, that art elicits a numinous awareness, which is experienced as a breach of time and space), there is one facet which strongly approaches a *succinct* definition and which Jung continually emphasised. That is, the symbol that is elicited by the work of art exists in the psyche of the artist and in the outer world. In the enclosure of his studio, the artist 'dreams' of the 'fox' and this turns out to be a mirroring of the 'fox' of the surrounding culture. In some or other way, there is a mirroring of similar and simultaneous processes which did not cause each other directly.

Especially in "modern art", Jung noticed how a similar process is present in the individual psyche of the artist as well as in the timeframe wherein he lives. Take for example the schizophrenic images in a painting and the schizophrenia of the *Zeitgeist*: "In the modern artist it is not produced by any disease in the individual but is a collective manifestation of our time. (...) Just because it is a collective phenomenon it bears identical fruit in the most widely separated realms, in painting as well as literature, in sculpture as well as architecture."[400]

It is important to remember that according to Jung, creative processes, such as the origination of art, are not about 'nature' but about 'culture'. There are processes within the person which are only the consequence of natural, causal processes, and there are processes which carry within them a concealed purposeful meaning and make a sort of unnatural, contingent, creative jump forward.[401] Whereas the natural processes are mediated by instinctive, causal laws of nature, the latter are mediated by spontaneous immaterial principles which also present themselves instinctually and synchronistically, such as in dreams or visions.[402]

Finally, a remark about the two works of art which Jung described explicitly: his *Stone* and *Noyé indifférent* by Tanguy. It is fascinating to read how Jung described his 'stone' synchronistically. Isn't he allowing us to sense how the stone, which came sailing into his life 'out of nowhere' and without him thinking about it instinctively received its form by Jung's hands, reflects as much the (non-psychic) place as well as what is happening in the psyche of the artist? Is Jung not allowing us to sense that the stone received its form because of *both processes*? Jung was afraid that Oakes would overlook this *participation synchronistique*, a *participation* in which subject and object are a unity.

In describing Tanguy's painting, Jung continually spoke about an 'objective psyche', clumsily called the 'subjective factor', which dwells both in the psyche

399 Jung 1930/1978: 105 (italics mine).
400 Jung 1932/1978b: 117.
401 See Jung 1921/1990: 478.
402 See Jung 1928/1960a: 48.

of the artist as well as in his surrounding culture. The UFOs which appear in the artist's psyche are not causally related to those which appear as objects for the post-war modern person. The time span between them is too big; but it is small enough to speak of simultaneity. It is the same archetype that appeared in Tanguy's psyche as well as in the culture after the Second World War. It is so evident that one can speak of a 'meaningful concurrence'. Jung wrote that an archetypal ordering principle lies at the basis of it; hence a synchronistic principle. They are "spontaneous products of the unconscious", completely contingent, discontinuous in character. They are creative acts in time.

Creation always originates from a mythic *illo tempore*, wherein time, space and cause are still included in the big synchronistic Chaos. Jung had always known and emphasised this. He will have the final word:

> The impact of an archetype, whether it takes the form of immediate experience or is experienced through the spoken word, stirs us because it summons up a voice that is stronger than our own. Whoever speaks in primordial images speaks with a thousand voices; he enthrals and overpowers, while at the same time he lifts the idea he is seeking to express out of the occasional and the transitory into the realm of the ever-enduring. He transmutes our personal destiny into the destiny of mankind, and evokes in us all those beneficent forces that ever and anon have enabled humanity to find a refuge from every peril and to outlive the longest night. That is the secret of great art, and of its effects upon us. The creative process, so far as we are able to follow it at all, consists in the unconscious activation of an archetypal image, and in elaborating and shaping this image into the finished work.[403]

403 Jung 1922/1978: 82 (italics mine).

References

Agnel, A., Cazenave, M., Dorly, C., Krakowiak, S., Letterier, M. and Thibaudier, V. (2005). *Le Vocabulaire de Carl Gustav Jung*. Paris: Ellipses.

Allesch, C. G. (2006). *Einführung in die psychologische Ästhetik*. Wien: WUV Facultas.

Bair, D. (2003). *Jung: A Biography*. New York/Boston: Back Bay Books/Little, Brown and Company.

Baumeister, T. (1999). *De Filosofie van de Kunsten: Van Plato tot Beuys*. Best: Damon.

Bishop, P. (1995). *The Dionysian Self: C. G. Jung's Reception of Friedrich Nietzsche*. Berlin/New York: Walter de Gruyter.

Bishop, P. (1998). Über die Rolle des Ästhetischen in der Tiefenpsychologie. Zur Schillerrezeption in der analytischen Psychologie C. G. Jungs. In *Jahrbuch der Deutschen Schillergesellschaft*. Göttingen: Wallerstein Verlag.

Bishop, P. (1999). Epistemological problems and aesthetic solutions in Goethe and Jung. In *The Goethe Yearbook*, Volume 4. New York: Boydell & Brewer (pp. 278–314).

Bishop, P. (2008). Psyche and imagination in Goethe and Jung: Or, living for love and loving life. In Rowland (2008), *Psyche and the Arts: Jungian Approaches to Music, Architecture, Literature, Painting and Film*. London/New York: Routledge.

Botton, A. de (2007). *The Architecture of Happiness*. London: Penguin Books.

Covington, C. and Wharton, B. (eds) (2003). *Sabina Spielrein: Forgotten Pioneer of Psychoanalysis*. Hove/New York: Brunner-Routledge.

Darwin, C. (1877). *The Descent of Man and Selection in Relation to Sex*. London: John Murray.

Draaisma, D. (2005). *Het Verdriet van de Kosmopoliet*. Retrieved from http://irs.ub.rug.nl

Eco, U. (ed.) (2004). *On Beauty*. London: Secker and Warburg.

Flournoy, T. (1900). *Des Indes à la Planète Mars: Étude sur un Cas de Somnambulisme avec Glossolalie*. Paris/Genève: Alcan/Eggimann.

Freud, S. (1930). *Three Contributions to the Theory of Sex*. New York: Plain Label Books.

Freud, S. and Jung, C. G. (1994). *The Freud/Jung Letters*. Princeton, NJ: Princeton University Press.

Gaillard, C. (1998). *Le Musée Imaginaire de Carl Gustav Jung*. Paris: Stock.

Gaillard, C. (2008). The Arts. In R. K. Papadopoulos (ed.), *The Handbook of Jungian Psychology: Theory, Practice and Applications*. London/New York: Routledge (pp. 324–376).

Goethe, J. W. von (1913). *Poetry and Truth from My Own Life*. London: G. Bell and Sons.

Gorsen, P. (1994). Zur Problematik der Archetypen in der Kunstgeschichte. Carl Gustav Jung und Aby Warburg. *Kunstforum International,* Band 127, 238–244.

Hannah, B. (1977). *Jung, his Life and Work: A Biographical Memoir.* London: Michael Joseph.

Hayman, R. (1999). *A Life of Jung.* London: Bloomsbury.

Hume, D. (1886). On the standard of taste. In D. Hume, *The Philosophical Works*, Volume 3. London: Little, Brown (pp. 266–284).

Jacobi, J. (1962). *The Psychology of Carl G. Jung: An Introduction with Illustrations.* New Haven, CT: Yale University Press.

Jaffé, A. (ed.) (1983). *C. G. Jung: Word and Image*. Princeton, NJ: Princeton University Press.

Jaffé, A. (1989). *From the Life and Work of C. G. Jung.* Einsiedeln: Daimon Verlag.

Jung, C. G. (1902/1957). On the psychology and pathology of so-called occult phenomena. In *Psychiatric Studies.* New York: Pantheon Books. Collected Works, Volume 1, 3–88.

Jung, C. G. (1905/1957). Cryptomnesia. In *Psychiatric Studies.* New York: Pantheon Books. Collected Works, Volume 1, 95–106.

Jung, C. G. (1907/1960). The psychology of dementia praecox. In *The Psychogenesis of Mental Disease.* New York: Pantheon Books. Collected Works, Volume 3, 3–151.

Jung, C. G. (1912/1944). *Psychology of the Unconscious: A Study of the Transformations and Symbolisms of the Libido. A Contribution to the History of the Evolution of Thought.* London: Kegan Paul, Trench, Trubner and Co.

Jung, C. G. (1913/1990). A contribution to the study of psychological types. In *Psychological Types.* Princeton, NJ: Princeton University Press. Collected Works, Volume 6, 499–509.

Jung, C. G. (1918/1964). The role of the unconscious. In *Civilization in Transition.* New York: Pantheon Books. Collected Works, Volume 10, 3–28.

Jung, C. G. (1918/1995). Über das Unbewusste. In *Zivilisation im Übergang*. Walter, Solothurn/Düsseldorf: Walter-Verlag. Gesammelte Werke, Band 10, 15–42.

Jung, C. G. (1921/1990). *Psychological Types.* Princeton, NJ: Princeton University Press. Collected Works, Volume 6.

Jung, C. G. (1922/1978). On the relation of analytical psychology to poetry. In *The Spirit in Man, Art, and Literature.* Princeton, NJ: Princeton University Press. Collected Works, Volume 15, 65–83.

Jung, C. G. (1922/1995). Über die Beziehungen der Analytischen Psychologie zum dichterischen Kunstwerk In *Über das Phänomen des Geistes in Kunst und Wissenschaft.* Solothurn und Düsseldorf: Walter-Verlag. Gesammelte Werke, Band 15, 75–96.

Jung, C. G. (1926/1989). *Analytical Psychology: Notes of the Seminar given in 1925 by Carl Gustav Jung.* Edited by William McGuire. Bollingen Series XCIX. Princeton, NJ: Princeton University Press.

Jung, C. G. (1927). *Analytische Psychologie und Erziehung: 3 Vorlesungen gehalten in London in Mai 1924.* Heidelberg: Niels Kampmann.

Jung, C. G. (1928/1960a). On psychic energy. In *The Structure and Dynamics of the Psyche.* New York: Pantheon Books. Collected Works, Volume 8, 3–66.

Jung, C. G. (1928/1960b). Analytical psychology and 'Weltanschauung'. In *The Structure and Dynamics of the Psyche.* New York: Pantheon Books. Collected Works, Volume 8, 358–381.

Jung, C. G. (1928/1964). The spiritual problem of modern man. In *Civilization in Transition.* New York: Pantheon Books. Collected Works, Volume 10, 74–94.

Jung, C. G. (1928/1966). The relations between the ego and the unconscious. In *Two Essays on Analytical Psychology.* New York: Pantheon Books. Collected Works, Volume 7, 123–241.

Jung, C. G. (1929/1966). The aims of psychotherapy. In *The Practice of Psychotherapy: Essays on the Psychology of the Transference and Other Subjects*. New York: Pantheon. Collected Works, Volume 16, 36–52.

Jung, C. G. (1930/1978). Psychology and literature. In *The Spirit in Man, Art, and Literature.* Princeton, NJ: Princeton University Press. Collected Works, Volume 15, 84–105.

Jung, C. G. (1932/1977). Is there a Freudian type of poetry? In *The Symbolic Life.* London/Henley: Routledge/Kegan Paul. Collected Works, Volume 18, 765–766.

Jung, C. G. (1932/1978a). Picasso. In *The Spirit in Man, Art, and Literature.* Princeton, NJ: Princeton University Press. Collected Works, Volume 15, 135–141.

Jung, C. G. (1932/1978b). "Ulysses": A monologue. In *The Spirit in Man, Art, and Literature.* Princeton, NJ: Princeton University Press. Collected Works, Volume 15, 109–134.

Jung, C. G. (1932/1978c). Sigmund Freud in his historical setting. In *The Spirit in Man, Art, and Literature.* Princeton, NJ: Princeton University Press. Collected Works, Volume 15, 33–40.

Jung, C. G. (1934/1960). A review of the complex theory. In *The Structure and Dynamics of the Psyche.* New York: Pantheon Books. Collected Works, Volume 8, 92–104.

Jung, C. G. (1934/1964). The meaning of psychology for modern man. In *Civilization in Transition.* New York: Pantheon Books. Collected Works, Volume 10, 134–156.

Jung, C. G. (1935/1977). The Tavistock Lectures. In *The Symbolic Life.* London/Henley: Routledge/Kegan Paul. Collected Works, Volume 18, 5–182.

Jung, C. G. (1938/1984). *Dream Analysis: Notes of the Seminar given in 1928–1930.* Edited by William McGuire. Princeton, NJ: Princeton University Press.

Jung, C. G. (1945/1964). After the catastrophe. In *Civilization in Transition.* New York: Pantheon Books. Collected Works, Volume 10, 194–217.

Jung, C. G. (1946/1954). Analytical psychology and education. In *The Development of Personality.* New York: Pantheon Books. Collected Works, Volume 17, 65–132.

Jung, C. G. (1949/1977). Foreword to harding: "Woman's mysteries". In *The Symbolic Life.* London/Henley: Routledge/Kegan Paul. Collected Works, Volume 18, 518–520.

Jung, C. G. (1950/1960). Synchronicity: An acausal connecting principle. In *The Structure and Dynamics of the Psyche.* New York: Pantheon Books. Collected Works, Volume 8, 419–531.

Jung, C. G. (1952/1956). *Symbols of Transformation: An Analysis of the Prelude to a Case of Schizophrenia.* New York: Pantheon Books.

Jung, C. G. (1954/1960). On the nature of the psyche. In *The Structure and Dynamics of the Psyche.* New York: Pantheon Books. Collected Works, Volume 8, 159–234.

Jung, C. G. (1955/1959). Mandalas. In *The Archetypes and the Collective Unconscious.* New York: Pantheon Books. Collected Works, Volume 9i, 387–390.

Jung, C. G. (1955–56/1963). *Mysterium Coniunctionis: An Inquiry into the Separation and Synthesis of Psychic Opposites in Alchemy.* New York: Pantheon/Books. Collected Works, Volume 14.

Jung, C. G. (1957/1960). The transcendent function. In *The Structure and Dynamics of the Psyche.* New York: Pantheon Books. Collected Works, Volume 8, 67–91.

Jung, C. G. (1957/1964). The meaning of self-knowledge. In *Civilization in Transition.* New York: Pantheon Books. Collected Works, Volume 10, 302–305.

Jung, C. G. (1958). *Ein moderner Mythus: Von Dingen, die am Himmel gesehen werden.* Zürich/Stuttgart: Rascher.

Jung, C. G. (1958/1964). Flying saucers: A modern myth of things seen in the skies. In *Civilization in Transition.* New York: Pantheon Books. Collected Works, Volume 10, 309–433.

Jung, C. G. (1961/1977). Symbols and the interpretation of dreams. In *The Symbolic Life.* London/Henley: Routledge/Kegan Paul. Collected Works, Volume 18, 185–264.

Jung, C. G. (1961/1989). *Memories, Dreams, Reflections.* Recorded and edited by Aniela Jaffé. New York: Vintage Books.

Jung, C. G. (1962/1997). *Erinnerungen, Träume, Gedanken von C. G. Jung.* Aufgezeichnet und herausgegeben von Aniela Jaffé. Zürich/Düsseldorf: Walter-Verlag.

Jung, C. G. (1972/1990). *Briefe I 1906–1945.* Freiburg im Breisgau: Walter, otten.

Jung, C. G. (1973). *Letters. Volume 1: 1906–1950.* Selected and edited by Gerhard Adler in collaboration with Aniela Jaffé. Princeton, NJ: Princeton University Press.

Jung, C. G. (1977). Letters on synchronicity. In *The Symbolic Life.* London/Henley: Routledge/Kegan Paul. Collected Works, Volume 18, 502–509.

Jung, C. G. (1977/1978). *C. G. Jung Speaking: Interviews and Encounters.* Edited by W. McGuire and R. F. C. Hull. London: Thames and Hudson.

Jung, C. G. (1983). *The Zofingia Lectures.* Princeton, NJ: Princeton University Press. Collected Works, Supplementary, Volume A.

Jung, C. G. (1988). *Nietzsche's Zarathustra: Notes of the Seminar given in 1934–1939 by Carl Gustav Jung.* Edited by James L. Jarrett. Two volumes. Bollingen Series XCIX. Princeton, NJ: Princeton University Press.

Jung, C. G. (1990). *Letters. Volume 2: 1951–1961.* Selected and edited by Gerhard Adler in collaboration with Aniela Jaffé. London: Routledge.

Jung, C. G. (1997). *Visions: Notes of the Seminar given in 1930–1934 by Carl Gustav Jung.* Edited by Claire Douglas. Two volumes. Bollingen Series XCIX. Princeton, NJ: Princeton University Press.

Jung, C. G. (2009). *The Red Book: Liber Novus.* Edited by Sonu Shamdasani. Philemon Series. A publication in arrangement with the Foundation of the Works of C. G. Jung, Zürich. New York/London: W. W. Norton and Company.

Kant, I. (2000). *Critique of the Power of Judgement.* Cambridge: Cambridge University Press.

Klingsöhr-Leroy, C. (2005). *Surrealisme.* London: Taschen.

Kortmann, F. (2000). Kunstenaarschap en geestesziekten. In *Maandblad Geestelijke Volksgezondheid* 6, 556–564.

Liard, V. (2007) *Carl Gustav Jung: Kulturphilosoph.* Paris: PUPS.

Maclagan, D. (2001). *Psychological Aesthetics: Painting, Feeling and Making Sense.* London/Philadelphia: Jessica Kingsley Publishers.

Maur, K. von (2000). Yves Tanguy oder "Die Gewissheit des Niegesehenen" Wandlungen des malerischen Oeuvres. In K. von Maur (2000) (ed.), *Yves Tanguy und der Surrealismus.* Ostfilderen/Ruit: Atje Cantz (pp. 11–133).

Mayo, D. H. (1995). *Jung and Aesthetic Experience: The Unconscious as Source of Artistic Inspiration.* New York: Peter Lang.

Molen, H. van der (ed.) (1997). *Klinische Psychologie: Theorieën en Psychopathologie.* Groningen: Wolters-Noordhoff.

Mulisch, H. (2001). *Voer voor Psychologen.* Amsterdam: De Bezige Bij.

Nietzsche, F. (1997). *Herwaardering van Alle Waarden.* Meppel/Amsterdam: Boom.

Nietzsche, F. (1999). *The Birth of Tragedy.* Cambridge: Cambridge University Press.
Nietzsche, F. (2001). *The Gay Science.* Cambridge: Cambridge University Press.
Nietzsche, F. (2005). *Thus Spoke Zarathustra: A Book for Everyone and Nobody*. Oxford: Oxford University Press.
Noll, R. (1994). *The Jung Cult: Origins of a Charismatic Movement.* Princeton, NJ: Princeton University Press.
Noll, R. (1997). *The Aryan Christ: The Secret Life of Carl Jung*. New York: Random House.
Oakes, M. (1987). *The Stone Speaks: The Memoir of a Personal Transformation.* Wilmette, IL: Chiron Publications.
Pamuk, O. (2006). *Istanbul: Memories and the City*. London: Faber and Faber.
Pérez-Reverte, A. (2008). *The Painter of Battles*. London: Phoenix.
Philipson, M. H. (1994). An *Outline of a Jungian Aesthetics*. Boston, MA: Sigo Press.
Read, H. (1960). *The Form of Things Unknown: Essays towards an Aesthetic Philosophy.* London: Faber and Faber.
Rowland, S. (1999). *C. G. Jung and Literary Theory: The Challenge from Fiction.* Basingstoke: Macmillan Press.
Rowland, S. (2005). *Jung as a Writer.* London/New York: Routledge.
Rowland, S. (2008). *Psyche and the Arts: Jungian Approaches to Music, Architecture, Literature, Painting and Film*. London/New York: Routledge.
Samuels, A., Shorter, B. and Plaut, F. (1987). *A Critical Dictionary of Jungian Analysis.* London/New York: Routledge & Kegan Paul.
Shamdasani, S. (1998a). *Cult Fictions: Carl Gustav Jung and the Founding of Analytical Psychology*. London/New York: Routledge.
Shamdasani, S. (1998b). The lost contributions of Maria Moltzer to analytical psychology. *Spring 64* (Fall and Winter), 103–119 [Including: The conception of the libido and its psychic manifestations (107–110); On the conception of the unconscious (111–119)].
Shamdasani, S. (1999). Memories, dreams, omissions. In Paul Bishop (ed.), *Jung in Contexts.* London/New York: Routledge (pp. 33–50).
Shamdasani, S. (2005a). *Jung and the Making of Modern Psychology: The Dream of a Science*. Cambridge: Cambridge University Press.
Shamdasani, S. (2005b). *Jung Stripped Bare by his Biographers, Even.* London/New York: Karnac.
Shamdasani, S. (2009). Introduction and editorial note. In Jung (2009), *Liber Novus: The "Red Book"* (pp. 193–226).
Sheppard, A. (1987). *Aesthetics: An Introduction to the Philosophy of Art.* Oxford/New York: Oxford University Press.
Spielrein, S. (1911). Über den psychologischen Inhalt eines Falles von Schizophrenie (dementia praecox). In *Jahrbuch für psychoanalytische und psychopathologische Forschungen III*, 329–400.
Spivey, N. (2005). *How Art Made the World: A Journey to the Origins of Art.* London: BBC Books.
Stein, M. (2006). *Jung's Map of the Soul: An Introduction.* Chicago, IL: Open Court/La Salle.
Timmer, M. (2001). *Van Anima tot Zeus: Encyclopedie van Begrippen uit de Mythologie, Religie, Alchemie, Cultuurgeschiedenis en Analytische Psychologie*. Rotterdam: Lemniscaat.

Vivas, E. (1974). On aesthetics and Jung. In *Modern Age*, Volume 18, Number 3, 246–256.

Wehr, G. (1989). *An Illustrated Biography of C. G. Jung*. Boston/Shaftesbury: Shambhala.

Worringer, W. (1980). *Abstraction and Empathy: A Contribution to the Psychology of Style*. New York: International Universities Press.

Zuch, R. (2004). *Die Surrealisten und Carl Gustav Jung: Studien zur Rezeption der analytischen Psychologie im Surrealismus am Beispiel von Max Ernst, Victor Brauner und Hans Arp*. Weimar: VDG.

Index

For Product Safety Concerns and Information please contact our EU representative GPSR@taylorandfrancis.com Taylor & Francis Verlag GmbH, Kaufingerstraße 24, 80331 München, Germany

Batch number: 10725812

Printed by Printforce, the Netherlands